INDUSTRIALISATION AND REGIONAL DEVELOPMENT

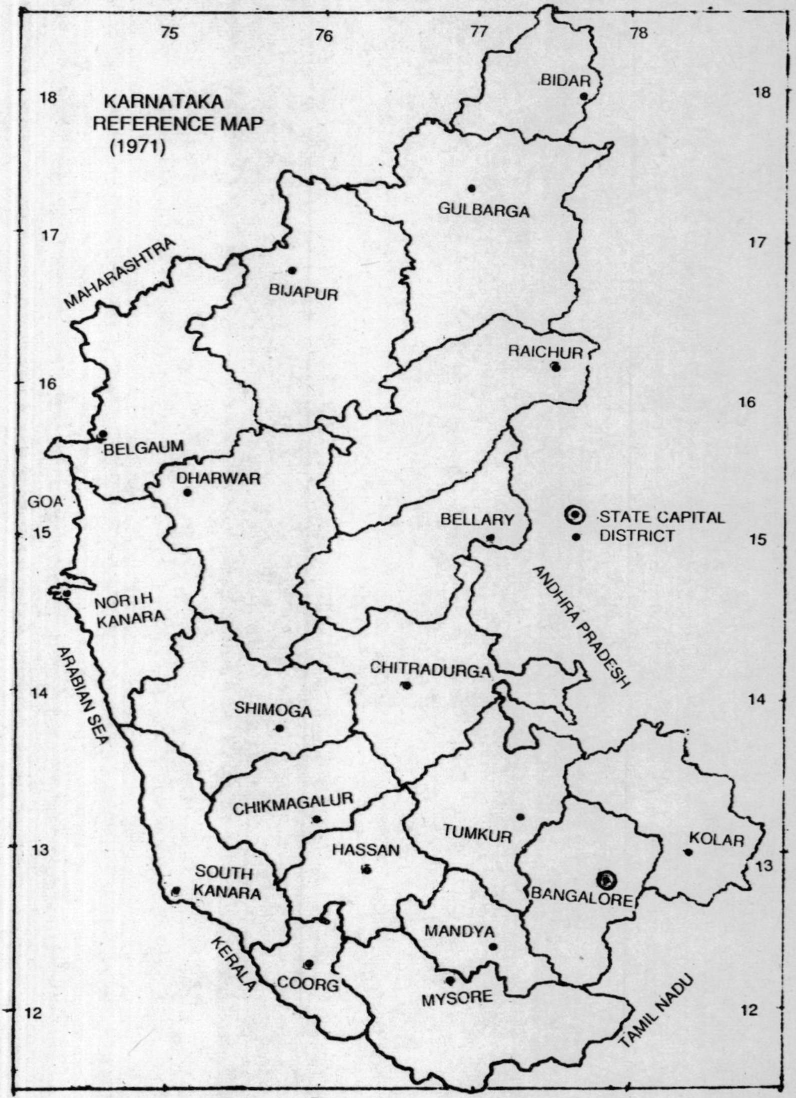

Map : Karnataka Reference Map (1971)

INDUSTRIALISATION AND REGIONAL DEVELOPMENT

B. SESHADRI

Foreword by
W.E. Hotchkiss

CONCEPT PUBLISHING COMPANY, NEW DELHI 110059

ISBN 81-7022-328-8

First Published 1991

Published and Printed by
Ashok Kumar Mittal
Concept Publishing Company
A/15-16, Commercial Block, Mohan Garden
NEW DELHI 110059 (India)

Lasertypeset by
Microtech Advance Printing Systems (Pvt.) Ltd.
H-13, Bali Nagar
NEW DELHI 110015

FOREWORD

DEVELOPMENT IS not merely a matter of economics. All paths to development have consequences for society in general, and some of these might be undesirable. As the structure of an economy changes different groups will be affected in different ways. There will be many gainers perhaps, but there might also be many losers. This is the stuff of which politics is made.

This book is the outcome of the author's Ph.D. thesis in which he analysed various development policy options which have been pursued in Karnataka. Based on an extensive study of the theoretical literature as it is, the applied nature of the work makes it valuable to those charged with the responsibility of future planning because the writer has brought out into the open the conflict between the development paths pointed out by "efficiency" and "equity". Only when the policy maker is aware of the likely consequences of specific measures can a balance between the conflicting demands be obtained.

The work adds to the sum of knowledge concerning Karnataka but, more importantly it increases the understanding of the effects of development measures in a way that has much wider application.

University of New South Wales W.E. HOTCHKISS

ACKNOWLEDGEMENTS

I CONSIDER it my duty to place on record my grateful thanks to all those who have helped me in successfully completing this work. While I sit to recollect the most important amongst them, quite a few intellectuals and institutions come to crowd my memory. It is a very difficult task indeed to reasonably evaluate the help, assistance and guidance rendered by them. And moreover, many of them wish to remain anonymous. But academic decency demands that I mention at least a few names which stand out as very near and dear.

To mention only a few to whom I owe a special debt of gratitude, I must begin with Dr. M.C. Kodli, under whose able guidance and supervision this thesis was prepared, and for whose help that transcends the confines of the norms of his accredited duties, I am deeply indebted. He did instill in me the much needed confidence, particularly at times when it threatened to desert me. And had it not been for his personal interest and perseverance, I would not have completed the task so easily. I owe to him all my unqualified gratitude.

I had the rare privilege of getting the kind counsel of the outstanding academics of the Centre of Advanced Study in Economics, Bombay, particularly of Dr. P.R. Brahmananda, Dr. J.C. Sandesara, Dr. P.R. Panchamukhi and Dr. S.P. Goswami during my stay at the Centre as a short term visiting fellow in 1983. They were kind enough to give me the much needed direction besides exposing me to the subtler aspects of research in Industrial Economics. I am highly indebted to them.

I am highly grateful to Dr. Abdul Aziz, Dr. (Mrs.) Hemalata Rao and Dr. R.S. Deshpande of the Institute for Social and Economic Change Bangalore, but for whose constant encouragement, suggestions and advice, I would not have completed my task in time. As a recipient of their unconditional help, I do find the influence of the valuable guidance of Dr. Abdul Aziz and Dr. R.S. Deshpande in almost every chapter of this work. I thank them very sincerely.

My well-wishers and academic associates, Dr. H. Basanna, Dr.

R.V. Dadibhavi, Dr. M.S. Kallur and Professor B.M. Hurkadli, richly deserve my grateful thanks for their continual encouragement and assistance. I am indebted to them.

Special mention is to be made of the tiring task of going through the manuscripts by Mr. M Thangaraj, Mr. Rajasekharan and Mr. Selvaraj, Ph.D. fellows of the Institute for Social and Economic Change, Bangalore. I did receive a lot of research assistance from Mr. A.M. Jose, Mr. Jose Thomas, Mr. Mohanasundaram and Mr. Gopinath Reddy of the same Institute. I am thankful to all these young intellectuals.

Mr. S. Pannaraj and Mr. A. Rudragouda, Chartered Accountants, Bellary, very richly deserve my gratitude. They helped me at all the stages of data processing and analysis. They really did a wonderful job for which I can only say a very big "Thank You".

Mr. M.B. Goud, Director of District and Regional Planning, and Mr. K. Sankar Rao, Research Officer, Special Studies Division, Department of Planning, Bangalore, did their best to procure and supply most of the data required for my work. The other gentlemen who helped me in the collection of data are Mr. Basavarajappa, Joint Director, and Mr. Manu, Deputy Director of the Directorate of Economics and Statistics, and Mr. Raghavendra Rao of the Census Directorate, Bangalore. I thank all of them very sincerely.

Libraries have a definite and determinant role in every research endeavour. In this regard, I must say with all sincerity that had it not been for the assistance I received from the Librarians of Karnatak University, Bombay University, Madras University, ISEC, RBI and IDBI libraries, my present work would not have acquired the academic authenticity which it has now. I am ever grateful to them and their staff.

Amongst the hundreds of individuals who crowd the columns of my memory in connection with my research endeavour, two of my colleagues, Mr. P. Gurubasappa and Mr. S. Jayanna, stand out very distinct and significant. If at all I could get relief from the diverse academic and mundane problems, it was only through the ready and unsolicited help that came to me from these two friends of mine. I am deeply indebted to them.

My sincere thanks are also due to Mr. Narayan of ISEC, Bangalore, and Mr. S.B. Pawar of Karnatak University, Dharwad, for doing the important job of typing the thesis well in time.

And finally, in a sentimental mood, I do feel that I would not have achieved anything worth in the academic field without the sacrifices made by my wife, Smt. B. Padmavathi. At the same time I cannot afford to forget the humble assistance rendered to me by my children, Madhavi, Ravi, Raghu and Giri. I thank them all with all my love and affection.

Dharwad B. SESHADRI

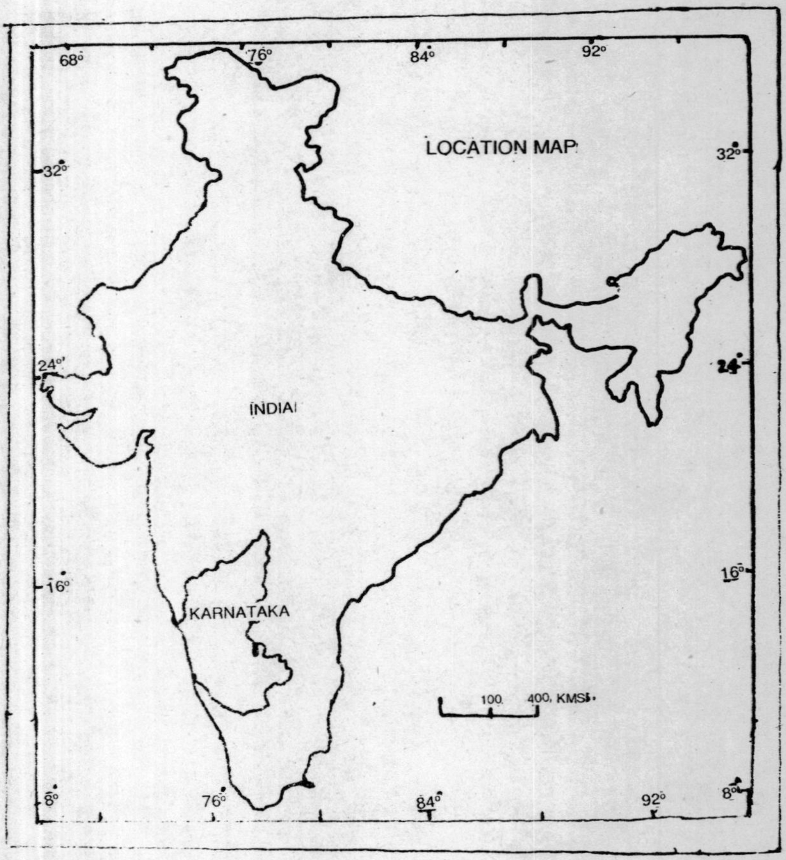

Map : Location Map

CONTENTS

LIST OF TABLES

LIST OF APPENDIX TABLES

LIST OF MAPS

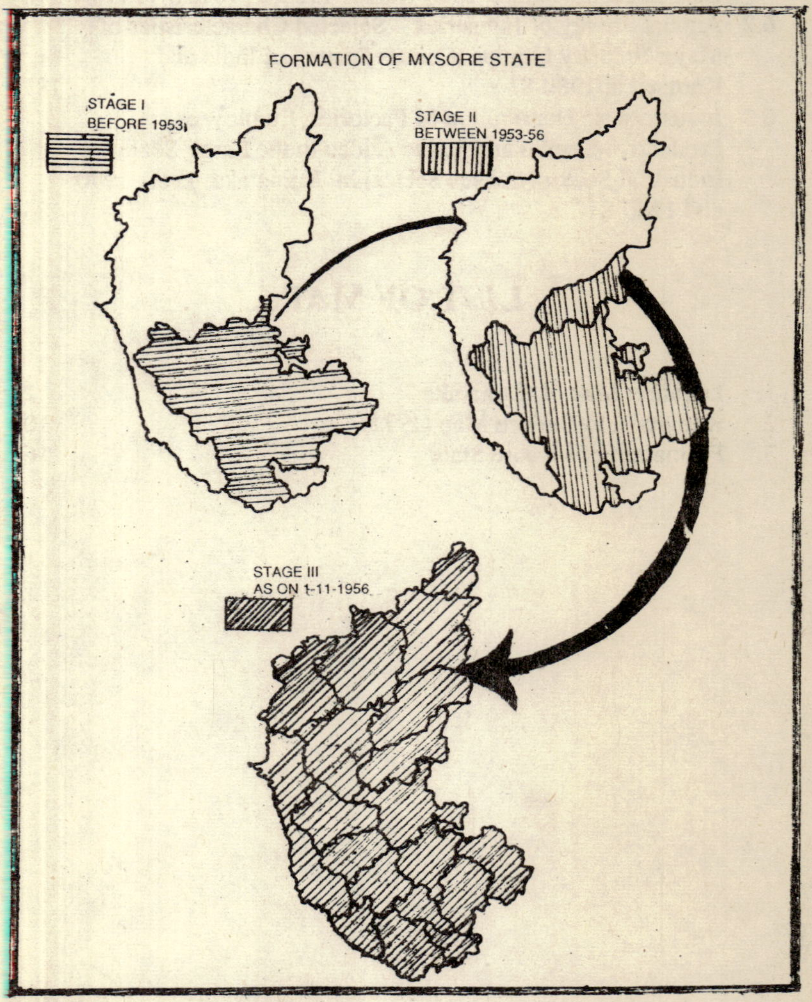

Map : Formation of Mysore State

1

INTRODUCTION

IN KEEPING with the academic intentions of "introduction" in social science research, a sincere attempt is made in this chapter to depict a succinct and suggestive portrayal of the inquiry in hand. Since "industrialisation" constitutes the core of the study, effort is made not only to trace the origin of modern industrialisation, but also to identify its dynamic role in the economic growth of developing economies. The most acceptable explanation for the unprecedented explosion of interest in industrialisation in the 19th and 20th centuries is discussed. The regional and structural dimensions of industrialisation at various spatial levels, and the diverse problems that go with them, are highlighted while presenting the problem of the study. And, above all, the dissertation design is also delineated in this chapter. This chapter consists of 10 sections. The first section gives a synoptic exposition of the unprecedented economic revolution that was heralded by the Industrial Revolution of the 18th century. Among other things, to identify the decisive role of industrialisation in the economic development of a region, a brief discussion of the 'industry-agriculture priority controversy' is presented in the second section. The third section reasons out the phenomenal explosion of interest in industrialisation. The fourth section provides a theoretical explanation of the precise ways in which industrialisation acts as a major ingredient of economic development. The problem of the study is stated in the fifth section; the genesis of regional disparities which are inherent in industrialisation and in the economic development through industrialisation, is identified; the nature of structural changes that generally take place in a tri-sectoral economy during the process of industrialisation is examined; and the diverse facets of the regional and structural problems which are found at various areal levels are brought out. The objectives and hypotheses of the study are stated and elucidated in the sixth and seventh sections respectively. The nature, scope and importance of the study are discussed in the eighth section.

The ninth section gives the methodology of the study. And the tenth section details the chapter scheme of the dissertation.

1.1 Some Reflections on Industrial Revolution

For the first time in the recorded history of mankind, a major breakthrough in the economic development and growth, which was destined to influence the very nature and course of the socio-economic and politico-cultural development of the world for centuries to come, came through the Industrial Revolution of the 18th century. The Industrial Revolution which had its birth in England, heralded altogether a new culture not only at the national level, but also at the global level. Considering the tremendous bearing that the Industrial Revolution technology had and continues to have on the economic changes and progress of nations, Hartwell calls it a "great discontinuity of history", and Polanyi calls it a "great transformation".[1] From a purely economic stand point, the Industrial Revolution is seen as an abrupt discontinuity in the rate of economic growth, and particularly in the rate of industrial growth.[2] In fact it marks a great divide between a world of slow growth with relatively static or semi-static economic structure in which population, output and real incomes were rising slowly (or not at all), and a world of much faster economic growth in which population has increased at an almost frightening rate, in which there have been sustained increases in the output and per capita real income.[3] Of course, if one scans through the development experiences of the industrialised countries of the North, one cannot fail to get the impression that it is indeed a dynamic historic innovation in the known history of mankind.

The unprecedented experience of the phenomenal growth initiated by the Industrial Revolution did not and could not get itself confined to the politico-geographical boundaries of England; through international economic connections which were quite necessary for the sustenance of the higher rates of growth of output and employment that were emerging in England, it came to embrace many other countries during the 19th and 20th centuries. David, F.Walker says that ever since the occurrence of the Industrial Revolution, a healthy dynamic manufacturing sector has been synonymous with progress and wealth, at least in the eyes of a substantial number of people.[4] There is also ample evidence to show this; by consciously employing the Industrial Revolution technology, the centrally planned economies like the

USSR, and the free enterprise economies like Japan have come to experience spectacular growth rates and increases in per capita real incomes and standards of living. *Inter alia*, the Industrial Revolution, by effecting significant changes in the economic structure, has been successful in accelerating the process of economic development.

However, the influence of the Industrial Revolution did not end up with revolutionising the growth rates; it went beyond them into the very thinking and sociology of knowledge of historians and economists. They had to revise their thinking, analysis and interpretation of growth-promoting factors. Among other things, there came into being a new belief that industrialisation is an indispensable means to cure the chronic disease of socio-economic stagnation, and to achieve and maintain higher growth rates, higher levels of employment and higher standards of living. And by passage of time, the experience of success of the North has made the policy-makers all over the world to equate "industrialisation" with "economic development". The new sociology of knowledge and thinking evolved out of the early phases of industrialisation started gaining international acceptance with the historic decolonisation in the 1940s. The countries which freed themselves, for the first time, from the callous clutches of socio-economic and political slavery, realised, to their shocking surprise, that they had been condemned to live in the maelstrom of poverty and stagnation for quite sometime. Political independence and sovereignty, perhaps, could not have any meaning to those economically crippled countries. So, they must have started a frantic search for some dependable and relatively infallible measures which could initiate and accelerate the process of liberation from the newly recognised underdevelopment trap. Probably, it was in such a psychological moment that the Industrial Revolution technology instantly caught the imagination of the less developed countries. And the earlier experiences helped a lot in re-emphasising faith in industrialisation. The belief that industrialisation leads to the path of progress follows directly from the historical experience of Europe and North America; equally it follows from the hot house pattern of development followed by the Soviet Union.

In the early 1940s itself P.N. Rosenstein Rodan argued that industrialisation is the way to achieve a more equal distribution of incomes between different areas of the world by raising incomes in depressed areas at a higher rate than in the rich areas. Later, in the early 1950s and 1960s. W.A. Lewis and Raul Prebisch urged for industrialisation of the Caribbean countries and Latin America respectively, as by far the best opportunity to capture the advantages of technical progress [5]. According to A.G. Mezerik, from almost the time of their independence, most underdeveloped countries recognised that they must develop manufacturing industries to serve home and, perhaps, foreign markets; towards this end they placed great emphasis on industrialisation, which they regarded from the first as a *sine qua non* of rapid economic development[6]. "It (industrialisation) is an effort", says Murrey, D. Bryce, "in which the underdeveloped countries place a major hope of finding a solution to their problems of poverty, insecurity and overpopulation, and ending their newly realised backwardness in the modern world".[7] In the second half of the sixties, the Third Cambridge Conference Report on "Industrialisation in Developing Countries" pointed out that everybody in the developing countries wants to industrialise swiftly. Industry glitters with promise. Nothing else seems to hold out much hope of fulfilling the expectations of new nationalism, winning economic independence and raising prosperity dramatically. Nothing else seems to cast off the millstones of population increase and falling prices for primary producers that, in spite of their doubled efforts, have made them worse off than before[8]. Jawaharlal Nehru, the first Prime Minister of independent India, while emphasising the decisive role of industrialisation, went to the extent of saying that real progress must ultimately depend on industralisation.[9] And Sir M. Visvesvaraya, the principal architect of industrial Mysore, while underlining the historic indispensability of industralisation, is stated to have said, "industrialise or perish".

1.2 Industry-Agriculture Priority Controversy

However, the excessive obsession for industralisation to initiate and accelerate higher growth rates should not make the policy-makers in developing countries to ignore the claims of agriculture in accelerating the growth process. In view of the fact that industrialisation is one of the determinants and not the sole determinant of development, and with a view to identifying the precise ways in which industralisation influences economic development, it is desirable to have some idea about "industry-first" or "agriculture-first" controversy. Here, it is necessary to note that industry and agriculture are not the alternative but the complementary tools of economic development. Ronald Robinson finds sharply divided opinion about the relative positions of industry and agriculture in the overall development plans; one school of thought backs the agricultural horse to pull the industrial cart; and the other, more radical school backs the industrial horse to draw the agricultural cart.[10]. There is also a third school which identifies a symbiotic relationship between the two.

The industry-first model has mostly emerged out of the socio-economic and demographic conditions obtaining in the developing countries of Asia. Harold Brookfield summarises this model thus: "The argument for industry-first strategy depends on the demonstrated or supposed ability of industry, and especially large-scale industry, to raise the national income per capita, create investment capital, and save foreign exchange through import substitution, much faster than any other method. In almost every industrialising country, the rate of growth of industrial output exceeds the rate of growth in other productive sectors. It is also argued that the social reorganisation accompanying industry forces the reconstruction of society as a whole. . . . For these reasons, industry can draw the unemployed and underemployed off the land, gainfully occupy them, and so create a market for the produce of an agricultural sector relieved of so many unproductive or less productive mouths to feed: this is an argument applied especially in the Asian situation. . . . But the strongest argument of all follows from the wider case for accelerated economic growth; if this will provide the resources with which to develop the whole economy, spread welfare and alleviate poverty, then the means which will accelerate growth the fastest are the means that should be employed first. And these, on the basis of a mass of empirical evidence, are to be found through industrialisation".[11]

On the other hand, equally forceful arguments are advanced to support the agriculture-first stand. Some arguments emphasise the ability of agriculture to provide the much needed surplus of labour, food and capital to the industrial sector; some others underline the favourable economic characteristics of agriculture in terms of the productivity of investment, the provision of employment, and the distribution of income; and yet others suggest the complementarity of agriculture and other sectors at the level of final and intermediate demand. Arthur Lewis argues that most certain way to promote industrialisation is to lay the foundation it requires by taking vigorous steps to raise food production per person engaged in agriculture. This is the surest way of producing the large and ever increasing demand for manufactures without which there can be little industrialisation.[12] In economies which are primarily agrarian, the purchasing power made available by agriculture determines the size of the home market for manufactures. Its food surpluses decide the number of workers that can be absorbed in non-agricultural sectors. It also provides the much needed capital and foreign exchange for industrialisation. Industry being capital intensive does not provide adequate employment, and this can only be generated on a sufficient scale in agriculture. Agricultural development is said to improve the distribution of income more than industrialisation. Above all, agriculture helps economic development by developing desirable linkages with other sectors at intermediate stages in the production process. Most of these arguments are advanced keeping in view the situation prevailing in Africa and Latin America.

Now it is universally recognised that *per se* neither industry nor agriculture can accelerate economic development on a long-run basis; both of them, being mutually reinforcing in the process of development, need be developed simultaneously, of course, by assigning different degrees of importance depending upon the resource endowment, stage of development, and development objectives of the countries concerned. And none can categorically deny their interdependence. Eugene Staley argues: "Improvement in the productivity of agriculture is one of the most solid means of promoting industrialisation; in fact, unless agriculture does modernise substantially, industrial expansion in most underdeveloped countries is likely to be cut short by lack of markets, for the great majority of the population will not have the necessary purchasing power. Conversely, agricultural improvements cannot go very far unless there is industrial development to take up the released manpower and to provide a solid technical base for the equipment and services essential to modernised agriculture."[13]

But, all societies are faced with the long-run desirability of industrialisation as a means of higher productivity and living standards; and to secure this, all societies need both accumulate industrial capital and solve the problem of food supplies to the industrial sector. All the arguments concerning the priority to be assigned to industry and agriculture, explicitly or implicitly point out one thing about industrialisation and economic development nexus, viz. that countries will not become rich unless at some stage they industrialise.[14]

1.3 Reasons for the Explosion of Interest in Industrialisation

The reasons for the unprecedented explosion of interest in

industrialisation for nearly 100 years are not hard to find. As the ensuing discussion unfolds, by far the most important reason for the incessant craze for rapid industrialisation in the underdeveloped and developing countries has been the identification of a positive nexus between industrialisation and economic prosperity. Samuel Lurie argues: "Industrialisation and poverty are two sides of the same medal. The most industrialised countries are the most prosperous, the least industrialised, almost without exception, poor. The nations of Europe plus Japan, the USSR, the USA and Canada, being the most industrialised countries reap the lion's share of the benefits. The 90 underdeveloped and developing countries account for but five per cent of the world's industrial output. In the industrialised nations live no more than 18 per cent of the world's population, yet they garner about 75 per cent of the world's income. All the other of the world's people are on the outside of charmed circle of industrialised societies. They are left to divide no more than a quarter of the world's income, and even this share decreases."[15] Being mainly the producers of the land-based products, the underdeveloped countries have come to notice a positive connection between wealth and standard of living of a country, and the extent of its industrialisation. For them, maldistribution of industrial activity seems to be a major cause for inter-regional disparities in the levels of development.

Another important reason for the explosion of interest in industrialisation is the phenomenal output of literature on both theoretical and empirical inquiries. The writings of economists like G. Myrdal came to confer international respectability on the belief about the historic necessity of industrialisation. Way back in the 1950s itself he said: "Manufacturing industry represents, in a sense, a higher stage of production. In advanced countries, the development of manufacturing industry has been concomitant with these countries' spectacular economic progress and rise in levels of living; many of its products are indeed almost symbolic of a high living standard. Not least in the underdeveloped countries, the productivity of manpower in industry tends to be considerably greater than in the traditional agricultural pursuits. Industrialisation, and the growth of that part of the working population that is engaged in industry, is therefore a means of raising national income per capita. In countries like India and Japan, with a high ratio of population to natural resources and, in particular, to land, manufacturing industry represents virtually the only hope of greatly increasing labour productivity and raising levels of living, however much is done to improve agriculture. But even in countries where population pressure is lower, as, for example, in many Latin American countries, the successful exploitation of a more favourable relation between population and natural resources requires mostly the growth of manufacturing industry."[16] Thus Myrdal emphasised the indispensability of industrialisation to achieve higher productivity, higher per capita real incomes and higher levels of living.

And the empirical studies of Simon Kuznets,[17] H.B. Chenery,[18] and H.B. Chenery and L. Taylor[19] further concretised the belief. If one scans through their studies, the impression becomes inescapable that no major country has yet become rich without having become industrialised, though the pace of industrialisation in relation to the rate of increase of per capita income varies significantly between different countries. T.C. Zacharia[20] and T.Y. Srinivas[21] in their doctoral dissertations have identified a definite and determinant role that industrialisation has in the development strategies of developing countries in general and that of India in particular.

Thus there are a number of expert expressions which recognise explicitly the direct nexus between industrialisation and economic development. Of course, today with a 200-year experience of industrialisation, nobody can afford to deny the fact that industrialisation is an integral part of the process of economic development, though one may refuse to consider it an indispensable instrument of economic development. According to R.B. Sutcliffe, the vast literature on industrialisation though does not prove that countries must industrialise to become rich, it does, however, suggest a connection; and a general presumption, if not exactly an argument in favour of immediate industrialisation, sometimes springs directly from such connection.[22] Today, most of the developing countries, including India, have been launching massive programmes of industrialisation not only as a means of achieving higher levels of development, but also as a means to ensure spatial equity in development; and such a measure does assume some kind of positive connection between industrialisation and economic development. In fact, in India, establishment of industries is one of the methods we have tried to adopt in improving the economic situation of backward areas.

1.4 Industrialisation-Economic Development Nexus

Very often, economists speak of a direct nexus between industrialisation and economic development. Of course, with the above background, it would not be difficult to comprehend the precise ways in which industrialisation accelerates economic development. Industrialisation affects economic development both as cause and effect of the latter. R.B. Sutcliffe opines: "Industrialisation is in one sense a process which has invariably been the outcome or accompaniment of economic development. In another sense, industrialisation denotes a set of policies which, more than any other broad set of policies, is seen as a means towards economic development."[23] Some of the important channels through which industrialisation promotes economic development are discussed below:

Among other things, economic development implies higher productivity per capita. And per capita productivity is relatively high in the industry-based secondary sector. As productivity increases through industrialisation, income increases and, as a consequence, the expenditure pattern undergoes a change; the demand for manufactured consumer goods, which has a higher income elasticity, tends to rise rapidly. Such a rise in demand for manufactured goods is likely to be particularly pronounced where development is accompanied by the transformation of a partial subsistence economy into a full market economy T.C. Zacharia argues that increased productivity in sectors outside as well inside the industry will call for an increased application of manufactured goods.[24]

Industrialisation accelerates economic development through structural transformation. Economic development implies significant changes in the sectoral composition of income and employment. And by definition industrialisation involves fundamental changes in the structure of an economy both in terms of output and occupational pattern of workforce. As a first step, industrialisation initiates a shift away from the land-based agriculture and allied activities to the man- and machine-based secondary and tertiary economic activities. Such a shift which moves workforce from the relatively low-productivity economic activities to the relatively high-productivity economic activities accelerates economic development. With some time-and region-based differences, such a structural change is found to have been taking place in the industrially advanced as well as in the currently industrialising economies.

Industrialisation promotes economic development by providing the much needed scaffolding for the accelerated development of agriculture which is an integral part of the dynamic process of economic development. Most of the critical inputs which increase the productivity of land are produced by the industrial sector. For instance, chemical fertilisers, pesticides and insecticides, and agricultural machinery are provided by industries. Similarly, large-scale commercial farming can be sustained only by developing irrigation projects, and extensive transport and communication networks; and industrialisation is necessary in developing these facilities. Thus industrialisation becomes necessary in initiating and sustaining higher productivity in agriculture, which in turn helps economic development.

Industrialisation has a direct bearing on the welfare content of economic development. Economic development is sought after, not because it is an end in itself, but because it acts as a major means in promoting the economic welfare of the people. It is generally said that the economic welfare of a society is reflected by the quantity and quality of the goods which are made available to the people. Experience shows that majority of the people in industrialised countries have access to a relatively larger number of goods of better quality – necessities, comforts and luxuries – than the people in developing countries.

Industrialisation is capable of administering shock treatment to the economies which have been suffering from the traditional disease of underdevelopment. To a great extent, it alone can break the vicious circle of poverty and stagnation in a relatively short period and thereby put a nation on the path of economic progress. Experience tells us that the vicious circle of poverty and backwardness can be broken decisively, and in a short period, only to the extent that the modern science and technology are extensively applied to use a country's resources both extensively and intensively to raise the per capita income levels; and this obviously calls for industrialisation.

Industrialisation promotes economic development by effecting that attitudinal change in the people which is conducive to rapid economic development. By and large, all the traditional societies are change-resistant. The change-resistant attitude reflects the anti-developmental mental make-up of the people. But industrialisation initiates such socio-economic changes which make people to accept change as a necessary condition of economic progress. Josef Bognar says that a society thinking in traditional categories is slow in accepting new norms. In a society based on tradition, events take place at an established inherited pace, whereas industrialisation activates forces alien to traditional community. Industrialisation gradually transforms the life of the regions, influences the aspirations and efforts of the people, their choice regarding training and education. It changes the very way of public thinking itself.[25]

Industrialisation promotes economic development through its intra-sectoral and inter-sectoral complementarity. Intra-sectorally or internally, the interdependence of consumer goods and capital goods industries accelerates economic development through the interaction of multiplier and accelerator. Inter-sectorally or externally, it induces a higher level of activity in the primary and tertiary sectors by consuming their output and providing their inputs. Owing to such internal and external complementarity, it is capable of providing strong growth stimuli to the stagnant and semi-stagnant agrarian economies.

Thus, the preceding discussion of this section shows that industrialisation is an integral part of the dynamic process of economic development, and it has a definite and determinant place in that process. Industrialisation by effecting a shift of workforce away from the relatively less productive and over-crowded primary sector to the secondary and tertiary sectors enables an economy to attain higher productivity per worker and higher net domestic product. By its very nature, it creates and enlarges sectoral inter-dependence which is highly conducive for higher economic activity. Industrialisation throws up opportunities for entrepreneurship and employment in the secondary and tertiary sectors. Above all, by making available a wide range of consumer goods and also higher purchasing power, it enables the people to attain a higher standard of living and a higher degree of economic welfare.

1.5 Statement of the Problem

Although nothing final can be said in precise terms to what extent the enthralling history of Industrial Revolution and the success story of industrialisation of the recent past would provide reliable guidance to the currently industrialising countries of the South in formulating and executing their industrialisation policies and programmes, one would be doing great injustice to the Industrial Revolution technology if one refuses to recognise its ability in sloughing of the dead skin of economic stagnation, and in ushering in an era of unprecedented sustained substantial growth rates. But, industrialisation brings with it a big train of socio-economic and politico-cultural problems. The present inquiry is designed to deal with only certain economic aspects of the regional and structural problems that generally go with industrialisation. As the dialectics of development would have it, industrialisation has given birth to an economically unsound, socially disastrous, morally indefensible and politically dangerous phenomenon, viz. regional disparities in development. And the structural changes that accompany industrialisation affect the inter-sectoral and intra-sectoral importance in terms of output, employment, productive capital, etc.

Spatially speaking, generally, regional disparities in development are a reflection of the structural situation prevailing in different regions. The North-South problem is not something peculiar to India as a nation, and Karnataka as a State; it is a global phenomenon. The highly industrialised North and the slowly industrialising South are alike confronted with the problem of regional disparities; the only difference is that the disparities seem to be more pronounced in the South than in the North. A.R. Pred says that the problem with industrialisation is that it seems to be inextricably bound up with an increase in spatial disparity.[26]

It is of interest of know that the roots of this phenomenon of spatial disparities are to be found not in the Industrial Revolution of the 18th century, but in the historic events that occurred in the 15th century. Almost 500 years ago, in the closing decade of the 15th century, two bold voyages from Iberia resulted in a chain of events that made the world one, but have not yet ceased to widen the disparities between areal groupings of mankind. Two types of European dominance, two types of dependence were initiated by these voyages. The Western voyage of Columbus opened the way for exploitative colonisation and the direct control of one society by another; the Eastern voyage of de-Gama began the more enduring commercial dominance/dependence relationship supported by sea-borne power. What began in so small a way in 1492 and 1498 was the process of "interdependent development". The sort of long-distance relationship that was created was new in the world history. The whole contemporary world problem that we call variously, that of "underdevelopment", "modernisation", or the "economic development of th Third World", is concerned at the base with a dominance/dependence relationship that is expressed in a great many ways. Most obviously it is expressed in the contrast between the rich and the poor countries, the former group enjoying per capita incomes 10 or 12 times larger than those of the latter group.[27]

And the areal economic dualism so initiated by geographical

discoveries has been very consistently perpetuated and accentuated by industrialisation; industrialisation has been successful in thickening the line of demarcation which separates the developed North from the underdeveloped and developing South. And by passage of time, the gap between the North and the South has been widening leading to unprecedented tensions at various spatial levels. The history of economic development provides ample evidence in support of the view that development through industrialisation leads to spatial disparities. Development, for diverse socio-economic and politico-demographic reasons, has a tendency to get itself concentrated in certain regions; it does not appear in all the regions of a nation or State simultaneously. And also, when once an area starts growing, it grows at a faster rate than the lagging regions through what Myrdal calls the "process of cumulative causation". Industrial development or economic development, *per se*, cannot spread evenly over any geographical region – be it a nation or a State. One general observation about the process of development is that the developed metropole feeds on the underdeveloped periphery. The highly industrialised regions, whether nations or States, have some underdeveloped segments, and the under-industrialised regions have developed segments in them.

Today almost every country is aware of the possible causes and the horrible consequences of spatial disparities. The potential danger of spatial disparities has found its forceful expression in the words of Simon Kuznets. He says, ". . .the stresses of the dislocation incident to early phases of industrialisation in the developed countries were sufficiently acute to strain the political and social fabric, force major political reforms, and sometimes result in civil war. . . . Can the frame-work of the underdeveloped societies withstand the strain which further widening of income inequality is likely to generate?"[28] Here it is worth recalling the prediction made by Robock, H. Stefan in 1959 about the Indian subcontinent in his capacity as a U.N. expert on Area Surveys. He said, "As a practical matter, regional factors underlie many of the pressing economic, political and social problems now being faced in a large number of underdeveloped countries. In Pakistan (East and West) and in Indonesia (Jawa versus outer islands), regional economic and political problems are so critical that they have at times threatened the long-run existence of the States itself."[29] (We know that today there is no united Pakistan; Bangladesh, the eastern part of Pakistan, has become an independent nation.)

India, with its politico-economic federal structure is not free from the North-South problem; the problem is found at two administratively strategic areal levels – inter-State and inter-district. Only a few States show high industrial development, and others suffer lamentable deficiency of industrial activities. Furthermore, even in the highly industrialised States, the picture is one of inter-district imbalances; only a few pockets are industrially developed, and the other areas have remained as backward as the most backward parts of the country.[30] The empirical inquiry made by S.A. Pandit way back in 1949 shows that India was not only industrially underdeveloped, but also exhibited all the evils of maldistribution and acute concentration of industrial activity.[31] The then existing maldistribution of industrial activity might have been, among other things, due to the relative free play of the market forces, and the absence of any kind of regional-equity-biased industrial policy during the British regime. But it is astonishing to note that such maldistribution persists in the Indian States despite the conscious implementation of regional policies.

Though the origin of regional policy in India can be traced back to the 1945 Report of the Economic Adviser to the Government of India, but an effective beginning was made only in the Fourth and Fifth Five Year Plans. While analysing regional policy in his doctoral dissertation, S.C. Patnaik says that mentioning of "regional balance" in the earlier plan documents was more casual and pious with a view to demonstrating the planners' awareness to the regional economic distress, rather than meant to be operational for removing that distress. Investment in the plan was mainly two-dimensional in allocation – sectoral and temporal. The spatial aspect of investment was never accepted as an additional dimension having any relevance to the development of the country. He also points out that the Government of India in their Fourth and Fifth Five Year Plans have accepted the goal of regional development more clearly, and have taken steps for setting up agencies and formulating policies having greater spatial orientation. And the orientation of central allocation of investment and financial grants to the constituent States on the basis of a composite index of economic and social backwardness are some of the measures of newly emerging regional policy to an otherwise "spaceless" temporal approach to investment planning.[32] Even then inter-State disparities persist in India.

It is heartening to note that Karnataka has the distinction of being a pioneer State in planned industrialisation. It has also a long history of regional policy. Right from the dawn of the present century, administrators and scholars have been alive to the gravity of the problem of regional disparities. The chief architects of industrial Karnataka – M. Visvesvaraya and Mirza Ismail – were not content with merely knowing the adverse consequences of regional imbalances, but they did plan for areally balanced industrial development. But, for reasons beyond their control, the mixed economy set up enabled the areal disparities to emerge and grow. And the areal disparities got a good grounding in 1956 when the State was reorganised and enlarged on linguistic basis. The Government of Karnataka, in keeping with the regional policy of the Centre, has been using its industrial dispersal policy and economic planning with a view to securing development without spatial disparities. But, even after the completion of the Sixth Five Year Plan, Karnataka continues to present a sad spectacle of maldistribution of industrial as well as economic activity across her districts.

The regional dispersal of industrial and economic activity involves some sort of conflict between the twin components of the growth objective, viz. efficiency and equity. Both the Centre and the State have been facing what may aptly be described as "dispersal dilemma". The path of faster economic growth may imply sharp geographic inequalities concentrating wealth and power in a few advanced centres, and condemning backward areas to lengthy periods of poverty. Conversely the policies of regional equalisation may slow down the growth of the entire economy. That means, accent on "efficiency" favours agglomeration, and accent on "equity" favours deglomeration. As such, the secret of successful industrial and economic planning lies in striking a judicious balance between "efficiency" and "equity".

Industrialisation has its structural dimension too. The economic structure of an economy undergoes a change the moment it begins to industrialise itself. It has been observed that economic development involves an inevitable shift away from the primary sector to the secondary and tertiary sectors. In fact such a structural change, which is the essence of economic development, is often referred to as industrialisation. T.Y. Srinivas argues that structural shift which results in a reduction in the share of agriculture in national income and employment, and a corresponding improvement in the share of manufacturing and service sectors is a historically observed fact of development.[33] The observed patterns of industrialisation indicate that usually in the initial stages, the primary sector is the dominant sector both in terms of output and employment; and as industrialisation gathers momentum, the secondary and tertiary sectors grow in importance, and the importance of the primary sector starts declining; in the second stage, among the non-primary sectors, the secondary sector becomes the dominant sector; and in the third stage, the tertiary sector gains an upper hand over the secondary sector and claims a relatively higher share of output and employment than the latter. But owing to some demographic and non-demographic reasons, majority of the currently industrialising countries in general, and India in particular, have not been exhibiting such an observed pattern. No doubt, industrialisation in these countries has been causing structural changes and noticeable shifts away from the primary to the non-primary sectors, but to start with itself the tertiary sector has come to be more predominant than the secondary sector. This type of sectoral leap is also observed in the State and district economies of Karnataka. Such an aberration from the normal pattern has been a cause of concern to planners at all spatial levels, because it engenders several problems that go with unplanned urbanisation.

Another facet of structural change is concerned with the changing importance of agro- and non-agro-based industries on the one hand, and that of consumer goods and capital goods industries, on the other. Generally, the initial stages of industrialisation are characterised by the predominance of the agro-based and consumer goods industries, whereas the mature stages of industrialisation are characterised by the predominance of non-agro-based and capital goods industries. But in some of the States in India, including Karnataka, the non-agro-based and capital goods industries seem to have been dominating the industrial activity even in the early phases of industrialisation. Such a deviation from the normal pattern was not experienced by early industrialisations; it may be the experience of latecomers. This new pattern is indicative of the fact that the latecomers can skip some of the stages of industrialisation. Of course, in that process, they may give rise to some new problems too.

Thus, the problem of industrialisation of Karnataka is viewed from two distinct but related angles, viz. regional and structural.

1.6 Objectives of the Study

Keeping in view the research effort that has so far gone into the regional and structural aspects of industrialisation and development in Karnataka since the 1930s, the researcher has set the following objectives for the inquiry on hand:

(i) To identify theoretically the precise ways in which industrialisation promotes economic development.
(ii) To get a thorough understanding of the directional and dimensional contours of inter-district disparities in industrialisation and economic development in Karnataka.
(iii) To know whether the inter-temporal trends in regional disparities have been favouring convergence or divergence.
(iv) To identify the localisation of the various large-scale industries in the State in the national perspective.
(v) To examine the inter-temporal growth of large-scale industries at the State level and of small-scale industries at the district level.
(vi) By examining the changing ratios of the consumer goods and capital goods industries, it is intended to identify the stages of industrialisation through which the State has been passing.
(vii) In order to get a proper comprehension of the dynamics of structural transformation that has been taking place in Karnataka – both at the State and district levels – the study wishes to make an in-depth examination of the inter-sectoral behaviour in the tri-sectoral economy of Karnataka.
(viii) Above all, the study wishes to highlight the policy implications which would be useful to the Government of Karnataka in formulating its regional development policy with a special accent on spatial equity and sectoral balance.

1.7 Hypotheses Proposed to be Tested in the Study

In the light of the objectives cited in the preceding section, the present study attempts to test the following hypotheses which are directly related to the regional and structural aspects of industrialisation in Karnataka.

1.7.1 Hypotheses Related to Regional Disparities

Geographically, growth is looked upon as essentially unbalanced. There is a widespread belief among development theorists that economic progress does not appear everywhere at the same time, and that once it appears, powerful forces make for a spatial concentration of economic growth around the initial points. It is more so in transitional societies. For a variety of reasons, in the early phases of industrialisation activities come to be concentrated in one or a few regions or centres. John Friedman and William Alonso opine that such centres grow so rapidly as to create problems of an entirely new order, but also act as suction pumps, pulling in the more dynamic elements from the more static regions. The remainder of the country is relegated to a second-class peripheral position. It is placed in a quasi-colonial relationship to the Centre, experiencing net outflows of people, capital and resources, most of which redound to the advantage of the Centre where economic growth will tend to be rapid, sustained and cumulative. As a result, income differences between the Centre and the periphery tend to widen.[34]

This geographically unbalanced nature of industrialisation and development has initiated a historic debate on the temporal pattern of the behaviour of divergence-convergence forces. The theoretical and empirical studies made so far reveal at least three distinct hypotheses on the possible behaviour of divergence-convergence forces in the process of development of an economy – be it a nation or a State. And all the three hypotheses[35] stated below are tested with specific reference to the inter-district disparities in industrialisation and development in Karnataka:

(i) The first one is the "self-perpetuation" hypothesis propounded by R.B. Hughes and found empirically valid by E.J.R. Booth. They hold the view that regional disparities diverge in the process of national economic development.

(ii) The second one is the "accordian effect" hypothesis propounded by F.A. Hanna, and found empirically valid by H.S. Perloff *et al.*, and F.A. Hanna. The proponents hold the view that regional disparities converge in the course of national economic development.

(iii) The third one is the well-known "concentration cycle" hypothesis propounded by Gunnar Myrdal, A.O. Hirschman, J.G. Williamson and William Alonso, and found empirically valid by J.G. Williamson and I.S. Koropeckyj. They hold the view that regional disparities diverge initially only to converge later on, and graphically the temporal behaviour of disparities traces an inverted "U".

1.7.2 Hypotheses Related to the Inter-Sectoral Aspects of Structural Transformation

A definite association between the levels of development and the sectoral shares of income and employment is identified by Colin Clark[36] and Simon Kuznets.[37] By and large, they hold the view that at low levels of economic development, most of the output comes from, and most of the workers are engaged in the primary sector. With development, the relative importance of the primary sector declines while that of the secondary and tertiary sectors increases, the increase in the latter being much more as development proceeds.[38] In most countries, the substantial decline in the share of the primary sector is compensated by a substantial rise in the share of the tertiary sector – not by a rise in the secondary sector.[39] An important aspect of structural transformation in countries like India is that while the share of the primary sector in national income has shown a perceptible fall, there has been no perceptible fall in the share of working population dependent on agriculture and related activities. Contrary to earlier expectations, modern industry has failed to generate large-scale employment opportunities.[40] In view of all these views, it is proposed to test the following hypotheses with specific reference to the inter-sectoral aspects of structural transformation in the State and district economies of Karnataka:

(i) There exists a definite association between the level of income and the sectoral shares. In the initial stages of development of an economy, its economic structure is characterised by the predominance of the primary sector in terms of its share of income and labour force; as economic development gathers momentum, the primary sector declines in importance, and such decline is duly compensated by the secondary and tertiary sectors. Statistically, there exists a negative correlation between the level of income and the share of the primary sector, whereas a positive correlation exists between the level of income and the shares of the non-primary sectors.

(ii) Among the non-primary sectors, with the decline in the importance of the primary sector, the secondary sector grows at a faster rate than the tertiary sector, but ultimately, the tertiary sector comes to excel the secondary sector.

(iii) There is a significant difference between the changes in the sectoral shares of income and labour force during the process of structural transformation. While the share of the primary sector in income shows a perceptible decline, no such perceptible decline in its share of labour force is noticeable; while it is the rise in the share of the secondary sector that largely compensates for the decline in the share of the primary sector as far as income is concerned, in the case of labour force, it is the rise in the share of the tertiary sector that largely compensates for the decline in the share of the primary sector.

1.7.3 *Hypotheses Related to the Inter-industry Aspects of Structural Transformation*

Inter-industry relations also undergo a change during the process of structural transformation. Some industries produce goods which are meant for immediate consumption, and some others for further production; and for inputs, some industries depend upon agricultural products, and some others on non-agricultural products. In the process of industrialisation, generally the consumer goods industries and agro-based industries come to dominate the industrial activity to start with, and later capital goods industries and non-agro-based industries come to figure predominantly in the industrial activity of an economy. In this regard, the following hypotheses are proposed to be tested with reference to the inter-industry aspects of structural transformation in the State of Karnataka:

(i) The consumer goods industries always develop first during the process of industrialisation, but the capital goods industries soon develop faster than the first group, and consequently the ratio of net output or value added in the consumer goods industries continually declines as compared with the net output of the capital goods industries.

(ii) In the initial stages of industrialisation, the agro-based industries figure more importantly than the non-agro-based industries, but, as industrialisation attains maturity, the latter come to figure more importantly than the former.

1.8 Nature, Scope and Importance of the Study

The present study, as its title suggests, is a study in regional economics with specific reference to industrialisation, and it examines the problem of industrialisation from two angles, viz. regional and structural. Spatially speaking, both the regional and structural analyses are mostly carried on at two areal levels – State and district. In the regional analysis greater accent is given to the study of the inter-temporal trends in regional disparities. The divergence-convergence trends are examined with reference to the per capita NDDP, spread of industries and industrial employment, and sectoral shares of income and labour force. Both the cross-section and inter-temporal analyses are employed in this empirical study. Structurally, the study focuses attention on the changes that have been taking place in the sectoral shares of income and employment in the State and district economies of Karnataka. The structural aspect also includes the analysis of the changing relative importance of the consumer goods and capital goods, and agro- and non-agro-based industries. The study also analyses the structure and growth of large-scale and small-scale industrial units in the State.

Temporally, by and large, the investigation is spread over two decades covering three points of time, viz. 1960-61, 1970-71 and 1980-81. The choice of the time cover – the initial and the terminal year – among other things, is governed by three important considerations. Firstly, though the enlarged State of Karnataka came into being on November 1, 1956, itself, all the districts that were brought under it came to be considered for planned development only with the commencement of the Third Five Year Plan. That is how 1960-61 is taken as the base year in the present study. Secondly, the secondary data on the various aspects of industrialisation and development are available from 1960-61 onwards. Thirdly, the choice of the terminal year 1980-81 is mainly governed by the census data; the latest census data available are for 1981. Geographically, the study embraces all the 19 districts of the State. They are: Bangalore, Belgaum, Bellary, Bidar, Bijapur, Chikmagalur, Chitradurga, Dakshina-Kannada, Dharwad, Gulbarga, Hassan, Kodagu, Kolar, Mandya, Mysore, Raichur, Shimoga, Tumkur and Uttar Kannada. In the present inquiry for the purpose of regional analysis, the districts are regarded as regions without going into the controversies that surround the concept of "region" in regional economics. And Karnataka State is chosen for study, among other things, for the reason that, research wise, Karnataka economy still continues to be a virgin field; there is vast scope for meaningful research inquiry. The accessibility to secondary data is also another consideration which prompted the researcher, who happens to be a native of Karnataka, to choose Karnataka for his study. And such an exclusive study, it is hoped, would provide a better understanding of the trends in industrialisation in the State of Karnataka.

At the global level, strictly speaking, "space" as a strategic dimension of industrial and development planning came to be recognised only after the Second World War. Of course, development planning is essentially a three-dimensional exercise; the other two dimensions, viz. "time" and "sector", are also equally important. Karnataka, as a consciously developing transitional economy, has been accommodating all the three dimensions in her planning. No doubt the time and sectoral dimensions were there even prior to the implementation of the Fourth Five Year Plan, but "space" to secure spatial equity in development made its entry in the Fourth Five Year Plan. With the time-bound space-centred sectoral planning, Karnataka has been striving to promote that pattern of sectoral development which would be effective in minimising areal disparities. But she has yet to go a long way to reach that goal of development with spatial equity.

The review of empirical studies made in Chapter II incidentally indicates that not much has been done to make an in-depth analysis of the regional and structural aspects of industrialisation in Karnataka. As such, the present study claims its importance by making a substantial addition to the existing understanding of the diverse facets of the dynamics of regional and structural situation obtaining in the State. The districts of Karnataka are at various levels of industrialisation and development with differing patterns of sectoral behaviour. A proper grasp of the changing inter-sectoral and intra-sectoral behaviour and a fuller comprehension of the trends in regional disparities are quite necessary in formulating meaningful district development plans. And it is here that the present work claims its importance by providing such knowledge. Another dimension of its importance lies partly in exploring the unexplored and underexplored facets of industrialisation and development in Karnataka, and partly in updating what has already been done in the field. The empirical findings and the policy implications derived therefrom, it is hoped, would be of much use to the planners in the State, and also to all those who are concerned with regional planning and development in other parts of the country.

1.9 Methodology

The present study is basically an empirical inquiry into the regional and structural aspects of industrialisation in Karnataka. However wherever necessary, adequate theoretical explanation is provided. The data are interpreted and evaluated keeping the principal objectives and hypotheses of the study at the centre of the analysis. The entire study is based on the secondary sources of data – both published and unpublished.

To give a quantitative touch to the empirical analysis, a few simple statistical tools are used. For measuring variations and trends in variations, range ratio, rank correlation, standard deviation, coefficient of variation and district relatives are generally used; and for identifying the nature of association between the functionally related variables, correlation coefficient is used. In the inter-industry analysis, economic ratios such as output-labour, capital-labour and capital-output are used. And location quotient is used to measure the degree of localisation of different industry groups in the State. In every core chapter, a section is devoted to highlight the findings, and the findings of all the core chapters are woven together in the concluding chapter.

In view of the manifold objectives, the data are obtained from more than one source. The data on Net State Domestic Product (NSDP) and Net District Domestic Product (NDDP) are collected from the published and unpublished records of the Directorate of Economics and Statistics, Government of Karnataka, Bangalore. The district wise data on the spread of industrial activity and factory employment are obtained from the Chief Inspector of Factories and Boilers, Government of Karnataka, Bangalore, and the Directorate of Economics and Statistics. The district wise data on small-scale industrial units are collected from the official records of the Directorate of Industries and Commerce, Government of Karnataka, Bangalore. The CSO publications of the Annual Survey of Industries (ASI) constitute the chief source for the Statewise and industrywise data on the large-scale industries (Census Sector). And so far as the data on population and workforce by industrial category are concerned, the study depends entirely on the census publications of the Government of India.

The data used in the study suffer from certain limitations, and they are discussed in some detail at appropriate places in the body of the thesis. Here it is to be pointed out that the limitations of the present study, to a great extent, are a reflection of the data limitations.

1.10 Chapter Scheme

Including this "Introduction", the work consists of seven chapters. The second chapter is designed to provide a relatively comprehensive theoretical and empirical frame-work for the analysis and interpretation of the data in the subsequent chapters. Most of the important theories in respect of regional disparities and structural transformation are discussed first, and the discussion is followed by a relatively extensive survey of the related empirical studies. The third chapter inquires into the nature and extent of inter-district disparities at three points of time – 1960-61, 1970-71 and 1980-81. Among other things, by employing both cross-section and inter-temporal analyses, this chapter, besides assessing the divergence-convergence trends at the district level, lays the foundation for the discussion of areal disparities in terms of the degree of industrialisation in the subsequent chapters. The fourth chapter examines the trends in inter-district disparities in registered manufacturing. It also carries on a similar exercise for the small-scale industrial units in the State. The fifth chapter deals with the structural transformation of State and district economies of Karnataka. It examines the inter-temporal changes in the sectoral composition of output and workforce. Incidentally, an attempt is also made to develop a typology of the districts taking the share of the non-primary sectors in output and workforce as the basis. The sixth chapter examines the localisation and growth of the large-scale industries covered by the Census Sector of the ASI in the State. The inter-temporal changes in the large-scale industrial structure are also inquired into. Above all, it deals with the changing relationship between the consumer goods industries and capital goods industries, and between the agro- and non-agro-based industries. The seventh chapter, being the last chapter, concludes the study by discussing and integrating all the principal findings and policy implications.

NOTES

1. Hartwell, R.M., *Industrial Revolution and Economic Growth*, Methuen and Company Ltd., London, 1971, p. 42.
2. Sutcliffe, R.B., *Industry and Underdevelopment*, Addison-Wesley Publishing Company, London, 1971, p.11.
3. Hartwell, R.M., op. cit., p. 42.

4. Walker, F. David, ed., *Planning Industrial Development*, John Wiley and Sons, New York, 1980, p. 1.
5. Quoted, Brookfield Harold, *Interdependent Development*, Methuen and Company Ltd., London, 1975, pp. 70-71.
6. Mezerik, A.G., *Industrialisation of Underdeveloped Countries*, UNIDO Symposium on Industrial Development, 1968, p. 2.
7. Bryce, D. Murrey, *Industrial Development*, McGraw Hill Book Company, New York, 1960, p. 3.
8. Quoted, James, E.M., "Some Determinants of Industrialisation in Small and Medium Size Economies: A Cross-Section Analysis", *The Indian Economic Journal*, Vol. 27, No. 2, Oct.-Dec. 1979, p. 82.
9. Nehru, Jawaharlal, *Speeches March 1953—August 1957*, New Delhi, 1958, p. 11.
10. Robinson, Ronald, (ed.), *Developing the Third World: the Experience of the Nineteen-Sixties*, University Press, Cambridge, 1971, p. 66.
11. Brookfield, Harold, op. cit., pp. 72-73.
12. Quoted, Robinson Ronald, op. cit., p. 66.
13. Staley, Eugene, *The Future of Underdeveloped Countries*, Harper and Brothers, New York, 1954, p. 304.
14. Sutcliffe, R.B., op. cit., p. 103.
15. Lurie, Samuel, "The International Symposium on Industrial Development", *UN Monthly Chronicle*, Vol. V, No. 1, Jan. 1968, p. 126.
16. Myrdal, Gunnar, *An International Economy*, Harper and Brothers, New York, 1956, p. 226.
17. Kuznets, Simon, "Quantitative Aspects of the Economic Growth of Nations" *Economic Development and Cultural Change*, July 1957.
18. Chenery, H.B., "Patterns of Industrial Growth", *American Economic Review*, Sept. 1960.
19. Chenery, H.B. and L. Taylor, "Development Patterns: Among Countries and Over Time", *Review of Economics and Statistics*, Nov. 1968.
20. Zacharia, T.C., *Role of Industrialisation in the Economic Development of a Country* (With special reference to India), Ph.D. thesis, Bombay University, 1966.
21. Srinivas, T.Y., *Industrialisation and Economic Development*, Ph.D. Thesis, Bombay University, 1975.
22. Sutcliffe, R.B., op. cit., pp. 69-71.
23. Ibid., p. 3.
24. Zacharia, T.C., op. cit., p. XXIV.
25. Bognar, Josef, *Economic Policy and Planning in Developing Countries*, Akadomiai Kiado, Budapest, 1959, pp. 295-296.
26. Pred, A.R., "Industrialisation, Initial Advantage and American Metropolitan Growth", *Geographical Review*, 55, 1965, pp. 158-185.
27. Brookfield, Harold, op. cit., p. 1.
28. Kuznets, Simon, *Presidential Address Delivered to the American Economic Association*, Dec. 29. 1954.
29. Stefan, R.H., "Regional and National Economic Development in India", *The Regional Science Association's Papers and Proceedings*, (Sixth Annual Meeting, 1959), Vol. VI, 1960, p. 66.
30. Goswami, S.P., *Location of Factories in Maharashtra — An Analysis of the Trends During 1960s*, Ph.D Thesis, University of Bombay, 1981, p. 3.

31. Pandit, S.A., *Regional Distribution of Industries in India*, Ph.D. Thesis, University of Bombay, 1949, p. 3.
32. Patnaik, S.C., *Economics of Regional Development and Planning in Third World Countries*, Associated Publishing House, New Delhi, 1981, pp. 20-23.
33. Srinivas, T.Y., op, cit. p. 22.
34. Friedman, John and Alonso, William, (eds.), *Regional Development and Planning: A Reader*, The M.I.T. Press, Cambridge, Massachussetts, 1972, p. 3.
35. For details, see Nair, K.R.G., *Regional Experience in a Developing Economy*, Wiley Eastern Ltd., New Delhi, 1982, p. 3 and also Chapter II of the present work.
36. Clark, Colin, *The Conditions of Economic Progress*, MacMillan and Company, London, 1957.
37. Kuznets, Simon, *Modern Economic Growth — Rate, Structure and Spread*, Yale University Press, London, 1969.
38. Nair, K.R.G., op. cit., p. 81.
39. Kuznets, Simon, "Quantitative Aspects of the Economic Growth of Nations II, Industrial Distribution of National Product and Labour Force", *Economic Development and Cultural Change*; Supplement to Vol. 4, July 1957, pp. 3-111. For the latest global level discussion on the issue, see, Quoted, Chandrasekhar, C.P., "An Event in Economics:, *Frontline*, Dec., 13-26, 1986, p. 18.
40. Excerpts from Manmohan Singh's Valedictory Address to the Eighth World Economic Congress, *The Economic Times*, Bangalore, Dec. 18, 1986. p. III.

2

THEORETICAL AND EMPIRICAL FRAME-WORK

2.1 Introduction

THE INTRODUCTORY chapter has made it explicitly clear that the present -inquiry is concerned with the regional and structural dimensions of industrialisation and economic development in Karnataka. As anywhere else in the world, in Karnataka too, industrialisation seems to have been showing a tendency to concentrate itself in certain regions. Industrial activity is not found uniformly spread in all the districts of the State. Similarly, in terms of economic development also there are wide variations among the districts. Added to this, there is also a tendency for the relatively developed districts to grow at a faster rate than the relatively less developed districts. In view of the differential natural and infrastructural advantages, inter-district disparities seem to persist in the State despite regional planning. Again, as elsewhere, in Karnataka too, industrialisation has been causing significant changes in the fundamental structure of the district economies. The structural change has been manifesting itself in quite a few directions. But the present inquiry is focusing attention on only two prominent facets of structural change, viz. inter-sectoral and intra-sectoral. The former is concerned with the changing importance of the primary and non-primary sectors in the process of industrialisation and economic development, and the latter with the changing importance of consumer goods and capital goods industries and agro-based and non-agro-based industries during the process of industrialisation. For diverse reasons, all the districts of Karnataka have not been showing a uniform pattern of structural transformation. And there appears to be some association between regional disparities and structural changes. As such any attempt to understand the dynamics of regional disparities cannot afford to ignore the analysis of the dynamics of structural transformation that accompanies industrialisation.

In view of the disastrous consequences that growing disparities hold in prospect, and in view of the close association that exists between regional development and structural transformation, quite a few economists in different parts of the world have made attempts to develop elaborate theories and hypotheses about regional disparities and structural transformation. And to lend authenticity and credibility to such theories, and also to test the related hypotheses, a number of economists have undertaken empirical investigations. The ultimate objective of such theoretical and empirical studies is to provide an operationally useful perspective of the regional and structural dimensions of industrialisation, so that the policy-makers can work out plans to secure development with spatial equity, which in turn is expected to ensure inter-personal economic equity. It is heartening to note that a few inter-State and intra-State studies have also been made in addition to a number of national- and international-level studies.

The review which follows is intended to provide the theoretical and empirical frame-work for the discussion that takes place in the subsequent chapters. Including the introductory section this chapter consists of five sections. The second and third sections discuss respectively the theories and empirical studies on regional disparities at various spatial levels. Of course, the discussion keeps "divergence-convergence" debate at its centre. The theories and empirical studies on the inter-sectoral aspect of structural transformation are examined in the fourth section. And the fifth section is devoted to the discussion of the theories and empirical studies pertaining to the changing relationship between the consumer goods industries and capital goods industries, and between agro-based and non-agro-based industries.

2.2 Theories on Regional Disparities

If the roots of areal dualism are to be found in the historic voyages of the 15th century, the roots of its awareness and the public concern about it are to be found in the economic crisis of the 1930's. The high level of unemployment and greater economic distress during the 1930s in Great Britain gave rise to such awareness and concern about the problems of the relatively lagging regions. As a consequence of that public awareness, the Barlow Commission was set up in 1936 by the

British Government. The U.S. Government also under similar circumstances, set up the TVA in 1941. These were the two major steps concerning regional problems having spatial dimensions.[1] These instances of regional development, however, did not make the world to accept "space" as a dimension of any significant relevance either in the theory of economic development or in public policy. Strictly speaking, the awareness about the existence and perpetuation of the "North-South problem"[2] is mostly a post-war phenomenon. The immediate cause for such universalisation of disparity consciousness was the North-South situation that rocked Italy. After the Second World War, to its shocking astonishment, Italy came to realise that it was virtually divided into two disparate halves – the developed industrial North and the backward agricultural South. Since then the problem of regional disparities has come to be known as North-South problem.[3] It is only in the recent past that the problem has been engaging the attention of the academics and policy-makers in the Third World countries.

In course of time, areal disparities came to induce economists to develop theories and hypotheses about the emergence, divergence and convergence of disparities. All the important theories agree that industrialisation involves spatial disparities; but they differ as to the causes of initial divergence, its perpetuation, and as to the timing of divergence and convergence in the growth path of a nation. William Alonso says: "Many have written during the last quarter century on the subject of regional imbalances in the process of national economic development. Some are of the opinion that regional disparities increase during the early stages of development, but that they will decline after some unspecified higher level of development because of greater integration of the national economy. Others, on the other hand, some think that regional inequality becomes a vicious circle of cumulative causation, with the centre gaining strength, and the periphery losing ground in infinite regress. Others say that regional disparities bear no fixed relation to the process of development as such, but rather that they are the artifact of the national political economy, which in turn reflects the world economic order."[4] Such differences have given rise to different hypotheses on regional disparities.

The classical economists who believe in the perfect mobility of factors in between places and employments, and who believe in the automatic functioning of the economic system, do not conceive the existence of spatial disparities in the long run. S.C. Patnaik says that the theories developed around the frame-work of pure capitalism maintain that the free play of the market forces ensures work to move where labour is available or labour to migrate where jobs are plentiful, and thus a harmonious balance is brought about between supply and demand in the long run; the disparities, if any, in profit, wages and employment between regions are considered only temporary and frictional which automatically tend to be eliminated by corresponding capital and labour movements.[5] Whereas, the Neo-Classical economists attribute spatial disparities to the malfunctioning of the equilibrium mechanism. In their view such malfunctioning is due to market imperfections and institutional bottlenecks which impede smooth factor and resource movements for bringing about an efficient regional allocation of resources. In their scheme, regional disparities tend to disappear in the course of economic growth process, when there is grater unification of markets and economic integration among regions. The same is the case with some of the location theories. S. Holland says that the location theories developed during the present century also fall within the Classical or Neo-Classical frame-work.[6] Thus the Classical and Neo-Classical analyses are not of much use in diagnosing and curing the economic malady of regional disparities.

The idea that growth by its very nature gives rise to regional inequalities can be traced back to the "Growth Pole Theory" which was initially developed by the French regional economists, particularly F. Perroux and Boudeville.[7] F. Perroux who developed the concept of "growth pole" in 1955 was the first to identify spatial disparities. He argues that development does not appear everywhere and all at once; it appears in points or development poles with variable intensities; it spreads along diverse channels and has varying terminal effects for the whole of the economy.[8] And Boudeville, in the process of developing the growth pole concept further, gives it a more geographical orientation. J.K. Singh says that the Perroux-Boudevillian formulation gives a dynamic concept of temporal changes in the emergence and development of growth poles; but it tells nothing about its relation to the space it occupies, and also about the inter-pole relationships.[9] Nevertheless, the idea that development is essentially unbalanced regionally emerges out of their formulation. However, the theorising on regional disparities got a major breakthrough in the writings of Gunnar Myrdal[10] A.O. Hirschman,[11] J.R. Hicks[12], J.G. Williamson[13] and William Alonso.[14]

Gunnar Myrdal happens to be the first to question the validity of the Classical and Neo-Classical wisdom in conferring the self-equilibrating capacity on the economic system. He particularly questions the effectiveness of the equilibrating mechanism in reducing regional disparities and in ensuring inter-regional parity in development. Myrdal argues that the play of the forces in the market normally tends to increase, rather than decrease the inequality between regions.[15] In his opinion, by nature, a free market system causes advanced regions to grow, at least in part, at the expense of other regions; and consequently, once income differences emerge, they tend to become self-perpetuating, unless some exogenous influence acts to offset market forces. Myrdal says: "If things were left to market forces unhampered by any policy interference, industrial production, commerce, banking, insurance, shipping and indeed almost all those economic activities which in a developing economy tend to give a bigger than average return – and in addition, science, art, literature, education and higher culture generally – would cluster in localities and regions, leaving the rest of the country more or less in backwater."[16] While discussing interregional growth differentials, Myrdal points out that once growth starts in a region, thereafter the ever increasing internal and external economies would fortify and sustain the continuous growth of the developing region at the expense of other localities and regions, where relative stagnation becomes the pattern. These views of Myrdal are well amplified by R.B. Hughes.[17]

Myrdal explains the process of cumulative causation which perpetuates interregional income differentials with two types of forces which are diametrically opposed to each other functionally. They are "Backwash Effects" and 'Spread Effects". The backwash effects refer to all those unfavourable forces which cause divergence or disparity, whereas the spread effects refer to all those favourable forces which bring about convergence or interregional parity. The spread effects are said to be favourable because they cause economic activities to be spread out among the different regions of the economy and thereby to the convergence among per capita regional incomes. The spread effects consist mainly of an increasing demand for the products of lagging or backward regions, and the diffusion of technology and knowledge. On the contrary, the backwash effects are said to be unfavourable because they cause concentration of economic activities in certain regions, and thereby cause greater disparities or divergence among regions. The backwash effects include the labour migration, capital movement, and trade which are detrimental to the growth of the backward regions. In short, backwash effects are those forces which ensure the growth of the North at the cost of the South, whereas spread effects are those forces which enable the South to grow by ensuring the transmission of growth-promoting forces from North to South. In Myrdal's opinion, spread effects are weaker than backwash effects. As such, in the absence of external influence, regional disparities continue to persist. And, on the basis of the results published in the Economic Survey of Europe in 1954, Myrdal draws two significant conclusions: (i) The regional inequalities are much wider in the poorer countries than in the richer countries; and (ii) while regional inequalities have been diminishing in the richer counties, the tendency has been the opposite in the poor countries.

A.O. Hirschman is another great name in this field of study. While inquiring into the manner in which growth can be communicated from one region or country to another, he says that it can be taken for granted that economic progress does not appear everywhere at the same time, and that, once it appears, powerful forces make for a spatial concentration of economic growth around the initial starting points.[18] Geographically speaking, for Hirschman, growth is necessarily unbalanced. He argues: "Whatever the reason there can be little doubt that an economy, to lift itself to higher income levels, must and will first develop within itself one or several regional centres of economic strength. This need for the emergence of "growing points" or "growth poles" in the course of the development process means that international and interregional inequality of growth is an inevitable concomitant and condition of growth itself."[19] However, he does not say that regional inequality is a permanent phenomenon. In the growth path, he notices chances for both divergence and convergence. The growth in a particular region is capable of affecting the growth of the regions around both favourably and unfavourbly.

Like Myrdal, Hirschman also identifies two sets of opposing forces emerging in the growth process; one set favouring convergence, and the other set, divergence. The first set consists of those forces which cause trickling down of Northern progress to the South, and he calls such forces "Trickling Down Effects". Hirschman says: "By far the most important of these effects is the increase of Northern purchases and investments in the South, and increase that is sure to take place, if the economies of the two regions are at all complementary. In addition, the North may absorb some of the disguised unemployed of the South and thereby raise the marginal productivity of labour and per capita consumption levels in the South."[20] On the other hand, he brands the divergence-causing forces as "Polarisation Effects". The unequal competition between the manufactures of the South and the North, and the undesirable internal migration of human resources, are by far the most important polarisation effects identified by Hirschman. Of all, he considers internal brain drain to be the most serious polarisation force. Hirschman observes: "A most serious and frequently observed polarisation effect consists in the kind of internal migration that may follow upon the economic advances of the North. Instead of absorbing the disguised unemployed, the Northern progress may denude South of its key technicians and managers as well as of the more enterprising young men. This type of migration may actually be undesirable not only from the point of view of the South, but also from that of the country as a whole, for the loss to the South due to the departure of these men may be higher than the gain to the North."[21] With all this, unlike Myrdal, he expresses his hope of North-South rapprochement. He feels confident that in the end the trickling down effects would gain the upper hand over the polarisation effects if the North had to rely to an important degree on the Southern products for its own expansion. But he considers deliberate economic policy to be an important influence in correcting interregional inequalities. He maintains:" . . . if the market forces that express themselves through the trickling down and polarisation effects result in a temporary victory of the latter, deliberate economic policy will come into play to correct the situation. Actually, of course, economic policy will be an important influence throughout the process."[22]

William Alonso,[23] while writing about urban and regional imbalances observes that Hirschman and Myrdal have arrived at fairly similar models of spatial polarisation of economies in the process of development; in the early stages of development, the polarisation or backwash effects become prominent and cause regional disparities; and after certain point, the trickling down or spread effects come to prominence and initiate the process of convergence. However, Myrdal appears to be more pessimistic than Hirschman about the eventual convergence as an economy approaches maturity. There are some significant differences between them as to the relative strength of these two sets of forces, and as to the final conclusions. According to Hirschman, sooner or later, the core or the developing region has to reduce its own congestion, overcome supply difficulties and expand home market. And he considers deliberate policy intervention to be an aspect of trickling down in his model. Myrdal, however, does not include government intervention as a part of his model, and holds to his theory of circular causation. In his opinion, the core will continue to experience a circular upward movement reinforcing favourable effects, and the periphery will have a reverse experience. Hirschman himself says: "I now find that Gunnar Myrdal has addressed himself to similar problems. . . and has had recourse to the same conceptual tools that are employed here: his 'backwash' and 'spread' effects correspond exactly to my 'polarisation' and 'trickling down' effects. Nevertheless, there are considerable differences in emphasis and conclusions".[24]

J.R. Hicks [25] has given a most reasonable explanation of the circumstances accounting for the emergence and perpetuation of regional disparities, and also for the ultimate reduction of disparities. He attributes the initial emergence of divergence to certain natural as well as man-made factors. He says, ". . . particular places within a country where wealth can grow most easily are marked out by geographical advantages, proximity to minerals or sources of power, or to areas particularly suitable for specialised crops; alternatively, they may have naturally good communications, so that their sources of supply are at a distance, they can be supplied from many sources rather easily."[26] In his view, once unequal rates of growth develop, they will tend to perpetuate themselves, or the disparity in growth rates might even increase because when industry and trade become more concentrated in a particular centre, they themselves give rise to that centre and an advantage for further development. And such growth of the dynamic area is capable of acting as a centrifugal force by trickling down the growth to the lagging regions; but it is also equally capable of acting as a centripetal force by draining the lagging regions of any growth potential they might have had. Hicks also expressed his confidence in the ability of government interference in reducing spatial inequalities. He says: "It is not difficult to induce the economic forces to move a little further or a little faster, than they would have done without interference."[27]

J.G. Williamson, as an effective preface to his pioneering empirical study[28] on regional inequalities, gives a crystal-clear theoretical analysis of the emergence of divergence and its final convergence. According to Williamson: "Given that significant economic growth first appears in one region of the national state, it should occasion no surprise that the absolute differential between rich and poor regions (North and South) should persist or even increase. Even if both the regions should grow at the same percentage rate after the fortuitous 'random shock' in the North, the absolute regional differential will not only persist but increase".[29] He considers divergence and convergence to be the two consecutive phases in the growth process of a nation; the centripetal forces which come to dominate the early stages of national development are bound to give way to the centrifugal forces at a later stage. He points out: ". . . that the early stages of national development generate increasingly large North-South income differentials. Somewhere during the course of development, some or all of the disequilibrating tendencies diminish, causing a reversal in the pattern of interregional inequality. Instead of divergence in interregional levels of development, convergence becomes the rule, with the backward regions closing the development gap between themselves and the already industrialised areas".[30] In short, he holds the view that regional disparities diverge initially only to converge later on. And he explains such behaviour of disparities with the help of four factors, viz., labour migration, capital migration, interregional linkages and Central Government policy.[31]

The foregoing discussion of some of the important theoretical works on regional inequalities brings out the salient aspects of the behavioural pattern of regional disparities. Most of the theorists agree that growth does not take place anywhere and everywhere at once, and, to start with, growth is necessarily unbalanced. They also accept that development process involves the operation of both the divergence-causing and convergence-causing forces. However, they do differ as to the relative strength of those two sets of opposing forces.

2.3 Empirical Studies on Regional Disparities

A number of attempts have been made in the past two decades to understand the patterns of regional inequalities at national and intra-national levels. A few studies have also been made with specific reference to India and Karnataka. Even then, very little progress seems to have been made in providing a generally acceptable explanation for the occurrence, accentuation and disappearance of areal disparities. The review made below includes the empirical inquiries made in capitalist economies, socialist economies and mixed economies. Here it needs to be emphasised that most of the empirical investigations centre round the "concentration cycle" hypothesis associated with the names of Gunnar Myrdal,[32] A.O. Hirschman,[33] J.G. Williamson,[34] and

William Alonso.[35]

Even before the "concentration cycle" hypothesis took its final shape, a sort of rudimentary empirical attempt was made by the United Nations. The UN while describing the problems of regional development and industrial location in Europe in its *Economic Survey of Europe 1954* noted that in Western Europe, disparities of income between one region and another were much wider in poorer countries than in the richer ones.[36]

But J.G. Williamson's article[37] is considered to be the pioneer empirical study to test the "concentration cycle" hypothesis, and even to this day, it remains the most comprehensive study of regional disparities available. He uses alternative techniques to test the hypothesis: first, an international cross-section analysis is pursued for 24 countries during the decades of the 1950s; second, the cross-section approach is applied to the U.S. Census Data (1950 and 1960) where countries are treated as regional units, and the States as nations, and third, the national time series analysis is applied to those few countries for which data are available. His inquiry shows that regional inequality in general is moderate in the high-income-group countries, high in the middle-income-group countries, but again declines as we move to countries in the lower-income-group. A perusal of the averages for each income class shows that the relationship between the level of development and the degree of regional inequality is quite significant; the severity of the North-South problem seems to be quite minor indeed among the mature economies.[38] His international cross-section study supports the hypothesis that regional inequalities tend to diverge in the early stages of development, but show a tendency towards convergence in the later stages. His analysis of the short-time time-series data for 16 countries, with the exception of Brazil, shows the co-efficient of variation to be stable or falling in all the developed countries, and increasing in developing countries like Japan, Yugoslavia and India. And the analysis of long-time historical time-series data supports the hypothesis that a "statistic" describing regional inequality will trace out an inverted "U" over the national growth path.[39] According to William Alonso, Williamson's empirical inquiry reveals that regional disparities are greater in less developed countries, and smaller in more developed; over time, regional disparities increase in the less developed countries, and decrease in the more developed; and these finds too suggest that regional inequality, if plotted against economic development, would result in a bell-shaped curve, with some peak being reached at the transition from the take-off to the mature stage.[40]

S. Elshaks' empirical study[41] also lends support to the "concentration cycle" hypothesis. He finds that a cross-section of the world's nations results in a near-normal curve of primacy on economic development. That is to say, primacy is rare in highly underdeveloped countries, rises during the take-off stage, and decreases thereafter. His time-series studies of developed countries also support this view, although not nearly as the cross-section data.[42] Baer Werner in his study of Brazil[43] points out that the North-eastern region which contains 25 per cent the population earns only 10 per cent of the national income, whereas the South which has 35 per cent of the population earns 50 per cent of the national income. His study reveals the existence of regional inequalities.[44]

I.S. Koropeckyj's empirical study of socialist countries[45] merits special attention. The study includes only the socialist countries of East Central Europe (including obviously the Soviet Union), and the emphasis is on the period since the Second World War. Koropeckyj investigates interregional inequality in terms of industrialisation as measured by industrial employment. He uses the coefficient of correlation for measuring the relationship between the NMP[46] (Net Material Product) per capita and industrial employment per 10,000 population, and weighted coefficient of variation to measure regional inequalities. His study confirms the close direct association between NMP per capita and industrial employment.

Incidentally, it is to be pointed out that there are also some empirical studies which support some other patterns of change in regional disparities other than the one indicated by the "concentration cycle" hypothesis. The study of E.J.R. Booth[47] lends support to the view contained in the "self-perpetuation" hypothesis that there is a tendency for regional disparities to diverge in the process of national economic development. On the other hand, the empirical work of H.S. Perloff *et al.*,[48] supports the view contained in the "accordian effect" hypothesis that there is a tendency for regional disparities to converge in the course of national economic development.

As far as India is concerned, S.A. Pandit's Study[49] is probably the pioneer empirical inquiry into the regional distribution of industries. His study reveals not only the existence of inter-State and intra-State disparities in industrialisation, but also their perpetuation. The study is significant for the reason that it gives the disparity position in India just on the eve of India's independence. As a part of his international exercise, J.G. Williamson, while measuring regional inequalities, comes to be conclusion that in India, the decade of the 1950s is characterised by his first phase, viz. the phase of increasing inequalities.[50] Inspired by Williamson's study, many scholars have attempted to study the trends in regional disparities in India. Some have used per capita incomes, and some others have used composite indices of development for measuring regional inequalities. There are also a few studies which have used levels of living, consumption expenditure, agricultural development, worker participation, value-added in manufacturing, industrial investment, industrial employment, PQLI (Physical Quality of Life Index), etc., for studying the trends in regional disparities.

O.P. Mahajan, basing his study on the exhaustive State income data, arrives at the conclusion that the decade of the 1950s is characterised by reduction in regional income inequalities.[51] This finding goes against the finding of J.G. Williamson for the same decade. S.K. Rao, who uses a composite index of development, does not notice any change in the relative positions of States between the 1950s and 1960s. His study suggests that regional disparities have not been reduced in the course of 15 years of planning.[52] R.K. Sampath's inquiry finds the existence of wide inter-State inequalities at the beginning of the planning era, and they declined steadily until 1964-65, but from then onwards up to 1970-71 they increased steadily.[53] V. Nath's study for the 1950s and 1960s notices the developed States growing at a faster rate than the less developed ones, and the tendency for more rapid growth in the developed areas is particularly marked in the industrial sector.[54] B.B. Tandon's study for the period from 1960-61 to 1970-71 arrives at certain important conclusions: there is a systematic relationship between rising regional disparities and economic development; despite differential rates of changes from year-to-year, the rank order of the States has not undergone any significant change; and there has been a pronounced widening of inter-State differentials.[55] D.N. Jha's study for the period from 1950-51 to 1970-71 reveals the widening of inter-State disparities.[56] K.R.G. Nair notices some decrease, but not very significant, in inter-State income differentials in the first decade of planning.[57] In another study, Nair finds some divergence in per capita NDP during the fifties.[58] His recent study which covers a period of three decades from 1950-51 emerges with certain interesting and intriguing findings. One interesting finding suggests that the inter-State disparities in per capita NDP were on the decline till the mid-sixties and are on the increase since then; the measures of disparity analysed here trace out a U-shaped curve over time, instead of an inverted U-shaped curve which is suggested in the concentration cycle hypothesis.[59] Perhaps the most intriguing finding of Nair is that while per capita differences in NDP are unchanged or have perhaps increased, there has been some convergence in the levels of personal consumption.[60] R.T. Tiwari's study[61] for the period from 1960-61 to 1968-69, and O.P. Mathur's study[62] for the period from 1960-61 to 1969-70 show that the inter-State disparities have recorded a rise. P.N. Dhar and D.U. Shastry who use power consumption data as proxy for the level of industrial development, S.Gupta who uses a measure based on concentration coefficients of income, R.K. Lahiri, who uses comparisons of proportionate distribution of population and industrial employment, and Hemalata Rao who uses factor analysis to construct composite indices of development, report reduction in regional disparities.[63] P. Venkataramaiah, who uses shift criterion for industrial income, does not find any narrowing down tendency, and even questions Dhar and Shastry's narrowing down conclusions.[64] M.D. Choudhary finds no change in the disparities between 1950 and 1970.[65] Ashok Mathur's recent study for the 1950s, 1960s and 1970s observes a downward, though fluctuating, movement of regional income inequalities up to the early sixties, and a sustained increase in inequalities since mid-sixties. His inquiry reveals that the trend of regional inequalities has acquired the nature of an upright rather than an inverted U-shaped curve.[66] S.P. Goswami's empirical study on Maharashtra reports not only the existence but also the widening of regional disparities in the industrial activity during the 1960s.[67] K. Ramakrishna Sharma's study on the industrial development of Andhra Pradesh shows that industrialisation in the State has not brought about any significant reduction in inter-district inequalities.[68]

Data-based disparity study in Karnataka is essentially a post-Reorganisation phenomenon. Though the works of V.L. D'Souza,[69] R. Balakrishna[70] and Y.S. Mahajan[71] carry a mine of information about the phases of industrialisation in Karnataka, they do not have anything worth to say about regional disparities. G.B. Baldwin's study[72] is probably the first attempt to bring the problems of industrial agglomeration in Mysore to surface. His investigation points out not only a tendency for the concentration of industries in and around Bangalore, but also a tendency for the industries to grow at a faster rate in Bangalore than in other parts of the State. M.C. Munshi's study reveals glaring regional inequalities not only in the princely State of Mysore but also in the districts that were added to it in 1956.[73] H.V. Shetty finds inter-regional variations in industrialisation[74], N.S. Hiremath finds regional disparities increasing between 1960-61 and 1970-71, and decreasing between 1970-71 and 1974-75.[75] K. Puttaswamaiah's massive work reveals the growth of regional disparities.[76] Gladys Sumitra's study for 1961, 1971 and 1981 reports a narrowing down tendency in regional disparities.[77] R.V. Dadibhavi's inter-taluka study reports the existence of spatial disparities in 1975-76.[78] His recent study reveals a convergence trend in income disparities over the period 1960-61 to 1975-76. But he says that the disparities are not too small to be ignored.[79]

2.4 Sectoral Aspects of Structural Transformation: Theory and Evidence

The sectoral theory is based on the belief that industrialisation and economic development invariably involve changes in the economic structure of an economy. The changes in the relative shares of different sectors in income and employment are by far the most important structural changes. Colin Clark[80] is said to be the first thinker to theorise the structural changes that take place in a trisectoral economy. He points out that low per capita real income is always associated with a low proportion of the working population engaged in non-primary production, and a high percentage in primary production. He also points out that high per capita real income is always associated with a high proportion of the working population in the non-primary sectors. In other words, he identifies a negative association between per capita income and the share of the primary sector in labour force, and a positive association between per capita income and the share of the secondary and tertiary sectors in labour force. Thus his theory establishes a definite relationship between the levels of economic development as measured by per capita income and sectoral importance; the primary sector dominates the economic activity of a nation in the initial stages of development, and in the mature stages of development, the secondary and tertiary sectors come to dominate. From this it can be inferred that economic development implies a gradual shift away from the primary sector to the secondary and tertiary sectors.

Simon Kuznets[81] adds very substantially to the sectoral theory. He interprets the changes in the relative importance of the sectors not only in terms of their shares in labour force, but also in terms of their shares in output. According to Simon Kuznets, the lower the product per capita, the larger the share of the A-sector (roughly equivalent to the primary sector) in output and labour force; the lower the product per capita, the smaller the share of the M-Sector (roughly equivalent to the secondary sector) and S-sector (tertiary sector) in output and labour force.

T.Y. Srinivas[82] has developed his sectoral theory on the basis of the observed patterns of industrial development. In the opinion of T.Y. Srinivas, in the initial stages of development, the primary sector is the dominant sector accounting for a major portion of the output and employment, and with development gathering speed, the secondary and tertiary sectors gain higher importance; and among the non-primary sectors, the secondary sector grows at a faster rate than the tertiary sector to start with, but only to be excelled by the tertiary sector ultimately. Thus, according to T.Y. Srinivas, economic development invariably involves a sure structural shift in production and employment patterns away from the primary sector, and towards the secondary and tertiary sectors.

K.R.G. Nair has made some meaningful addition to the sectoral theory in his recent study.[83] His interpretation of the sectoral changes in the process of development is based on the sound assumption that the distribution of workers among the various sectors of an economy has an important bearing on product per worker, and therefore on NDP. According to Nair: "At low levels of development, productivity in the primary sector as well as the domestic demand for non-primary products are so low that most of the output comes from, and most of the workers are engaged in the primary sector. With development, product per worker in the primary sector increases and so does the demand for non-primary products, as a result of both of which, the relative importance of the primary sector declines, while that of the secondary and tertiary sectors increases, the increase in the latter being much more as development proceeds".[84] Thus, Nair, while echoing the views of Colin Clark and Simon Kuznets, elucidates the causes for the shifting sectoral dominance in the development path of a nation.

So, the view that emerges from the writings of sectoral theorists is that, generally, the primary sector dominates the economic activity in the initial stages of development of a nation or region, and in the mature stages of development the secondary and tertiary sectors dominate the economic activity. As economic development proceeds, the primary sector loses its dominance, while the non-primary sectors gain importance; the decline in the share of the primary sector is duly compensated by the increase in the shares of the non-primary sectors; and among the non-primary sectors, when the primary sector's share declines it is the secondary sector that claims more than the tertiary sector to start with, but in the later stages, it is the tertiary sector that comes to claim an upper hand over the secondary sector.

Some empirical studies have been made to examine the changes in the relative importance of the sectors in the process of industrialisation and economic development.

Simon Kuznets' well-known article[85] is a most comprehensive pioneering empirical study about the changing sectoral importance. His cross-section analysis in terms of sectoral shares of output shows that as the level of per capita income drops, the share of agriculture in the national product rises; and, on the contrary, in the distribution by the share of the M-sector, the lower the level of per capita income, the lower the share of the M-sector in the national product. His findings confirm the well-known negative correlation between the level of income and the share of agriculture, and positive correlation between the level of income and the share of non-agricultural commodity production. His long-term trend study shows that in all the countries considered, without exception, the share of the A-sector declines with secular rise in product per capita; in all the countries except the Union of South Africa and New Zealand, the share of the M-sector in total product rises; but the trends in the S-sector are mixed – in some countries it moves downwards, and in some, it moves upwards.[86] His study in respect of the sectoral shares of labour force reveals a negative association between product per capita and the share of the A-sector, and a positive association between product per capita and the share of the M-sector; and a distinct positive association between product per capita and the share of the S-sector. His long-term trend study reveals that the sectoral behaviour in terms of labour force differs from that of the sectoral behaviour in terms of income. In most countries, the substantial decline in the share of the A-sector is compensated by a substantial rise in the share of the S-sector, and not by a rise in the share of the M-sector[87] T.Y. Srinivas' cross-section analysis[88] shows the inverse relationship between per-capita national income and the share of agriculture in both labour force and GNP. He says: "As we move from less developed countries to developed ones the share of agriculture in both GNP and labour force falls. In other words, a negative correlationship exists between the per capita national income and the share of agriculture in labour force, and also between the per capita national income and the share of agriculture in GNP."[89] K.R.G. Nair's cross-section studies of Indian States for the years 1951, 1961 and 1971 reveal a general tendency for the primary sector to be much more prominent in the economies of low per-capita NDP States than in high per capita NDP ones, the reverse being the case of the relative importance of the secondary sector, and also to some extent of the tertiary sector.[90] On the other hand, his inter-temporal analysis does not give any conclusive evidence about the said relationships.

Some studies have also been made about the structural transformation in Karnataka. R.V. Dadibhavi's cross-section studies of the districts of Karnataka for the years 1960-61, 1970-71 and 1975-76 reveal a positive correlation between the district per capita income and the share of the primary sector in the total output and a negative correlation between the district per capita income and the shares of the secondary and tertiary sectors in total output. His inter-temporal study shows that with the rise in product per capita, the share of the primary sector has been declining and that of the secondary and tertiary sectors has been increasing. Of course, he does not find conclusive evidence.[91] The Project Formulation Division of the Planning Department in Karnataka, in its recent study, provides evidence of the shift in importance from the primary sector to the secondary and tertiary sectors in terms of their share in the State income. The primary sector's share in the State income recorded a fall from 61 per cent in 1960-61 to 50 per cent in 1981-82, whereas the shares of the secondary and tertiary sectors recorded a rise from 15 per cent and 24 per cent in 1960-61 to 22 per cent and 28 per cent in 1981-82, respectively.[92] A similar inter-sectoral shift in terms of sectoral shares of income and employment is noticed in another study of the Planning Department of Karnataka.[93] A recent empirical study provides adequate evidence to the sectoral shift. The study shows that not only the State income originating from the primary sector, but also the proportion of workforce engaged in agriculture is going down in Karnataka. However, the rate of decline in the proportion of workforce in agriculture is much lower compared to the rate of decline in the share of the primary sector's income. The study also indicates that the share of income and also workforce in the primary sector are negatively associated with the development index.[94]

2.5 Inter-Industry Aspects of Structural Transformation: Theory and Evidence

The inter-industry aspects of structural change have also received some attention in the recent past. There have been a number of attempts to establish detailed patterns of growth within the industrial sector. The present study is concerned mainly with two of the variants of such study, viz. the changing importance of the consumer goods and capital goods industries and of the changing importance of the agro-based and non-agro-based industries.

The well-known work in the case of the consumer goods and capital goods industries is associated with the name of Walter Hoffmann.[95] According to Hoffmann, the relative shares of consumer goods industries and capital-goods industries in the industrial output undergo a change during the process of industrialisation; initial stages of industrialisation are characterised by the predominance of consumer goods industries, whereas the capital goods industries come to predominate the industrial activity in the mature stages of industrialisation. He says: ". . . the structure of the manufacturing sector of the economy has always followed a uniform pattern. The food, textile, leather and furniture industries – which we define as 'consumer goods industries' – always develop first during the process of industrialisation. But the metal-working, vehicle-building, engineering and chemical industries – the 'capital goods industries' – soon develop faster than the first group. This can be seen throughout the process of industrialisation. Consequently, the ratio of the net output (value added) in the consumer goods industries continually declines as compared with the net output of the capital goods industries".[96] Though Hoffmann argues that it is a gradual process, in his analysis he divides it into a number of stages. In stage I, the ratio of consumer goods output to capital goods output is 5($\pm$1) to 1; Stage II, has a ratio of 2.5($\pm$1) to 1; and Stage III has a ratio of 1($\pm$0.5) to 1. Thus, in all these stages, the output of capital goods, starting from a much smaller base, rises faster than consumer goods output until in Stage IV capital goods output is higher than consumer goods output. In other words, consumer goods industries come to dominate Stage I; capital goods industries become increasingly important and have nearly half as great as consumer goods industries in Stage II; and in

Stage III, a balance is found between the two with a tendency for the capital goods industries to expand rather more rapidly than the consumer goods industries.

Walter Hoffmann himself has provided empirical evidence in support of his hypothesis. The downward movement in the ratio of the net output of consumer goods industries to that of capital goods industries is observable for a wide range of countries which are included in the empirical study of Hoffmann.[97] The older industrialised countries like Belgium, Great Britain, France and Switzerland are found to have passed Stage I before the end of the 19th century; Brazil, Chile, Mexico, Argentina, India and New Zealand are found to have passed it during 1906-48; and countries like Great Britain, France, Switzerland, Denmark, Belgium, Italy, Sweden, the USA, Germany, Canada, Australia and South Africa are found to have reached Stage III by the middle of the 20th century.[98] K. Ramakrishna Sharma's empirical study[99] which inquires into the industrialisation process of Andhra Pradesh during 1960-71 also lends support to the theory of Hoffmann. The study reveals that Andhra Pradesh is found to have entered Stage III of industrialisation visualised by Hoffmann.[100]

Not much seems to have been done either to theorise or to test empirically the changing relationship between the agro-based and non-agro-based industries. However, it is not very difficult to reason out the changing relationship between the two during the process of industrialisation, which, while causing several other structural changes, also causes changes in the inter-industry relations of this kind. Generally, when a region is industrially backward, the traditional and agro-based industries claim a relatively higher share in industrial employment, capital and output. A greater part of the industrial income generated in such a backward region comes from the traditional industrial sector, which is predominantly agro-based. But as the process of industrialisation gains momentum with greater emphasis on the development of the basic and capital-intensive industries, the industrial structure of the region gets diversified, and the share of the agro-based industries naturally falls in the total employment, capital and output.[101] All this is to say that in the initial phases of industrialisation, generally, the agro-based industries come to dominate the industrial activity, and in the mature stages of industrialisation, the non-agro-based industries come to dominate the industrial activity. And over a period of time, during the process of industrialisation, there is a tendency for the agro-based industries to decline in importance, and for the non-agro-based industries to increase in importance.

K. Ramakrishna Sharma[102] lends support to the above-cited hypothesis. The study which covers one decade – from 1960 to 1971 – provides conclusive evidence to the reduction in the importance of agro-based industries in the State of Andhra Pradesh. The proportion of workers in the agro-based industries declined from 83.57 per cent in 1960 to 76.41 per cent in 1971; and their share in the fixed capital declined from 56.77 per cent in 1960 to 26.28 per cent in 1971; and their share in the total value added declined from 72.76 per cent in 1960 to 45.76 per cent in 1971.[103] At the same time the inquiry also provides evidence to the continued dominance of the agro-based industries in the State economy particularly in terms of their share in industrial employment.

NOTES

1. Patnaik, S.C., *Economics of Regional Development and Planning in Third World Countries*, Associated Publishing House, New Delhi, 1981, pp. 16-17.
2. *Note:* Throughout this work, purely for literary simplification, the terms such as North-South Problem and "Regional Dualism" are used interchangeably with "Regional Disparities", "Spatial Disparities" and "Areal Disparities".
3. Lutz, U., *Italy: A Study of Economic Development*, Oxford University Press. London, 1962.
4. Quoted, Nair, K.R.G., *Regional Experience in a Developing Economy*, Wiley Eastern Ltd., New Delhi, 1982, p, viii.
5. Patnaik, S.C., *op. cit.*, (1981), p.1.
6. Holland, S., *Capital versus Regions*, Macmillan, London, 1976.
7. Singh, Jiwitesh Kumar, *Regional Economics*, Bharathi Prakashan, Varanasi, 1978, p, 38.
8. Quoted, *Ibid.*, p.38.
9. *Ibid.*, p.38.
10. Myrdal, G., *Economic Theory and Underdeveloped Regions*, Gerald Duckworth, 1957.
11. Hirschman, A.O., *The Strategy of Economic Development*, New Haven, Yale University Press, USA, 1958.
12. Hicks, J.R., *Essays in World Economics*. Clarendon Press, Oxford, 1958.
13. Williamson, J.G. "Regional Inequality and the Process of National Development: A Description of the Patterns", *Economic Development and Cultural Change*. Vol. XIII, No. 4, Part II, July 1965.
14. Alonso, William, "Urban and Regional Imbalances in Economic Development", *Economic Development and Cultural Change*. Vol. 17, No. 1, October 1968.
15. Myrdal, G., *Economic Theory and Underdeveloped Regions*, Vora and Co. (P) Ltd., Bombay, 1958, p. 38.
16. *Ibid.*, p.38.
17. For details see Hughes, R.B., "Interregional Income Differences:

Self-perpetuation", *Southern Economic Journal.* Vol. 28, No. 1, July 1961, pp.42-44.
18. Hirschman, A.O., *op. cit.*, (1958), p. 183.
19. *Ibid.*, pp. 183-184.
20. *Ibid.*, pp. 187-188.
21. *Ibid.*, p. 188.
22. *Ibid.*, p. 190.
23. Alonso, William, *op. cit.*, (1968), pp. 8-9.
24. Hirschman, A.O., *op. cit.*, 1958, p. 187.
25. Hicks, J.R., *op. cit.*, 1958.
26. Quoted, Baer Werner, "Regional Inequality and Economic Growth in Brazil", *Economic Development and Cultural Change*, Vol. XII, No. 1, October 1963, p. 269.
27. *Ibid.*, pp. 270-271.
28. Williamson, J.G., *op.cit.*, (1965).
29. *Ibid.*, p. 4.
30. *Ibid.*, p. 9.
31. For details, see *Ibid.*, pp. 5-9.
32. Myrdal, G., *op. cit.*, (1958).
33. Hirschman, A.O., *op. cit.*, (1958).
34. Williamson, J.G., *op. cit.*, (1965).
35. Alonso, William, *op. cit.*, (1968).
36. Quoted, Singh, A.K., *Patterns of Regional Development: A Comparative Study*, Sterling Publishers (P.) Ltd., New Delhi, 1981, pp. 2-3.
37. Williamson, J.G., *op. cit.*, (1965).
38. *Ibid.*, p. 14.
39. Dadibhavi, R.V., *Inter-District Variations in Income, Productivity and Industrial Structure in Karnataka State*, Ph.D., Thesis, M.S. University of Baroda, 1983, pp. 11-12.
40. Alonso, William, *op. cit.*, (1968), p. 9.
41. Quoted, *Ibid.*
42. *Ibid.*, p. 9.
43. Werner, Baer., *op. cit.*, 1963.
44. *Ibid.*, pp. 271-272.
45. Koropeckyj, I.S., "Equalisation of Regional Development in Socialist Countries", *Economic Development and Cultural Change*. Vol. 21, No. 1, October 1972.
46. *Note*: NMP (Net Material Product) includes only the net value added in material production branches (industry, agriculture, construction, freight transportation, the production-serving communication, trade and public catering, material and technical supply, procurements and others) and excludes the net value added in service and government sectors.
47. Booth, E.J.R. "Interregional Income Differences", *Southern Economic Journal*, Vol. 31. No. 1, July 1964.
48. Perloff, H.S., Dunn, Jr. E.S., Lampard, E.E., and Muth, Richard. F., *Regions, Resources and Economic Growth, Resources for the Future*. John Hopkins Press, Baltimore, 1960.
49. Pandit, S.A., *Regional Distribution of Industries in India*, Ph.D. Thesis, University of Bombay, 1949, pp. 60-61.
50. Williamson, J.G., *op. cit.*, (1965).

51. Quoted, Mathur, Ashok, "Regional Development and Income Disparities in India: A Sectoral Analysis", *Economic Development and Cultural Change*, Vol. 31, No. 3, April 1983.
52. Rao, S.K., "A Note on Measuring Economic Distances Between Regions in India", *Economic and Political Weekly*, Vol. VIII, No. 17, April 28, 1973, p. 799.
53. Sampath, R.K., "Inter-State Inequalities in Income in India: 1951-71", *Indian Journal of Regional Science*, Vol. IX, No. I, 1977, p. 8.
54. Nath, V., "Regional Development in Indian Planning" *Economic and Political Weekly*, Vol. v, Nos. 3, 4 and 5. Annual Number, January 1970, p. 259.
55. Tandon, B.B., "Inter-State Income Disparities since 1960-61", *The Asian Economic Review*, April and August 1982, pp. 49-54.
56. Jha, D.N., "Regional Imbalances in India (1951-1971)", *Southern Economist*, Annual Number, May 1, 1978, pp. 25-32.
57. Nair, K.R.G., "Inter-State Income Disparities in India", *Indian Journal of Regional Science*, Vol. III(2), 1971, p. 49.
58. Nair, K.R.G., "A Note on Inter-State Differentials in India, 1950-51 to 1960-61", *Journal of Development Studies*, July 7, 1973, pp. 441-447.
59. Nair, K.R.G. *op. cit.*, 1982, pp. 24-25.
60. Quoted, *Ibid.*, p. VII-VIII.
61. Tiwari, R.T., "Inter-regional Disparities in Levels of Development (Indian Experience)", *Man and Development*, Vol. VI, No. 1, March, 1984, p. 24.
62. Mathur, O.P., "The Problem of Interregional Disparities: The Indian Background", *Indian Journal of Regional Science*, Vol. V. No. 1, 1973, p. 90.
63. Quoted, Mathur, Ashok, *op. cit.*, (1983), p. 476.
64. Venkataramaiah, P., "Inter-State Variations in Industry, 1951-61: A Comment", *Economic and Political Weekly*, 4, August 1969, p. 1281.
65. Quoted, Mathur, Ashok, *op. cit.*, (1983), p. 476.
66. *Ibid.*, pp. 478-479.
67. Goswami, S.P., *Location of Factories in Maharashtra — An Analysis of the Trends During 1960s*, Ph.D. Thesis, University of Bombay, 1981, pp. 2-4.
68. Sharma Ramakrishna, K., *Industrial Development of Andhra Pradesh — A Regional Analysis*, Himalaya Publishing House, Bombay, 1982, p. 132.
69. D'Souza, V.L. *Economic Development of Mysore State*, Bangalore Press, 1937.
70. Balakrishna, R., *Industrial Development of Mysore*, Bangalore Press, 1940.
71. Mahajan, Y.S. *Industrialisation of Karnataka*, Karnataka Chamber of Commerce, Hubli, 1950.
72. Baldwin, B. George., *Industrial Growth in South India*, The Free Press, Glencoe, Illinois, 1959.
73. Munshi, M.C. *Location of Industries in Mysore State*, Indian Statistical Institute, Calcutta, 1962.
74. Shetty, H.V., *Industrial Problems of Mysore State (with special reference to location and regional balance)*, Ph.D. Thesis, Karnatak University, 1964.
75. Hiremath, N.S., *Economic Planning and Development in Karnataka*, Ph.D. Thesis Karnatak University, 1978.
76. Puttaswamaiah, K., *Economic Development of Karnataka; A Treatise in Continuity and Change*, Oxford and IBH, 1980.
77. Sumitra, Gladys, "Some Aspects of Regional Development in Karnataka — An Inter-District Analysis", paper presented at the UGC Seminar on "Regional Dispersal of Industries in Karnataka", held at B.R. Project, P.G. Centre,

University of Mysore, in January 1984.
78. Dadibhavi, R.V., "An Analysis of Inter-Taluka Disparity and Backwardness in Karnataka State, 1975-76", *Indian Journal of Regional Science*, Vol. XIV, No. 2, 1982.
79. Dadibhavi, R.V., *Inter-District Variations in Income, Productivity and Industrial Structure in Karnataka State*, Ph.D. Thesis, M.S. University, Baroda, 1983.
80. Clark, Colin, *The Conditions of Economic Progress*, (1st Edition) London, 1940.
81. Kuznets, Simon, "Quantitative Aspects of the Economic Growth of Nations: II Industrial Distribution of National Product and Labour Force", *Economic Development and Cultural Change*, Suppl. to Vol. No. 4, July, 1957. pp. 16-22.
82. Srinivas, T.Y., *Industrialisation and Economic Development*, Ph.D. Thesis, Bombay University, 1975, pp. 76-104.
83. Nair, K.R.G., *op. cit.*, (1982).
84. *Ibid.*, pp. 81-82.
85. Kuznets, Simon., *op. cit.*, (1957).
86. *Ibid.*, pp. 8-17.
87. *Ibid.*, pp. 19-32.
88. Srinivas., T.Y. *op. cit.*, (1957).
89. *Ibid.*, p.59.
90. Nair, K.R.G., *op. cit.*, 1982, p. 90.
91. Dadibhavi, R.V., *op. cit.*, 1983, pp. 86-87.
92. Planning Department (Project Formulation Division), *Background Paper on Planning in Karnataka: Performance and Strategy*, Government of Karnataka, Bangalore, Jan. 1984, pp. 163-165.
93. Planning Department, *An Approach to Karnataka's Seventh Five Year Plan 1985-90*, Government of Karnataka, Bangalore, June, 1984, pp. 222-223.
94. Venkataraman, L.S., Prahladachar, and Deshpande, R.S., *Dynamics of Rural Transformation in Karnataka, 1956-76*, ISEC, Bangalore, 1985, p. VI-2 and pp. 18-28.
95. Hoffmann, Walter, *The Growth of Industrial Economies*, Manchester, 1958.
96. Quoted, Sutcliffe, R.B., *Industry and Underdevelopment*, Addison Wesley Publishing Company, London, 1971, pp. 33-34.
97. Hoffmann, Walter, *op. cit.*, (1958).
98. For details, see Sutcliffe, R.B., *op. cit.*, (1971), pp. 33-40.
99. Sharma, Ramakrishna, K., *op. cit.*, 1982.
100. *Ibid.*, p. 69.
101. *Ibid.*, p. 59.
102. *Ibid.*, pp. 55-66.
103. *Ibid.*, pp. 60-62.

3

NET DISTRICT DOMESTIC PRODUCT AND INTER-DISTRICT DISPARITIES IN KARNATAKA

3.1 Introduction

THE FIRST two chapters, besides locating the roots of regional disparities, have also shown that industrialisation and development, left to themselves, have a very natural tendency to engender areal disparities. They also make it explicitly clear that spatial disparities, which are a potential threat to the unity and integrity of a nation, can be minimised mainly, if not entirely, through an effective Government intervention. *Inter alia*, we come to know that regional disparities are a global phenomenon, and they exist at various spatial levels in almost every country irrespective of the fact whether a particular country is a member of the North or of the South. India as a nation and Karnataka as a State have been experiencing the problem of areal disparities for quite some time. At the national level we have inter-State disparities and at the State level, we have inter-district disparities. With the express intention of narrowing down the inter-regional disparities, the planners and administrators in India have been converting their concern into action through a variety of region-specific policies and programmes. Here it is to be pointed out that any regional policy to be effective needs to be based on a thorough knowledge of the directional and dimensional contours of regional disparities, which the planning authorities can afford to have only if they can measure regional development with some operationally meaningful criteria. In India, as in some other parts of the world, attempts have been made to measure regional economic progress by using devices such as composite index of economic development, composite index of levels of living, levels of NDP, value added in manufacturing, spread of industrial activity, industrial employment, sectoral shares of output and workforce, PQLI, regional spread in the structural diversification, and so on. Of late, per capita NDP has come to be accepted as a relatively reliable measure of development. There seems to be very wide agreement among economic statisticians that the per capita NDP constitutes the most appropriate index with which to measure or compare growth, despite all the well-known and acknowledged imperfections that attended upon it. It does measure in a rough sort of way the average welfare of the citizens.[1]

In the present study which is confined to the State of Karnataka, the nature, extent and trends in inter-district disparities are examined with reference to the levels of NDP, spread of industrial activity, and regional spread in the structural diversification, as measured by the sectoral shares of income. And the present chapter devotes itself to an analysis of inter-district disparities as measured by NDP and sectoral shares of income. A part of the purpose of this chapter is to obtain an overall image of the dynamics of regional inequalities in the State, and a part of the purpose is to provide a useful background for a critical examination of industrialisation in Karnataka – regional and structural – that follows in the ensuing chapters. And the disparity analysis in terms of NDP may also help us to find out whether inter-district disparities in industrialisation have any bearing on inter-district disparities in development. With this given focus in view, including this introductory section, this chapter is split into 11 sections. The estimation of NDDP and the limitations that go with it, with special reference to Karnataka, are discussed in the second section. The third section, by using cross-section analysis, assesses the extent of inter-district disparities in per capita NDDP for the years 1960-61, 1970-71 and 1980-81. The fourth section, by using intertemporal analysis, examines the disparity behaviour between 1960-61 and 1980-81; it lays special emphasis on the much debated divergence-convergence trends over time. The fifth and sixth sections undertake both the cross-section and inter-temporal analyses of inter-district inequalities in terms of the per capita NDDP of the primary sector; the seventh and eighth sections, of the secondary sector; and the ninth and tenth sections, of the tertiary sector. The analysis which is being made in sections five to ten pertains to the regional spread of the structural diversification of different districts as measured by the proportion of income from each sector which is also an indicator of the level of development. The analysis of these sections is comparable with that of the preceding sections. And the eleventh section concludes the discussion by recording the main findings.

3.2 Estimation of NDDP in Karnataka

The estimation of NDDP, as is being done by the State Income Division of the Directorate of Economics and Statistics, is based on the concept of "income originating" rather than on "income accruing". The "income originating" concept of NDDP refers to the income generated within the geographical and administrative boundaries of a district in a given year, whereas the "income accruing" concept refers to the income received by the residents of a district in a given year. These concepts of income estimation are also found in the estimation of national income in India; NDP reflects the "income originating" and the Net National Income at Factor Cost reflects the "income accruing". In this regard, the Planning Commission opines that for a comparative study of the level of industrial and economic development of regions, it is sufficient to have income originating within a region.[2] The present study uses the NDDP data based on the "income originating" concept for measuring the economic progress of the districts of Karnataka, for two reasons. First, the principal purpose of the present chapter is to examine the inter-district disparities, and as such, it suits the purpose. Second, the NDDP estimates prepared by the Directorate of Economics and Statistics, the only source available, are based on the "income originating" concept. Of course, the "income originating" concept is beset with some statistical and conceptual problems.[3]

Recently the Directorate of Economics and Statistics, Bangalore, brought out a revised series of NDDP at factor cost by industry origin for some selected years. For the purpose of estimating NDDP by industry origin, the district economy is divided into 16 sectors, which are further compressed into three broad sectors, namely, the primary, secondary and tertiary.[4] The sum total of the economic value of all the goods and services produced during a given year, at factor cost, within the geographical boundaries of a district is regarded as NDDP. Depending upon the nature of the available data, production and apportionment methods are adopted to arrive at the Net District Sectoral Output.[5]

The way that the present study uses the NDDP data is partly governed by the nature of the data made available by the Directorate of Economics and Statistics, and partly by the purpose of the study. The available data do not enable us to undertake a time-series analysis; the data on NSDP of Karnataka at factor cost by industry origin are available right from 1970-71, but no such data are available for NDDP; the NDDP data at factor cost by industry origin are available for 1960-61 and 1970-71 at current prices, and for 1975-76, 1980-81, 1982-83 and 1983-84 at current as well as constant prices (i.e. 1970-71 prices). In view of these limitations, the present study resorts to inter-temporal and cross-section analysis of the NDDP data which, to a great extent, serves the purpose of the study. At this juncture, it is pertinent to point out that in order to get a realistic account of inter-district variations in NDDP, it becomes necessary to neutralise the effects of rising prices on NDDP. But we do not have any appropriate price indices to convert the 1970-71 and 1980-81 data to 1960-61 prices. However, the Directorate of Economics and Statistics has reduced the sectoral composition of NSDP up to 1977-78 in terms of 1960-61 prices. In the present study, the deflator implicit in the sectoral income by industry origin provided by DES is used to deflate the sectoral incomes of the districts to suit our purpose. Of course, such an exercise assumes a nearly uniform price movement among the districts between 1960-61 and 1980-81.

In the present study, the per capita NDDP for all the 19 districts of Karnataka for the years 1960-61, 1970-71 and 1980-81 is derived by dividing each district's NDDP by its population as per the 1961, 1971 and 1981 censuses respectively. And the per capita NDDP for all the three points of time is expressed at constant prices, i.e., at 1960-61 prices.

3.3 Per Capita NDDP and Inter-District Disparities: A Cross-Section Analysis

The cross-section analysis undertaken in this section, *inter alia*, is designed partly to ascertain an idea as to the magnitude of regional disparities in the levels of development at three different points of time in Karnataka, and partly to provide the disparity information necessary for the inter-temporal analysis that follows in the next section. The per capita NDDP data of all the 19 districts for 1960-61, 1970-71 and 1980-81 are furnished in Table 3.1. Table 3.1 reveals the existence of wide inter-district variations in the levels of development in the State.

In 1960-61, on the one extreme there is Kodagu, the highest per capita NDDP district, with Rs. 721, and on the other extreme there is Bidar, the lowest per capita NDDP district, with Rs. 197. If this inter-district development distance is viewed with reference to the per capita NDP of the State of Rs. 293, the magnitude of the divergence becomes clear. Kodagu's per capita NDDP is higher than the State's per capita NDP by 146 per cent, and, on the other hand, the per capita NDDP of Bidar is lower than the State's per capita NDP by 33 per cent. The disparity situation may also be understood by classifying the districts into two groups – relatively developed and relatively less developed – by taking the per capita NSDP as the basis. As per this criterion, seven districts, namely, Kodagu, Shimoga, Uttara Kannada, Chikmagalur, Dakshina Kannada, Bellary and Hassan, come under the classification of the relatively developed districts, and the remaining 12 districts come under the classification of the relatively less developed districts.

TABLE 3.1: Per Capita NDDP of Karnataka: 1960-61, 1970-71 and 1980-81 (at 1960-61 prices)

Sl. No.	Districts	1960-61		1970-71		1980-81	
		(in Rs.)	Rank	(in Rs.)	Rank	(in Rs.)	Rank
1	2	3	4	5	6	7	8
1.	Kodagu	721	1	1,172	1	979	1
2.	Shimoga	572	2.5	442	4	442	4
3.	Uttara Kannada	572	2.5	390	6	338	13
4.	Chikmagalur	475	4	580	2	569	2
5.	Dakshina Kannada	354	5	363	10	400	5.5
6.	Bellary	303	6	445	3	385	8
7.	Hassan	299	7	364	9	389	7
8.	Tumkur	281	8	257	18	301	16
9.	Chitradurga	272	9	366	8	400	5.5
10.	Belgaum	264	10	307	15	340	12
11.	Mysore	257	11	347	11	364	11
12.	Mandya	256	12	315	14	373	9
13.	Dharwad	255	13	319	13	333	14
14.	Bangalore	254	14	382	7	501	3
15.	Kolar	236	15	265	17	199	19
16.	Raichur	225	16	413	5	370	10
17.	Gulbarga	221	17	338	12	305	15
18.	Bijapur	201	18	249	19	234	18
19.	Bidar	197	19	270	16	296	17
	Karnataka	293	—	357	—	374	

Note: The districts are arranged in the descending order of per capita NDDP in 1960-61.

Source: Derived from Appendix Tables 3.1, 3.2 and 3.3.

The disparity situation in 1970-71 is not materially different from the earlier one; wide variations do exist. Kodagu with Rs. 1,172 is the highest per capita NDDP district, and Bijapur with Rs. 249 is the lowest per capita NDDP district. The per capita NDDP of Kodagu is higher than the per capita NSDP by 228 per cent, and the per capita NDDP of Bijapur is lower than the per capita NSDP by 30 per cent. On the basis of the per capita NSDP of Karnataka, 10 districts, namely, Kodagu, Shimoga, Uttar Kannada, Chikmagalur, Dakshina Kannada, Bellary, Hassan, Chitradurga, Bangalore and Raichur, can be regarded as relatively developed, and the remaining nine districts as relatively less developed.

Inter-district disparities in the levels of development are found in 1980-81 also. Kodagu with Rs. 979 claims the position of the highest per capita NDDP district in the State, whereas Kolar with Rs. 199 becomes the lowest per capita NDDP district. Kodagu's per capita NDDP is higher than the per capita NSDP of Rs. 374, by 162 per cent, and Kolar's per capita NDDP is lower than the per capita NSDP by 47 per cent. And in 1980-81, only eight districts, namely, Kodagu, Shimoga, Chikmagalur, Dakshina Kannada, Bellary, Hassan, Chitradurga and Bangalore, with their per capita incomes higher than the per capita income of the State, claim the position of relatively developed districts, and the remaining 11 districts, with their per capita incomes lower than the State's, attract for themselves the positions of relatively less developed districts.

Thus, the data presented in Table 3.1 reveal the existence of inter-district disparities in the levels of development at all the three points of time – 1960-61, 1970-71 and 1980-81. Further, to give quantitative touch to such disparities, range ratio, standard deviation and coefficient of variation are calculated for the per capita NDDP for all the three points of time. They are presented in Table 3.2.[6]

TABLE 3.2: **Range Ratio, Standard Deviation, and Coefficient of Variation of Per Capita NDDP of Karnataka : 1960-61, 1970-71 and 1980-81**

Years	Range Ratio	Standard Deviation	Coefficient of Variation
1	2	3	4
1960-61	0.57	143.55	43.88
1970-71	0.65	197.89	49.58
1980-81	0.66	160.30	40.51

Source: Derived from Table 3.1.

The values of some of the measures of dispersion presented in Table 3.2 very clearly indicate the existence of areal disparities in all the three points of time considered in the present study. Two recent studies[7] on Karnataka also reveal the presence of inter-district variations in the levels of development.

3.4 Per Capita NDDP and Inter-District Disparities: An Inter-Temporal Analysis

The principal aim of the inter-temporal analysis here is to find out the behaviour pattern of spatial disparities over time; it also helps us to know whether the inter-district disparities have been converging or diverging during the period considered in the present study; and incidentally it also indicates whether the area-specific programmes designed by the Government of Karnataka to minimise areal disparities have been effective in doing so. One important fact that emerges from the second chapter, in which a number of empirical studies are reviewed, is that there is no single view about the inter-temporal behaviour of regional disparities; different studies for different areal units have provided evidence to different hypotheses on convergence-divergence trends. In view of such divergent evidences, an attempt is made in this section to closely examine the disparity trends in per capita NDDP in Karnataka, between 1960-61 and 1970-71, and between 1970-71 and 1980-81. In this direction some of the simple statistical tools are used to analyse the disparity trends.

Table 3.1 itself presents the ranks of all the 19 districts in 1960-61, 1970-71 and 1980-81. If we read in-between columns 4, 6 and 8, we get to know that, with a few exceptions, there have been very few changes in the ranks of the districts over time. And to verify the empirical validity of this view the rank correlation coefficients are worked out. The rank correlation coefficients turn out to be +0.65 for the first decade (1960-61 to 1970-71), +0.83 for the second decade (1970-71 to 1980-81), and +0.66 for the two decades put together (1960-61 to 1980-81). These coefficients indicate that the ranks of the districts are almost identical between 1960-61 and 1970-71, 1970-71 and 1980-81, and between 1960-61 and 1980-81. No doubt there are a few shifts, but they are not very significant when compared to the overall pattern of stability. The glaring exceptions for the initial and terminal years of the study are Uttara Kannada, Tumkur, Bangalore, Kolar and Raichur. Bangalore, which holds the 14th rank in 1960-61, claims the 3rd in 1980-81; Raichur, which holds the 16th rank in 1960-61, claims the 10th rank in 1980-81; on the other hand, Uttara Kannada, which holds the rank between the 2nd and 3rd in 1960-61, goes down to the 13th rank in 1980-81; Tumkur, which holds the 8th rank in 1960-61, moves down to the 16th rank; and Kolar, which holds the 15th rank in 1960-61, moves down to the 19th rank in 1980-81. However, the correlation coefficients do not provide any useful evidence about the convergence-divergence trends. The relative stability in the ranks of the districts roughly suggests the presence of regional disparities.

The values of standard deviation and coefficient of variation of per capita NDDP for 1960-61, 1970-71 and 1980-81 are already presented in Table 3.2. These values give us some idea as to the inter-temporal behaviour of convergence-divergence trends. The values of both the standard deviation and coefficient of variation for the first decade (1960-61 to 1970-71) indicate an increasing trend of inter-district inequalities, whereas their values for the second decade (1970-71 to 1980-81) indicate a declining trend of disparities. The standard deviation moves up from 143.55 in 1960-61 to 197.89 in 1970-71, and then moves down to 160.30 in 1980-81. Similarly, the coefficient of variation moves up from 43.88 per cent in 1960-61 to 49.58 per cent in 1970-71 and then moves down to 40.51 per cent in 1980-81. If this inter-temporal inter-district disparity trend is projected on a graph, it traces out an inverted "U". Here, it is interesting to note that this finding lends support to the concentration cycle hypothesis propounded by G. Myrdal.[8], A.O. Hirschman,[9] J.G. Williamson,[10] william Alonso,[11] and found empirically valid by J.G. Williamson[12] and I.S. Koropeckyj.[13] But, it is equally intriguing to note that the inter-temporal study of R.V. Dadibhavi on Karnataka[14] lands support to the accordian effect hypothesis.[15]

To get further insight into the divergence-convergence trends, the district per capita income relatives are calculated for two points of time – 1960-61 and 1980-81. The district per capita income relatives are obtained for both the years – initial and terminal – by expressing each district's per capita income as a percentage of the State per capita income. Such per capita income relatives and the changes registered by them between 1960-61 and 1980-81 are presented in Table 3.3.

Two vital facts about inter-district disparities emerge out of the data presented in Table 3.3. First of all, the data show the existence of inter-district disparities in both the years under consideration. In

TABLE 3.3: Variations in District Per Capita Income Relatives in Karnataka: 1960-61 and 1980-81

Sl. No.	Districts	District Per Capita Income Relatives		% Change in 1980-81 over 1960-61
		1960-61	1980-81	
1	2	3	4	5
1.	Kodagu	246.08	261.77	+6.38
2.	Shimoga	195.22	118.18	-39.46
3.	Uttara Kannada	195.22	90.37	-53.71
4.	Chikmagalur	162.12	152.14	-6.16
5.	Dakshina Kannada	120.82	106.95	-11.48
6.	Bellary	103.41	102.94	-0.46
7.	Hassan	102.05	104.01	+1.92
8.	Tumkur	95.90	80.48	-16.08
9.	Chitradurga	92.83	106.95	+15.21
10.	Belgaum	90.10	90.91	+0.90
11.	Mysore	87.71	97.33	+10.97
12.	Mandya	87.37	99.73	+14.15
13.	Dharwad	87.03	89.04	+2.31
14.	Bangalore	86.69	133.96	+54.53
15.	Kolar	80.55	53.21	-33.94
16.	Raichur	76.79	98.93	+28.83
17.	Gulbarga	75.43	81.55	+8.11
18.	Bijapur	68.60	62.57	-8.79
19.	Bidar	67.24	79.14	+17.70
	Karnataka	100	100	—

Note: The districts are arranged in the descending order of per capita NDDP in 1960-61.

Source: Derived from Appendix Tables 3.1 and 3.3.

1960-61, at the top there is Kodagu with 246.08 as its per capita income relative, and at the bottom there is Bidar with 67.24 as its per capita income relative. Similarly, in 1980-81 Kodagu continues to be at the top with 261.77 as its per capita income relative, and at the bottom we find Kolar with only 53.21 as its per capita income relative. The spread between the per capita income relative of the district at the top and of the district at the bottom indicates the existence of disparities. Secondly, there are also indications in the table as to the convergence trend. During the period under study, the district per capita income relative has moved up by more than 10 per cent in the case of six districts, namely, Chitradurga, Mysore, Mandya, Bangalore, Raichur and Bidar. Here it is to be pointed out that all these districts were classified (in the preceding section) as relatively less developed districts on the basis of their 1960-61 per capita NDDP. On the other hand, district per capita income relative has moved down by more than 10 per cent in the case of five other districts, namely, Shimoga, Uttara Kannada, Dakshina Kannada, Tumkur and Kolar. Of the five, the first three were in the list of relatively developed districts, and the last two were in the list of relatively less developed districts in 1960-61. These changes – the higher-per-capita-income districts recording a decline, and the lower-per-capita income districts recording an increase – roughly indicate a trend of convergence.

The correlation coefficient (r) between the district per capita income relatives of 1960-61 and the percentage changes in 1980-81 over 1960-61 is also worked out. The "r" turns out to be –0.18. This value of "r" indicates the existence of an inverse association between the district per capita income relatives of 1960-61 and the percentage change in the relatives between 1960-61 and 1980-81. However, this value of "r" does not provide any conclusive evidence in support of the converging trend, since it is very negligible.

3.5 Per Capita Primary NDDP and Inter-District Disparities: A Cross-Section Analysis

Ashok Mathur in his recent study[16] has used the per capita sectoral incomes to examine the trends in inter-State disparities in India. In the present study, the per capita sectoral incomes are derived by dividing each sector's income in the districts by the total population of the respective districts. And for deriving the per capita figures for 1960-61, 1970-71 and 1980-81, the population figures of 1961, 1971 and 1981 censuses are used respectively. The data in respect of per capita primary income are given in Table 3.4

Columns 3, 5 and 7 very clearly exhibit the existence of wide variations in the per capita primary NDDP in all the three points of time. Kodagu claims the highest per capita primary income, whereas Bangalore claims the lowest per capita primary income in all the three points of time considered.

The spread between the shares of the two districts is very wide; as against Kodagu's claim of Rs. 608, Rs. 1,003 and Rs. 799 for 1960-61, 1970-71 and 1980-81 respectively, Bangalore claims Rs. 77, Rs. 79 and Rs. 60 respectively for the same years.

TABLE 3.4: Per Capita Primary NDDP in Karnataka : 1960-61, 1970-71 and 1980-81 (at 1960-61 Prices)

Sl. No.	Districts	1960-61 (in Rs.)	1960-61 Rank	1970-71 (in Rs.)	1970-71 Rank	1980-81 (in Rs.)	1980-81 Rank
1	2	3	4	5	6	7	8
1.	Kodagu	608.00	1	1,003.0	1	799.00	1
2.	Uttara Kannada	442.00	2	246.0	7	190.00	10
3.	Shimoga	379.00	3	293.5	5	264.00	3
4.	Chikmagalur	364.00	4	461.0	2	421.00	2
5.	Dakshina Kannada	228.50	5	181.0	13	176.50	12
6.	Hassan	220.00	6	259.0	6	259.00	4
7.	Tumkur	201.00	7	169.5	15	169.00	14
8.	Bellary	183.00	8	305.0	4	222.00	8
9.	Mandya	178.00	9	227.5	9	246.00	6
10.	Belgaum	174.00	10	183.0	12	193.00	9
11.	Chitradurga	159.00	11	232.0	8	235.00	7
12.	Kolar	152.00	12	162.0	17	96.50	18
13.	Mysore	144.00	13	197.5	11	177.00	11
14.	Dharwad	136.50	14	166.0	16	165.00	15
15.	Raichur	135.00	15	306.0	3	249.50	5
16.	Gulbarga	122.00	16	218.5	10	161.00	16
17.	Bidar	107.00	17	172.0	14	176.00	13
18.	Bijapur	103.00	18	141.0	18	111.00	17
19.	Bangalore	77.00	19	79.0	19	60.00	19
	Karnataka	179.50		209.50		183.50	

Note: The districts are arranged in the descending order of per capita primary income in 1960-61.

Source: Derived from the Appendix Tables 3.1, 3.2 and 3.3.

A better picture of disparity can be obtained by comparing the per capita primary income of each district with that of the State's per capita primary income. The per capita primary income of the State is Rs. 179.50 in 1960-61. Kodagu's per capita primary income is higher than the State's by 239 per cent, and on the other extreme, Bangalore's per capita primary income is lower than the State's by 57 per cent. If we classify the districts into two categories – those whose per capita primary income is higher than the State's and those whose per capita primary income is lower than the State's – by using the State's per capita income as the dividing line, eight districts, namely, Kodagu, Uttara Kannada, Shimoga, Chikmagalur, Dakshina Kannada, Hassan,

Tumkur and Bellary, come under the first category, and the remaining 11 districts come under the second category. This division of districts, among other things, shows the inter-district disparities in per capita primary income.

Inter-district disparities in per capita primary income are also found in the year 1970-71 in which the State's per capita primary income works out to Rs. 209.50. The per capita primary income of Kodagu, which tops the list, is higher than the State's by 279 per cent, whereas the per capita primary income of Bangalore, which occupies the last position, is lower than the State's by 62 per cent. In this year, 10 districts, namely, Kodagu, Uttara Kannada, Shimoga, Chikmagalur, Hassan, Bellary, Mandya, Chitradurga, Raichur and Gulbarga, have their per capita primary incomes higher than the State's and the remaining nine districts have per capita primary incomes lower than the State's. Thus the data for 1970-71 also show that there are inter-district disparities in per capita primary income.

A similar disparity situation also exists in 1980-81. At one end of the scale there is Kodagu whose per capita primary income exceeds the State's per capita primary income by 335 per cent, whereas, on the other end of the scale, there is Bangalore whose share lags behind the State's share by 67 per cent. In this year we have 10 districts, namely, Kodagu, Uttara Kannada, Shimoga, Chikmagalur, Hassan, Bellary, Mandya, Belgaum, Chitradurga and Raichur, whose per capita primary income is higher than the State's, and in the case of the remaining nine districts, their per capita primary income is lower than the State's.

To lend statistical support to the finding that inter-district disparities in per capita primary income exist, the range ratio, standard deviation and coefficient of variation are calculated and presented in Table 3.5.

TABLE 3.5: Range Ratio, Standard Deviation, and Coefficient of Variation of Per Capita Primary Income of Karnataka : 1960-61, 1970-71 and 1980-81

Years	Range Ratio	Standard Deviation	Coefficient of variation
1	2	3	4
1960-61	0.78	133.01	61.45
1970-71	0.85	191.76	72.83
1980-81	0.86	153.57	66.76

Source: Derived from Table 3.4

The values of the measures of dispersion presented in Table 3.5 do indicate the existence of regional disparities in the per capita primary income in the State. Ashok Mathur's inter-State study also finds such disparities in the 1950s, 1960s and 1970s.[17] And his study appears to be a pioneer study in this direction in India.

Thus, the cross-section analysis of regional disparities indicates that inter-district disparities in per capita primary income exist in all the three points of time considered in the present study.

3.6 Per Capita Primary NDDP and Inter-District Disparities: An Inter-Temporal Analysis

The cross-section analysis has confirmed the existence of inter-district disparities in per capita primary income in the years under study. And now in this section an inter-temporal analysis is conducted to know whether the disparities have been converging or diverging. In this regard, the rank correlation coefficient is worked out to know the stability or otherwise of the ranks of the districts in between 1960-61 and 1980-81. The standard deviation and coefficient of variation are worked out for 1960-61, 1970-71 and 1980-81, to examine the divergence-convergence trends. And to supplement these measures of dispersion the district per capita primary income relatives are calculated for the initial and terminal years of the present study.

The details in respect of the ranks allotted to all the districts of Karnataka for 1960-61, 1970-71 and 1980-81 are already presented in Table 3.4. The rank correlation coefficients for the first decade (1960-61 to 1970-71), second decade (1970-71 to 1980-81), and for the two decades put together (1960-61 to 1980-81) are 0.64, 0.91 and 0.69 respectively. These values indicate the relative stability of the ranks during the period under consideration. The first and the last ranks are consistently held by Kodagu and Bangalore respectively in all the three points of time. Of course, there are a few significant shifts. Uttara Kannada, which held the 2nd rank in 1960-61, moved down to the 10th rank in 1980-81; Dakshina Kannada, which held the 5th rank in 1960-61, moved down to the 12th rank in 1980-81; Tumkur, which held the 7th rank in 1960-61, moved down to the 14th rank in 1980-81; Kolar, which held the 12th rank in 1960-61, moved down to the 18th rank in 1980-81; but, on the contrary, Raichur, which held the 15th rank in 1960-61, moved up to the 5th rank in 1980-81. But for these shifts, there is reasonable stability in the ranks of the districts. And such stability indicates that the disparity situation has not undergone any material change between 1960-61 and 1980-81.

The values of standard deviation and coefficient of variation are already furnished in Table 3.5. They provide indisputable evidence about the inter-temporal trends in inter-district disparities in the per capita primary income. The absolute dispersion, as measured by standard deviation, records a rise from 133.01 in 1960-61 to 191.76 in 1970-71, and then records a fall to 153.57 in 1980-81. In the same way, the relative dispersion, as measured by coefficient of variation, records a rise from 61.45 in 1960-61 to 72.83 in 1970-71, and then records a fall of 66.76 in 1980-81. So far as convergence-divergence trends are concerned, these values lend themselves to more than one interpretation. If we consider their values only for 1960-61 and 1980-81, ignoring 1970-71, they lend support to the "self-perpetuation" hypothesis, propounded by R.B. Hughes[18] and found empirically valid by E.J.R. Booth,[19] according to which the regional disparities diverge in the process of national economic development. But, an altogether different picture emerges if all the three points of time are considered. When their values are considered for all the three points, they lend support to the "concentration cycle" hypothesis, and the per capita primary income displays an inverted U-shaped behaviour of inter-district disparities. That means the first interpretation shows the trend of divergence, whereas the second one, the trend of convergence. Here is is to be noted that in Ashok Mathur's inter-State study, the primary sector displays an upright U-shaped behaviour, rather than an inverted U-shaped behaviour.[20]

To further our understanding of disparity trends, the district per capita primary income relatives are worked out for 1960-61 and 1980-81. Table 3.6 provides all the details about the district relatives. It also shows the percentage change in the district relatives in 1980-81 over 1960-61.

Table 3.6 reveals a clear declining trend in regional disparities. Column 3 shows that the first eight districts have their relatives higher than 100, and the remaining 11 districts have their relatives lower than 100 in 1960-61. Of the 11, nine districts have come to register a sizeable increase in their relatives in 1980-81. On the other hand, of the eight higher relative districts, four districts have come to record a substantial fall in their relatives in 1980-81. These inter-temporal movements of district relatives are indicative of the convergence trend.

TABLE 3.6: Variations in District Per Capita Primary Income Relatives in Karnataka : 1960-61 and 1980-81

Sl. No.	Districts	District Per Capita Primary Income Relatives		% Change in 1980-81 over 1960-61
		1960-61	1980-81	
1	2	3	4	5
1.	Kodagu	338.72	435.42	+28.55
2.	Uttara Kannada	246.24	103.54	-57.95
3.	Shimoga	211.14	143.87	-31.86
4.	Chikmagalur	202.79	229.43	+13.14
5.	Dakshina Kannada	127.30	96.19	-24.44
6.	Hassan	122.56	141.14	+15.16
7.	Tumkur	111.98	92.10	-17.75
8.	Bellary	101.95	120.98	+18.67
9.	Mandya	99.16	134.06	+35.20
10.	Belgaum	96.94	105.18	+8.50
11.	Chitradurga	88.58	128.07	+44.58
12.	Kolar	84.68	52.59	-37.90
13.	Mysore	80.22	96.46	+20.24
14.	Dharwad	76.05	89.92	+18.24
15.	Raichur	75.21	135.97	+80.79
16.	Gulbarga	67.97	87.74	+29.09
17.	Bidar	59.61	95.91	+60.90
18.	Bijapur	57.38	60.49	+5.42
19.	Bangalore	42.90	32.70	-23.78
	Karnataka	100	100	—

Note: The districts are arranged in the descending order of per capita primary income in 1960-61.

Source: Derived from Table 3.4.

The correlation coefficient (*r*) is worked out to identify the nature of functional relationship between 1960-61 district per capita primary income relatives and the percentage change in 1980-81 over 1960-61. The correlation coefficient which turns out to be -0.28 indicates an inverse relationship the two variables.

Thus, most of the statistical tools used to measure the inter-temporal trends in disparities show that there has been a tendency towards the reduction of inter-district disparities in per capita primary NDDP in Karnataka.

3.7 Per Capita Secondary NDDP and Inter-District Disparities: A Cross-Section Analysis

The data in respect of the per capita secondary income for 1960-61, 1970-71 and 1980-81 are furnished in Table 3.7.

TABLE 3.7: Per Capita Secondary NDDP in Karnataka: 1960-61, 1970-71 and 1980-81 (at 1960-61 prices)

Sl. No.	Districts	1960-61		1970-71		1980-81	
		(in Rs.)	Rank	(in Rs.)	Rank	(in Rs.)	Rank
1	2	3	4	5	6	7	8
1.	Shimoga	126.00	1	70.50	3	88.00	4
2.	Bangalore	74.00	2	163.00	1	256.00	1
3.	Uttara Kannada	51.50	3	54.50	8	46.00	12
4.	Dakshina Kannada	51.00	4.5	85.50	2	101.00	2
5.	Chikmagalur	51.00	4.5	40.00	13	42.00	14
6.	Chitradurga	49.00	6	63.00	6	79.00	5
7.	Bellary	45.00	7	54.00	9	59.50	9
8.	Mysore	42.50	8	68.00	4.5	88.50	3
9.	Kodagu	42.00	9	68.00	4.5	66.00	6
10.	Bijapur	38.00	10	36.00	15	41.00	16
11.	Dharwad	36.00	11	56.00	7	61.50	7
12.	Gulbarga	33.00	12	45.25	11	58.00	10
13.	Mandya	30.50	13	30.50	17	36.50	17
14.	Tumkur	30.00	14.5	27.50	18	49.00	11
15.	Belgaum	30.00	14.5	52.00	10	60.00	8
16.	Raichur	29.00	16	37.00	14	41.25	15
17.	Kolar	25.00	17.5	34.00	16	27.50	19
18.	Bidar	25.00	17.5	25.00	19	34.00	18
19.	Hassan	22.00	19	44.00	12	44.00	13
	Karnataka	44.50	–	63.50	–	85.50	–

Note: The districts are arranged in the descending order of per capita Secondary Income in 1960-61.

Source: Derived from the Appendix Tables 3.1, 3.2 and 3.3.

A close scrutiny of the data in columns 3, 5 and 7 reveals the existence of wide variations in the per capita secondary income in all the three points of time. In 1960-61, there is Shimoga on the one extreme with Rs. 126, and on the other extreme, there is Hassan with Rs. 22; and the spread between the two works out to Rs. 104.

Shimoga's per capita secondary income is higher than the State's by 183 per cent, whereas, Hassan's per capita secondary income is lower than the State's by 51 per cent. The distance between the State's per capita secondary income and that of the districts' indicate the extent of spatial disparities. As per the data in Column 3, the first seven districts, namely, Shimoga, Bangalore, Uttara Kannada, Dakshina Kannada, Chikmagalur, Chitradurga and Bellary have their per capita shares higher than the State's, and the remaining 12 districts have their per capita shares lower than the State's. These economic distances of the districts are indicative of the existence of inter-district disparities.

Inter-district disparities in the per capita secondary income are also found in 1970-71. At the apex, there is Bangalore with Rs. 163, and at the bottom, there is Bidar with Rs. 25, and the spread between the two works out to Rs. 138. They are at great variance from the State's per capita secondary income. Bangalore's per capita share of the sector is higher than the State's by 157 per cent, whereas, Bidar's is lower than the State's by 61 per cent. In 1970-71, only five districts, namely, Shimoga, Bangalore, Dakshina Kannada, Mysore and Kodagu, have their per capita secondary incomes higher than the States, whereas, the remaining 14 districts have their shares lower than the State's.

The disparity situation in 1980-81 does not seem to be materially different from the one obtaining in 1960-61 and 1970-71. At the one end of the scale there is Bangalore with a per capita secondary income of Rs. 256 and, at the other, there is Kolar with Rs. 27.50, and the spread between the two comes to Rs. 228.50. Bangalore's per capita secondary income is higher than the State's by 199 per cent, whereas, Kolar's per capita secondary income is lower than the State's by 68 per cent. In this year, quite a few districts are at variance from the State's per capita secondary income. Column 7 shows that only four districts, namely, Shimoga, Bangalore, Dakshina Kannada and Mysore, have their per capita secondary incomes higher than the State's, and the remaining 15 districts have their figures lower than the State's.

To quantify the above findings about inter-district disparities in the per capita secondary income in Karnataka, the range, ratio, standard deviation and coefficient of variation are calculated and presented in Table 3.8.

A close perusal of the data in the table reveals the existence of inter-district disparities in the per capita secondary income in all the three points of time considered. Similar disparities in the per capita secondary income in 1950s, 1960s and 1970s are also noticed by

Ashok Mathur in his inter-State Study.[21]

TABLE 3.8: Range Ratio, Standard Deviation and Coefficient of Variation of Per Capita Secondary Income of Karnataka: 1960-61, 1970-71 and 1980-81

Years	Range Ratio	Standard Deviation	Coefficient of Variation
1	2	3	4
1960-61	0.70	22.98	52.57
1970-71	0.73	29.97	54.04
1980-81	0.81	48.65	72.29

Source: Derived from Table 3.7.

3.8 Per Capita Secondary NDDP and Inter-District Disparities: An Inter-Temporal Analysis

The previous section has shown that inter-district disparities in the per capita secondary income existed in 1960-61, 1970-71 and 1980-81. And the main purpose of the present section is to find out the inter-temporal behaviour of those disparities. In order to know whether the trend is in favour of convergence or divergence, some of the statistical tools such as rank correlation coefficient, standard deviation, coefficient of variation and district per capita relatives are used.

The data relating to the relative positions of the various districts in terms of their ranks in 1960-61, 1970-71, and 1980-81 are already presented in Table 3.7. The value of rank correlation coefficient turns out to be 0.74 for the first decade (1960-61 to 1970-71), 0.92 for the second decade (1970-71 to 1980-81) and 0.65 for the two decades put together (1960-61 to 1980-81). And these values indicate the relative stability of the ranks during the period under consideration. Of course, there are a few significant shifts. Uttara Kannada, Chikmagalur and Bijapur, which held the 3rd, 4.5th and 10th ranks in 1960-61, went down to the 12th, 14th and 16th ranks respectively in 1980-81; on the other hand, Belgaum which held the 14.5th rank in 1960-61 scaled up to the 8th rank in 1980-81. Except for these shifts, there is reasonable stability in the ranks of the districts. However, these rank correlation coefficients cannot say anything definite about the divergence-convergence trends.

The values of standard deviation and coefficient of variation help us to identify whether the inter-temporal trend has been favouring convergence or divergence. These values which are already presented in Table 3.8, unlike those of the per capita primary income, lend themselves to only one interpretation, whether we consider the first decade alone or the second decade alone, or the two decades together. The value of standard deviation records a consistent increase; it increases from 22.98 in 1960-61 to 29.97 in 1970-71, and further to 48.65 in 1980-81. It is also the case with the value of coefficient of variation; it increases from 52.57 in 1960-61 to 54.04 in 1970-71, and on to 72.29 in 1980-81. These values of standard deviation and coefficient of variation show that, inter-temporally, the trend has been in favour of divergence rather than convergence. Thus this finding lends full support to the "self-perpetuation" hypothesis. Incidentally, it is to be pointed out that Ashok Mathur's study reveals an inverted U-shaped behaviour of the inter-State disparities in the per capita secondary income.[22]

The district per capita secondary income relatives are worked out for the initial and terminal years of the study, to supplement the results of standard deviation and coefficient of variation in identifying the trends in regional disparities over time. The particulars of district relatives and of percentage change in 1980-81 over 1960-61 are given in Table 3.9.

The data show a clear trend of divergence. It is so because, most of the districts which claim lower district per capita relatives in 1960-61 have come to record a further fall in 1980-81. Of the 12 districts which claim less than 100 as their district per capita relatives in 1960-61 nine districts have come to record a further fall in 1980-81, and the remaining three districts have recorded a rise, but the increase is negligible. At the other end, of the seven districts which claim more than 100 as their district relatives in 1960-61, only Bangalore and Dakshina Kannada register an increase, and the rest register a fall in 1980-81. But the overall trend is indicative of divergence.

The correlation coefficient (r) which is worked out to identify the nature of association between the 1960-61 district per capita income relatives and the percentage change in 1980-81 over 1960-61 turns out to be -0.073 which indicates an inverse association between the two variables in question. Here it is to be pointed out that the correlation coefficient is statistically not significant. However, *per se*, it does not help us to say anything conclusively on the divergence-convergence trends.

TABLE 3.9: Variations in District Per Capita Secondary Income Relatives in Karnataka: 1960-61 and 1980-81

Sl. No.	Districts	District Per Capita Income Relatives		% Change in 1980-81 over 1960-61
		1960-61	1980-81	
1	2	3	4	5
1.	Shimoga	283.15	102.93	-63.65
2.	Bangalore	166.29	299.42	+80.06
3.	Uttara Kannada	115.73	53.80	-53.51
4.	Dakshina Kannada	114.61	118.13	+3.07
5.	Chikmagalur	114.61	49.12	-57.14
6.	Chitradurga	110.11	92.40	-16.08
7.	Bellary	101.12	69.60	-31.17
8.	Mysore	95.51	103.51	+8.38
9.	Kodagu	94.38	77.19	-18.21
10.	Bijapur	85.39	47.95	-43.85
11.	Dharwad	80.90	71.93	-11.09
12.	Gulbarga	74.16	67.84	-8.52
13.	Mandya	68.54	42.69	-37.72
14.	Tumkur	67.42	57.31	-15.00
15.	Belgaum	67.42	70.18	+4.09
16.	Raichur	65.17	48.25	-25.96
17.	Kolar	56.18	32.16	-42.76
18.	Bidar	56.18	39.77	-29.21
19.	Hassan	49.44	51.46	+4.09
	Karnataka	100	100	—

Note: The districts are arranged in the descending order of per capita secondary income in 1960-61.

Source: Derived from Table 3.7.

3.9 Per Capita Tertiary NDDP and Inter-District Disparities: A Cross-Section Analysis

The data pertaining to the per capita tertiary income for 1960-61, 1970-71 and 1980-81 are presented in Table 3.10.

The data in columns 3, 5 and 7 show the existence of inter-district disparities in per capita tertiary income in all the three points of time. In 1960-61, at the one end of the scale, there is Bangalore with a per capita tertiary income of Rs. 103, and at the other end, there is Mandya with a per capita tertiary income of Rs. 47.50, and the spread between the two comes to Rs. 55.50. Bangalore's figure is higher than the State's by 49 per cent, whereas, Mandya's is lower than the State's by 31 per cent. Column 3 shows that only the first seven districts in Table 3.10, namely, Bangalore, Dharwad, Uttara Kannada, Bellary, Dakshina Kannada, Kodagu and Mysore, have their per capita tertiary incomes higher than the State's, and the remaining 12 districts have their per capita tertiary incomes lower than the State's.

TABLE 3.10: Per Capita Tertiary NDDP in Karnataka: 1960-61, 1970-71 and 1980-81 (at 1960-61 prices)

Sl. No.	Districts	1960-61 (in Rs.)	1960-61 Rank	1970-71 (in Rs.)	1970-71 Rank	1980-81 (in Rs.)	1980-81 Rank
1	2	3	4	5	6	7	8
1.	Bangalore	103.00	1	140.00	1	185.00	1
2.	Dharwad	82.50	2	97.00	3	106.50	4
3.	Uttara Kannada	78.50	3	89.50	5	102.00	7
4.	Bellary	75.00	4	86.00	6	103.50	6
5.	Dakshina Kannada	74.50	5	96.50	4	122.50	2
6.	Kodagu	71.00	6	101.00	2	114.00	3
7.	Mysore	70.50	7	81.50	7	98.50	8
8.	Shimoga	67.00	8	78.00	9	90.00	10
9.	Gulbarga	66.00	9	74.25	10	86.00	13.5
10.	Bidar	65.00	10	73.00	11	86.00	13.5
11.	Chitradurga	64.00	11	71.00	14	86.00	13.5
12.	Raichur	61.00	12	70.00	15	79.25	18
13.	Belgaum	60.00	14	72.00	12.5	87.00	11
14.	Bijapur	60.00	14	72.00	12.5	82.00	17
15.	Chikmagalur	60.00	14	79.00	8	106.00	5
16.	Kolar	59.00	16	69.00	16	75.00	19
17.	Hassan	57.00	17	61.00	17	86.00	13.5
18.	Tumkur	50.00	18	60.00	18	83.00	16
19.	Mandya	47.50	19	57.00	19	90.50	9
	Karnataka	69.00	—	84.00	—	105.00	—

Note: The districts are arranged in the descending order of per capita tertiary income in 1960-61.

Source: Derived from Appendix Tables 3.1, 3.2 and 3.3.

Wide variations amongst districts exist in 1970-71 also. At the top there is Bangalore with Rs. 140, and at the bottom, there is Mandya with Rs. 57, and the spread between the two is Rs. 83. Bangalore's per capita tertiary income comes to exceed the State's by 67 per cent, and that of Mandya's lags behind the State's by 32 per cent. There are only six districts, namely, Bangalore, Dharwad, Uttara Kannada, Bellary, Dakshina Kannada, and Kodagu, whose per capita tertiary income is higher than the State's, and the per capita tertiary income of the remaining 13 districts is lower than the State's. These figures indicate the economic distance between the State and the Districts.

In terms of inter-district disparities in per capita tertiary income, 1980-81 does not seem to be very much different from 1960-61 and 1970-71; areal disparities do exist in 1980-81. Again Bangalore tops the list by claiming a per capita tertiary income of Rs. 185, and Kolar comes to occupy the lowest position by claiming a per capita tertiary income of Rs. 75, and the spread between the two comes to Rs. 110. Bangalore's claim is higher than the State's by 76 per cent, whereas Kolar's claim is lower than the State's by 29 per cent. In this year, the State's figure stands at Rs. 105. In all, there are five districts, namely, Bangalore, Dharwad, Dakshina Kannada, Kodagu, and Chikmagalur, whose per capita tertiary income is higher than the State's and the per capita tertiary income of the remaining 14 districts is lower than the State's. Thus, the data for 1980-81 also confirm the existence of economic distances between the State and the Districts.

And to give quantitative precision to the inter-district variations in per capita tertiary income, the range ratio, standard deviation and coefficient of variation are calculated. Their values are presented in Table 3.11.

TABLE 3.11: Range Ratio, Standard Deviation and Coefficient of Variation of Per Capita Tertiary Income of Karnataka: 1960-61, 1970-71 and 1980-81

Years	Range Ratio	Standard Deviation	Coefficient of Variation
1	2	3	4
1960-61	0.37	12.24	18.29
1970-71	0.42	18.55	23.07
1980-81	0.42	23.83	24.23

Source: Derived from Table 3.10.

The data in the Table 3.11 reveal the existence of inter-district disparities in per capita tertiary income in all the three points of time – 1960-61, 1970-71 and 1980-81.

3.10 Per Capita Tertiary NDDP and Inter-District Disparities: An Inter-Temporal Analysis

The cross-section analysis of the preceding section has shown that there exist inter-district disparities in per capita tertiary income in 1960-61, 1970-71 and 1980-81. And now the present section attempts to explain whether the disparities have been heading towards convergence or divergence, with the help of an inter-temporal analysis. And in this regard, the rank correlation coefficient, standard deviation, coefficient of variation and district per capita relatives are used.

All the particulars related to the ranking of the districts in all the three points of time are already furnished in Table 3.10. The rank correlation coefficients for the first decade (1960-61 to 1970-71), second decade (1970-71 to 1980-81) and for the two decades put together (1960-61 to 1980-81) turn out to be 0.92, 0.82 and 0.69 respectively. The values of the coefficients indicate the relative stability of the ranks of the districts during the period under study. There are only a few significant shifts; Uttara Kannada and Raichur which held the 3rd and 12th ranks respectively in 1960-61, moved down to the 7th and 18th ranks respectively in 1980-81; and Chikmagalur and Mandya, which held the 14th and the 19th ranks respectively in 1960-61, moved up to 5th and 9th ranks respectively in 1980-81. However, the rank correlation coefficient *per se* cannot tell anything conclusively about the divergence-convergence trends.

The values of standard deviation and coefficient of variation of the per capita tertiary income, already presented in Table 3.11, like those of the per capita secondary income, lend themselves to only one interpretation as far as inter-temporal trends in disparities are concerned. The values in Table 3.11 show that the inter-district disparities in per capita tertiary income, both in absolute and relative terms, have been consistently increasing between 1960-61 and 1980-81. The value of a standard deviation increased from 12.24 in 1960-61 to 18.55 in 1970-71, and then on to 23.83 in 1980-81. In the same fashion, the value of the coefficient of variation increased from 18.29 in 1960-61 to 23.07 in 1970-71, and on to 24.23 in 1980-81. This finding also lends empirical support to the "self-perpetuation" hypothesis referred to in the preceding section.

In order to gain further understanding of the inter-temporal trends in disparities, the district per capita tertiary income relatives are worked out. The data pertaining to them for 1960-61 and 1980-81 are presented in Table 3.12.

TABLE 3.12: Variations in District Per Capita Tertiary Income Relatives in Karnataka: 1960-61 and 1980-81

Sl. No.	Districts	District Per Capita Relatives		% Change in 1980-81 over 1960-61
		1960-61	1980-81	
1	2	3	4	5
1.	Bangalore	149.28	176.19	+18.03
2.	Dharwad	119.57	101.43	-15.17
3.	Uttara Kannada	113.77	97.14	-14.62
4.	Bellary	108.70	98.57	-9.32
5.	Dakshina Kannada	107.97	116.67	+8.06
6.	Kodagu	102.90	108.57	+5.51
7.	Mysore	102.17	93.81	-8.18
8.	Shimoga	97.10	85.71	-11.73
9.	Gulbarga	95.65	81.91	-14.36
10.	Bidar	94.20	81.91	-13.05
11.	Chitradurga	92.75	81.91	-11.69
12.	Raichur	88.41	75.48	-14.63
13.	Belgaum	86.96	82.86	-4.71
14.	Bijapur	86.96	78.10	-10.19
15.	Chikmagalur	86.96	100.95	+16.09
16.	Kolar	85.51	71.43	-16.47
17.	Hassan	82.61	81.91	-0.85
18.	Tumkur	72.46	79.05	+9.10
19.	Mandya	68.84	86.19	+25.20
	Karnataka	100	100	—

Note: The districts are arranged in the descending order of per capita tertiary income in 1960-61.

Source: Derived from Table 3.10.

If we scrutinise the data presented in Table 3.12, the impression becomes inescapable that the trend has been in favour of divergence. Majority of the lower district per capita relative districts have registered a further fall during the period under study. Of the 12 districts whose district per capita tertiary income relative is less than 100 in 1960-61, nine districts have come to register a fall in 1980-81, and only three of them have recorded a rise. On the other hand, of the seven districts whose district per capita tertiary income relative is higher than 100, four have come to register a fall and three, an increase. However, the overall impact of these changes is in favour of divergence rather than convergence.

The correlation coefficient (*r*) which turns out to be -0.045 shows that the district relatives of 1960-61 and the percentage change in 1980-81 over 1960-61 are inversely associated. But the value of the coefficient is so small that it is hardly useful in assessing the convergence-divergence trends.

3.11 Main Findings

(i) The cross-section analysis has revealed the existence of inter-district disparities in the levels of development, as measured by per capita NDDP, in all the three points of time considered in the Study – 1960-61, 1970-71 and 1980-81. And the inter-temporal analysis has shown that the spatial disparities increased between 1960-61 and 1970-71, but declined between 1970-71 and 1980-81. Thus, the trend in regional inequalities in Karnataka has come to acquire the well-known inverted U-shape.

(ii) No uniformity in the behaviour of inter-district disparities in per capita sectoral incomes is noticed. The convergence-divergence trends exhibited by the primary and non-primary sectors are quite divergent. On the one hand, the regional disparities in per capita primary income increase between 1960-61 and 1970-71, but decline between 1970-71 and 1980-81, and thus the primary sector has come to display an inverted U-shaped behaviour of regional disparities. On the other, in the case of the secondary and tertiary sectors, the regional disparities increase consistently right from 1960-61 to 1980-81.

(iii) The per capita NDDP and the per capita primary income have come to display similar trends in regional disparities. Both of them register an increase between 1960-61 and 1970-71, and a decline between 1970-71 and 1980-81. As such both of them have come to display a broadly inverted U-shaped pattern of inter-district disparities. Here it is pertinent to know that in view of its continued predominance in the State economy, the primary sector has come to influence the aggregative behaviour of spatial per capita income disparities in the State.

NOTES

1. Rudra, Ashok, "The Rate of Growth of Indian Economy", E.A.G. Robinson and Michèl Kindran (eds), *Economic Development in South Asia*, MacMillan and Company Ltd., 1970.
2. Planning Commission, *Third Five Year Plan*, Government of India, 1961.
3. For details, see Houchwald, W., "Conceptual Issues of Regional Income Estimates" in NBER's *Regional Income (Studies in Income and Wealth*, Vol. 21), Princeton University Press, 1957, p. 4.
4. Directorate of Economics and Statistics, *Estimates of District Income in Karnataka for Selected Years*, Government of Karnataka, Bangalore, 1986.
5. For details in respect of the methodology, see Bureau of Economics and Statistics, *Estimates of District Income in Karnataka — 1974-75*, Government of Karnataka, Bangalore, 1976.
6. The Standard Deviation is given as
   $SD = \sqrt{X^2/N}$, and coefficient of variation as
   $CV = \sigma/X \times 100$
7. Dadibhavi, R.V., *Inter-District Variations in Income, Productivity and Industrial Structure in Karnataka State*, Ph.D. Thesis, M.S. University of Baroda, 1983, pp. 56-61, and Sumitra, Gladys, "Some Aspects of Regional Development in Karnataka — An Inter-District Analysis", Paper presented at the UGC Seminar on Regional Dispersal of Industries in Karnataka, B.R. Project, P.G. Centre, University of Mysore, Jan. 1984, p. 19.
8. Myrdal, G., *Economic Theory and Underdeveloped Regions*, Vora, Bombay, 1958.
9. Hirschman, A.O., *The Strategy of Economic Development*, Yale University Press, New Haven, 1961.
10. Williamson, J.G., "Regional Inequality and Process of National Development", *Economic Development and Cultural Change*, Vol. 13, No. 4, Part II, July 1965.
11. Alonso, William, "Urban and Regional Imbalances in Economic Development", *Economic Development and Cultural Change*, Vol. 17, No. 1, October 1968.
12. Williamson, J.G. *op. cit.*, (1965).
13. Koropeckyj, I.S., "Equalisation of Regional Development in Socialist Countries", *Economic Development and Cultural Change*, Vol. 21, No. 1, October 1972.
14. Dadibhavi, R.V. *op. cit.*, (1983), p. 66.
15. For more details about the various hypotheses and empirical studies on regional disparities, see Chapter II of the present work.
16. Mathur, Ashok, "Regional Development and Income Disparities in India: A Sectoral Analysis," *Economic Development and Cultural Change*, Vol. 31, No. 3, April 1983.
17. Mathur, Ashok, *op. cit.*, (1983), p. 481.
18. Hughes, R.B., "Inter-regional Income Differences: Self-Perpetuation, *Southern Economic Journal*, Vol. 28, No. 1, July 1961, pp. 41-45.
19. Booth, E.J.R., "Inter-regional Income Differences", *Southern Economic Journal*, Vol. 31, No. 1, July 1964, pp. 44-51.
20. Mathur, Ashok, *op. cit.*, (1983), p. 481.
21. *Ibid.*, p. 481.
22. *Ibid.*, p. 481.

APPENDIX TABLE 3.1: Sectoral Composition of District Income of Karnataka : 1960-61 (at 1960-61 Prices)

(In Rs. lakhs)

Sl. No.	Districts	Agriculture	Forestry & logging	Fishing	Mining	Manufacturing Registered	Manufacturing Unregistered	Construction	Electricity gas & water supply	Railways	Transport by other means & storage	Communication	Trade Hotels & Restaurants	Banking & Insurance	Real Estate ownership of dwellings & Bussiness services	Public administration	Other services	Net Domestic product	Population as per 1961 Census	Per capita Income (in Rs.)
1	2	3	4	5	6	7	8	9	10	11	12	13	14	15	16	17	18	19	20	21
1.	Bangalore	1853	59	11	—	1003	241	541	75	77	216	55	1127	126	216	334	432	6366	25,04,462	254
2.	Belgaum	3301	144	1	—	205	255	139	7	33	65	22	532	78	170	68	225	5245	19,83,811	264
3.	Bellary	1481	115	1	83	81	98	209	22	38	51	5	282	43	79	44	141	2773	9,15,261	303
4.	Bidar	704	4	—	—	10	120	39	1	9	18	4	218	7	56	35	84	1309	6,63,172	197
5.	Bijapur	1645	62	4	7	118	358	149	4	19	45	9	472	65	143	51	189	3340	16,60,178	201
6.	Chikmagalur	2060	110	2	5	53	38	205	8	6	24	6	139	15	51	46	70	2838	5,97,305	475
7.	Chitradurga	1650	65	6	21	124	162	240	12	9	33	6	327	4	94	75	147	2975	10,94,284	272
8.	Dakshina Kannada	3276	167	128	—	422	206	160	13	13	85	22	589	51	135	59	208	5534	15,63,837	354
9.	Dharwad	2573	84	3	—	224	248	219	11	103	142	21	717	126	167	76	256	4970	19,50,362	255
10.	Gulbarga	1656	28	5	18	108	257	95	3	70	47	8	408	10	120	70	190	3093	13,99,457	221
11.	Hassan	1940	19	6	5	57	57	78	9	32	24	27	152	35	76	65	97	2679	8,95,847	299
12.	Kodagu	1860	102	1	—	37	12	85	2	—	14	3	94	2	27	36	53	2328	3,22,829	721
13.	Kolar	1558	51	6	345	75	126	102	18	18	40	7	335	14	111	84	154	3044	12,90,144	236
14.	Mandya	1585	13	3	—	72	80	99	23	5	15	5	142	39	77	56	88	2302	8,99,210	256
15.	Mysore	2157	234	12	1	219	243	223	25	56	94	14	512	24	144	128	204	4290	16,71,399	257
16.	Raichur	1430	10	1	42	40	141	133	3	31	37	6	279	12	94	73	144	2476	11,00,895	225
17.	Shimoga	3713	110	13	22	186	64	990	41	17	48	5	285	7	86	98	137	5822	10,17,368	572
18.	Tumkur	2695	33	11	9	72	196	122	17	4	24	4	280	15	118	85	151	3836	13,67,402	281
19.	Uttara Kannada	2304	627	87	29	101	88	162	5	23	30	9	223	15	59	41	141	3944	6,89,549	572
	Karnataka State	39441	2037	301	587	3207	2990	3990	299	563	1052	238	7113	688	2023	1524	3111	69164	235,86,772	293

Sources: 1. Bureau of Economics and Statistics, Government of Karnataka, Bangalore.
2. *Census of India* 1961, Vol. XI, Mysore, Part II-A, General Population Tables, 1964, pp. 17-18.

APPENDIX TABLE 3.2: Sectoral Composition of District Income of Karnataka : 1970-71 (at 1960-61 Prices)

(In Rs. lakhs)

Sl. No.	Districts	Agriculture	Forestry & logging	Fishing	Mining	Manufacturing Registered	Manufacturing Unregistered	Construction	Electricity gas & water supply	Railways	Transport by other means & storage	Communication	Trade Hotels & Restaurants	Banking & Insurance	Real Estate ownership of dwellings & Bussiness services	Public administration	Other services	Net Domestic product	Population as per 1971 Census	Per capita Income (in Rs.)
1	2	3	4	5	6	7	8	9	10	11	12	13	14	15	16	17	18	19	20	21
1.	Bangalore	2563	63	35	2	3535	757	1130	73	121	561	174	1634	534	304	740	629	12,855	3365515	382
2.	Belgaum	4261	158	13	8	439	272	543	12	75	115	52	684	86	200	239	286	7,443	2423342	307
3.	Bellary	3190	96	15	121	223	109	262	14	72	109	23	323	32	109	121	174	4,993	1122686	445
4.	Bidar	1405	8	5	1	36	36	128	7	31	48	7	244	14	70	72	116	2,228	824059	270
5.	Bijapur	2701	68	21	14	179	223	300	12	70	103	28	558	50	182	173	265	4,947	1985591	249
6.	Chikmagalur	3225	143	19	7	50	61	182	6	34	37	17	199	23	67	57	147	4,274	736647	580
7.	Chitradurga	3137	69	32	6	378	143	354	11	42	74	18	417	37	125	101	174	5,118	1397456	366
8.	Dakshina Kannada	3233	197	77	1	635	495	512	16	6	155	39	888	161	163	140	323	7,041	1939315	363
9.	Dharwad	3780	92	21	1	597	231	457	22	106	237	59	963	114	199	234	354	7,467	2342213	319
10.	Gulbarga	3678	58	15	46	199	169	405	13	78	103	15	518	35	161	152	228	5,873	1739220	338
11.	Hassan	2788	40	21	6	84	66	324	9	47	53	4	226	24	94	73	150	4,009	1102370	364
12.	Kodagu	3674	111	9	1	29	37	188	3	—	22	10	138	26	33	56	96	4,433	378291	1172
13.	Kolar	2187	56	15	196	145	140	212	17	84	60	24	395	47	145	116	182	4,021	1516646	265
14.	Mandya	2586	19	20	1	135	71	125	18	22	33	19	228	31	92	82	150	3,632	1154374	315
15.	Mysore	3805	265	30	3	458	211	731	20	42	161	43	644	91	172	196	345	7,217	2077238	347
16.	Raichur	4209	26	9	86	167	82	262	14	36	79	17	383	28	139	137	170	5,844	1415740	413
17.	Shimoga	3593	174	36	15	430	108	348	30	39	79	29	411	51	113	118	173	5,747	1301485	442
18.	Tumkur	2675	38	27	20	47	127	257	15	31	59	21	367	34	154	101	206	4,179	1627721	257
19.	Uttara Kannada	1321	681	70	18	165	96	191	8	14	77	18	273	26	74	114	164	3,310	849105	390
	Karnataka State	58011	2362	490	553	7931	3434	6911	320	950	2165	617	9493	1444	2596	3022	4332	104,631	29299014	357

Sources: 1. Computed from: (i) Sectoral Composition of District Income of Karnataka, 1970-71 (at 1970-71 prices — Revised) and (ii) State Income for 1970-71 (at 1960-61 prices), Bureau of Economics and Statistics, Government of Karnataka, Bangalore.

2. *Census of India*, 1971, Series — 14 Mysore Part II-A, General Population Tables, 1973.

APPENDIX TABLE 3.3: Sectoral Composition of District Income of Karnataka : 1980-81 (at 1960-61 Prices)

(In Rs. lakhs)

Sl. No.	Districts	Agriculture	Forestry & logging	Fishing	Mining	Manufacturing Registered	Manufacturing Unregistered	Construction	Electricity gas & water supply	Railways	Transport by other means & storage	Communication	Trade Hotels & Restaurants	Banking & Insurance	Real Estate ownership of dwellings & Bussiness services	Public administration	Other services	Net Domestic product	Population as per 1981 Census	Per capita Income (in Rs.)
1	2	3	4	5	6	7	8	9	10	11	12	13	14	15	16	17	18	19	20	21
1.	Bangalore	2852	45	47	6	10021	954	1492	202	169	912	433	2571	1459	525	2326	781	24,802	49,47,610	501
2.	Belgaum	5632	102	9	5	515	512	716	46	107	194	81	981	140	273	458	361	10,132	29,80,440	340
3.	Bellary	3068	62	34	140	364	143	347	29	161	98	26	632	48	154	218	204	5,728	14,89,225	385
4.	Bidar	1743	9	2	—	51	93	169	22	39	85	7	313	26	100	139	146	2,944	9,95,691	296
5.	Bijapur	2579	44	4	43	90	439	396	55	98	172	47	785	59	238	284	288	5,621	24,01,782	234
6.	Chikmagalur	3732	95	5	5	40	91	240	12	45	83	38	319	45	98	171	172	5,191	9,11,769	569
7.	Chitradurga	4101	43	23	15	675	232	467	26	62	118	41	625	57	179	221	218	7,103	17,77,499	400
8.	Dakshina Karnada	3920	123	140	14	665	1017	676	35	52	310	143	1078	426	221	310	373	9,503	23,76,724	400
9.	Dharwad	4791	60	5	1	701	445	606	57	155	382	104	1155	225	275	437	397	9,794	29,45,487	333
10.	Gulbarga	3239	37	5	71	426	202	535	42	58	174	26	659	38	220	351	267	6,350	20,80,643	305
11.	Hassan	3438	28	18	25	58	90	428	22	81	131	31	378	54	141	169	180	5,272	13,57,014	389
12.	Kodagu	3617	72	2	—	12	35	248	8	—	28	27	176	41	56	108	90	4,520	4,61,888	979
13.	Kolar	1637	38	16	151	29	173	279	42	86	77	40	509	46	194	248	233	3,798	19,05,492	199
14.	Mandya	3451	13	20	1	190	114	165	46	40	52	45	370	41	148	414	175	5,285	14,18,109	373
15.	Mysore	4375	177	36	4	574	702	965	51	58	318	97	897	139	273	393	384	9,443	25,95,900	364
16.	Raichur	4341	25	9	77	182	162	347	44	51	91	25	609	42	192	203	200	6,600	17,83,822	370
17.	Shimoga	4164	175	15	14	749	193	459	58	61	106	66	569	61	166	250	214	7,320	16,56,731	442
18.	Tumkur	3281	24	20	17	343	257	339	36	47	140	16	689	49	216	227	256	5,957	19,77,854	301
19.	Uttara Karnada	1528	440	39	28	131	90	253	22	22	128	40	329	78	108	212	174	3,622	10,72,034	338
	Karnataka State	65489	1612	449	617	15816	5944	9125	855	1392	3606	1333	13644	3074	3777	7139	5113	138,985	371,35,714	374

Sources: 1. Computed from: (i) Sectoral Composition of District Income of Karnataka, 1980-81 (at 1970-71 prices — Revised) and (ii) State Income for 1970-71 (at 1960-61 prices), Directorate of Economics and Statistics, Government of Karnataka, Bangalore.

2. *Census of India* 1981, Series-9 Karnataka Part II-B (ii) *Primary Census Abstract*, 1983.

4

INTER-DISTRICT VARIATIONS IN INDUSTRIALISATION IN KARNATAKA

4.1 Introduction

IN A WAY, this chapter is a sequel to the first three chapters. The preceding chapters have shown that growth does not take place anywhere and everywhere at once, and, to start with, growth is necessarily unbalanced – both regionwise and sectorwise. It is more so in the case of industrialisation which invariably involves structural transformation. Industrialisation has an inherent tendency to get itself concentrated only in certain regions of a nation or of a State. The tendency for rapid growth to remain within the developed areas is particularly marked in the industrial sector. The increase in concentration brings out one feature of the process of Industrialisation, which is that growth generates further growth.[1] And when once areal disparities emerge in the normal course of Industrialisation for diverse socio-economic, political and demographic reasons, they tend to accentuate themselves unless some deliberate external force is administered to arrest such trend. Most of the theoretical and empirical studies[2] on regional industrialisation and development have come to identify the emergence and operation of two sets of opposing forces, namely, divergence-causing and convergence-causing, during the process of modern economic development which invariably implies industrialisation. It is the relative strength of such forces that determines whether the trend is in favour of divergence or convergence. But as to their relative strength and the timing of their operation in the growth process, there is no unanimous opinion or evidence. However, most of the studies agree that government intervention is necessary to ensure spatial equity in industrialisation and development. In view of the close association between industrial development and economic development, of late, there has come into existence a feeling that the maldistribution of industrial activity is a major cause for regional disparities in development. Giving due consideration to such a feeling quite a few governments have been using industrial dispersal policies as a major instrument in narrowing down inter-State and inter-district disparities in development. The Indian Government at the national level and the Karnataka Government at the State level have been very consciously using industrial dispersal policies to narrow-down the inter-State and inter-district inequalities respectively. Here it is to be noted that equi table dispersal of industrial activity regionally is only a means, but not an end in itself; the end is spatial equity in development and levels of living of the people. In Chapter 3, we have made an in-depth analysis of the inter-district disparities in development in Karnataka. In that process, the inter-temporal trends in regional disparities have also been examined. In this chapter, we continue the discussion of disparities with special reference to the spatial distribution of industrial activity, which constitutes a significant, if not the sole, determinant of development. And it is in this sense that this chapter is a sequel to all the preceding chapters in general and to Chapter 3 in particular.

The discussion of this chapter which centres round such things as the distribution of registered manufacturing activity and small-scale industrial activity across the 19 districts of the State, and the inter-temporal behaviour of inter-district disparities in industrial development, would be of immense use to the policy-makers in planning for regional equity. The utility of such analysis gains much more significance in States like Karnataka where "deliberate industrialisation" and "controlled expansion of industrial activity" have come to be used as highly dependable devices to ensure development with spatial justice. They are also used to resolve the "dispersal dilemma" by attempting to reconcile the twin seemingly conflicting components of the growth objectives, namely "efficiency" and "equity". Including this introductory section, this chapter consists of eight sections. The second section attempts to identify the circumstances in which inter-district disparities in industrial development emerged in Karnataka. It takes us back to the second half of the 1950s when the State was reorganised and enlarged on a linguistic basis. The third section describes the nature and limitations of the data used in this chapter. A cross-section analysis of regional disparities in registered manufacturing is undertaken in the fourth section. The fifth section makes an inter-temporal analysis of inter-district disparities in registered manufacturing activity in terms of "factories", "workers" and "NDDP from registered manufacturing". In doing so, it throws light on the behavioural pattern of regional disparities between 1960-61 and 1980-81. The sixth and seventh sections are devoted to the study of the small-scale industrial units in Karnataka; the sixth section, besides examining the spread of small-scale industrial activity among the districts, makes a cross-section analysis to find out the existence or otherwise of inter-district disparities in small-scale industrial activity in the State; and the seventh section undertakes an inter-temporal analysis to know whether the trend has been favouring convergence or divergence. And the eighth section concludes the discussion by presenting the main findings.

4.2 Origins of Inter-District Disparities in Industrialisation in Karnataka

The roots of regional disparities in industrial activity can be traced back to the 1950s when the enlarged State of Mysore (now called Karnataka) was created by bringing together all the districts, inhabited by Kannada-speaking people, which had been scattered across the States and provinces surrounding the then princely State of Mysore. Prior to 1953, the Old Mysore State had only nine districts, namely, Bangalore, Mysore, Kolar, Mandya, Tumkur, Chitradurga, Shimoga, Hassan and Chikmagalur. In October 1953, Bellary district, which was in the then Madras State, was transferred to the Old Mysore State under the Andhra Act, 1953. And on November 1, 1956, four districts, namely, Belgaum, Bijapur, Dharwad and Uttara Kannada, from the then Bombay State, three districts, namely, Gulbarga, Raichur and Bidar from the then State of Hyderabad, one district, namely, Dakshina Kannada, from the then State of Madras, and one more district, namely, Kodagu from part C State of Coorg, were transferred to the Old Mysore State.[3]

The reorganisation of the State as per the States Reorganisation Act, 1956 has very much to do with the emergence of regional disparities in industrial activity in the State. On the eve of the reorganisation of the State, not only the two halves – Old Mysore consisting of 10 districts, and New Mysore consisting of nine districts – were at variance industrially, but within those halves also, the different districts – were at different levels of industrial development. Thus, for the enlarged State of Karnataka, regional disparities are almost congenital.

The maldistribution of industrial activity in the State is evident from the fact that before 1956, Bangalore and mysore districts alone had 77.26 per cent of the factories then existing in Old Mysore; and the remaining 22.74 per cent of the factories were distributed among the remaining eight districts. Similar maldistribution of industrial activity was also found in New Mysore; Dakshina Kannada and Belgaum districts alone had 65.64 per cent of the factories then operating in New Mysore; and the remaining 34.36 per cent of the factories were distributed among the remaining seven districts.[4] In 1956, both the halves together had 1.64 thousand factories and 1.72 lakh workers. The Old Mysore had 945 factories (i.e. 57.80 per cent) and 118,860 workers (i.e. 69.05 per cent), whereas, New Mysore had the remaining 690 factories (i.e. 42.20 per cent) and 53,258 workers (i.e. 30.95 per cent). These figures show that the two halves, which were brought together to form the enlarged State of Karnataka in 1956, were at different levels of industrial activity; the former was decidedly at a higher level of industrial activity than the latter. The techno-economic survey made by the NCAER brings out this fact of maldistribution of industrial activity in the State. The Survey specifically points out that interregional imbalances were observed immediately after the Reorganisation due to the merger of some totally industrially backward regions with the erstwhile Mysore State.[5] The maldistribution of industrial activity in Karnataka on the eve of its reorganisation, and immediately after that, has been reported in some works, particularly in those of V.B. Angadi,[6] N.S. Hiremath,[7] D.M. Nanjundappa,[8] K. Munirathna Naidu.[9] So, historically, Karnataka had to begin its process of planned industrialisation in the 1960s with all the evils of North-South regional mix.

4.3 The Data Used

The disparity-discussion of this chapter is entirely based on secondary sources of data – both published and unpublished. The data on the regional spread of registered manufacturing activity are collected from the records of the Chief Inspector of Factories and Boilers, Government of Karnataka, Bangalore. In this source, the regional spread of industrial activity is viewed from only two angles, namely, number of factories and number of workers. No comparable data on investment and value added are available for the period from 1960-61 to 1980-81. However, the districtwise data on the contribution of registered manufacturing to NDDP found in the District Income Estimates of the Directorate of Economics and Statistics, Government of Karnataka, Bangalore, are used in the present analysis. So, as far as the spread of registered manufacturing is concerned, based on the data limitations, the present study limits itself to the analysis of the regional disparities only in terms of "factories", "workers", and "contribution of registered manufacturing segment to NDDP".

The data on the districtwise distribution of small-scale industrial activity are collected from the records of the Directorate of Industries and Commerce, Government of Karnataka, Bangalore. Periodwise, comparable data are available from 1969-70 onwards. The available data enable us to gauge the regional spread of small-scale industrial activity in terms of three characteristics, namely, "units", "workers" and "investment". And hence, based on the nature of the data available, the inter-district disparities in small-scale industrial activity are examined with reference to units, workers and investment. And the inter-temporal analysis takes only two points of time – 1970-71 and 1980-81.

The Directorate of Industries and Commerce does not have districtwise comparable data on the large-scale industrial activity for all the districts for the period under consideration. Similar data are also not available for the said period in the CSO publications of the Annual Survey of Industries. As such, a separate analysis of regional disparities in large-scale industrial activity is not undertaken in the present chapter. This is indeed a major limitation of the study.

4.4 Registered Manufacturing and Inter-District Disparities: A Cross-Section Analysis

The second section of this chapter has shown that there was some industrial activity in all the 19 districts which were brought together in 1956. It has also made it clear that there was maldistribution of industrial activity spatially; a major proportion of the industrial activity was concentrated only in a couple of districts, and all the rest had only very little industrial activity. Being quite alive to this history of regional disparities in industrial development, the Government of Karnataka has been following the policy of controlled expansion to achieve, among other things, spatial parity in industrial development.

But, the efforts do not seem to be commensurate with the enormity of the problem . Inter-district disparities persist. Some districts have been growing at a faster rate than others, and thereby perpetuating regional disparities. The primary aim of this section is to identify the economic distances that exist amongst districts in terms of registered manufacturing activity at three points of time – 1960-61, 1970-71 and 1980-81.

The districtwise data of factories, workers and NDDP from registered manufacturing are presented in Table 4.1. The table, in general, reveals that the industrial activity, judged from all the three characteristics, is spread over the entire State, but there are wide disparities in the development of industry among the different districts of the State.

In 1960-61, a substantial proportion of the industrial activity is concentrated in Bangalore. Bangalore claims for itself 26.12 per cent of the factories, 42.39 per cent of the workers, and 31.28 per cent of the NDDP from registered manufacturing. On the other extreme, there is Bidar with insignificant industrial activity. Bidar's share in the State's registered manufacturing activity is just 0.32 per cent in terms of factories, 0.06 per cent in terms of workers and 0.31 per cent in terms of NDDP from registered manufacturing. The glaring gap between Bangalore and Bidar is indicative of the existence of very wide inter-district variations in industrial development. The magnitude of disparity can be visualised from another angle also. The five top-scoring districts, namely Bangalore, Belgaum, Dakshina Kannada, Dharwad and Mysore claim for themselves 67.24 per cent of the factories, 74.02 per cent of the workers and 64.64 per cent of the NDDP from registered manufacturing, and the remaining 14 districts together claim only 32.76 per cent of the factories, 25.98 per cent of the workers and 35.36 per cent of the NDDP from registered manufacturing.

The data for 1970-71 also show the existence of considerable variations in industrial activity among the districts. Again, Bangalore has the distinction of claiming the highest share in the State's factories, workers and the NDDP from registered manufacturing, whereas the least claim goes to Kodagu. Bangalore claims 35.40 per cent of the factories, 49.82 per cent of the workers and 44.57 per cent of the NDDP from registered manufacturing. At the other end of the scale, there are districts with marginal industrial activity like Kodagu, which claims only 0.73 per cent of the factories, 0.32 per cent of the workers,

TABLE 4.1: Selected Characteristics of Registered Manufacturing in Karnataka: 1960-61, 1970-71 and 1980-81

Sl. No.	District	Number of Factories			Number of Workers			NDDP from Registered Manufacturing (in Rs. Lakhs)		
		1960-61	1970-71	1980-81	1960-61	1970-71	1980-81	1960-61	1970-71	1980-81
1	2	3	4	5	6	7	8	9	10	11
1.	Bangalore	575	1350	4460	72040	137430	230991	1003	3535	10021
		(26.12)	(35.40)	(44.86)	(42.39)	(49.82)	(41.94)	(31.28)	(44.57)	(63.36)
2.	Belgaum	231	310	1210	11764	14897	72544	205	439	515
		(10.50)	(8.13)	(12.17)	(6.92)	(5.40)	(13.17)	(6.39)	(5.54)	(3.26)
3.	Bellary	75	155	258	4419	7147	17832	81	223	364
		(3.41)	(4.06)	(2.60)	(2.60)	(2.59)	(3.24)	(2.53)	(2.81)	(2.30)
4.	Bidar	7	29	52	102	1141	2445	10	36	51
		(0.32)	(0.76)	(0.52)	(0.06)	(0.41)	(0.44)	(0.31)	(0.45)	(0.32)
5.	Bijapur	120	141	432	3727	4302	15380	118	179	90
		(5.45)	(3.70)	(4.35)	(2.19)	(1.56)	(2.79)	(3.68)	(2.26)	(0.57)
6.	Chikmagalur	30	36	86	913	1540	5638	53	50	40
		(1.36)	(0.94)	(0.87)	(0.54)	(00.56)	(1.02)	(1.65)	(0.63)	(0.25)
7.	Chitradurga	65	102	226	10783	13252	12807	124	378	675
		(2.95)	(2.67)	(2.27)	(6.35)	(4.80)	(2.33)	(3.87)	(4.76)	(4.27)
8.	Dakshina Kannada	248	373	737	17635	19392	46203	422	635	665
		(11.27)	(9.78)	(7.41)	(10.38)	(7.03)	(8.39)	(13.16)	(8.01)	(4.20)
9.	Dharwad	255	373	588	12305	17421	36314	224	597	701
		(11.58)	(9.78)	(5.91)	(7.24)	(6.32)	(6.59)	(6.98)	(7.53)	(4.43)

Contd.

TABLE 4.1 *Contd.*

1	2	3	4	5	6	7	8	9	10	11
10.	Gulbarga	69	101	215	3741	6209	11101	108	199	426
		(3.13)	(2.65)	(2.16)	(2.20)	(2.25)	(2.02)	(3.37)	(2.51)	(2.69)
11.	Hassan	22	54	125	1018	2441	6464	57	84	58
		(1.00)	(1.41)	(1.26)	(0.60)	(0.89)	(1.17)	(1.78)	(1.06)	(0.37)
12.	Kodagu	20	28	58	528	882	3272	37	29	12
		(0.91)	(0.73)	(0.58)	(0.31)	(0.32)	(0.59)	(1.15)	(0.37)	(0.08)
13.	Kolar	36	75	105	959	4879	6491	75	145	29
		(1.64)	(1.97)	(1.06)	(0.56)	(1.77)	(1.18)	(2.34)	(1.83)	(0.18)
14.	Mandya	18	52	104	2492	4119	6193	72	135	190
		(0.82)	(1.36)	(1.05)	(1.47)	(1.49)	(1.12)	(2.24)	(1.70)	(1.20)
15.	Mysore	171	196	481	12040	14729	27260	219	458	574
		(7.77)	(5.14)	(4.84)	(7.09)	(5.34)	(4.95)	(6.83)	(5.77)	(3.63)
16.	Raichur	137	271	334	4114	6162	22660	40	167	182
		(6.22)	(7.11)	(3.36)	(2.42)	(2.23)	(4.11)	(1.25)	(2.11)	(1.15)
17.	Shimoga	60	69	278	6741	13272	14476	186	430	749
		(2.73)	(1.81)	(2.80)	(3.97)	(4.81)	(2.63)	(5.80)	(5.42)	(4.74)
18.	Tumkur	33	51	60	974	1529	5369	72	47	343
		(1.50)	(1.34)	(0.60)	(0.57)	(0.55)	(0.98)	(2.24)	(0.59)	(2.17)
19.	Uttara Kannada	29	48	133	3631	5128	7366	101	165	131
		(1.32)	(1.26)	(1.33)	(2.14)	(1.86)	(1.34)	(3.15)	(2.08)	(0.83)
	Karnataka	2201	3814	9942	169926	275872	550806	3207	7931	15816
		(100)	(100)	(100)	(100)	(100)	(100)	(100)	(100)	(100)

Source: Derived from Appendix Table 4.1.

and 0.37 per cent of the NDDP from registered manufacturing, and Bidar, which claims only 0.76 per cent of the factories, 0.41 per cent of the workers, and 0.45 per cent of the NDDP from registered manufacturing. This wide spread between Bangalore, on the one hand, and Kodagu and Bidar, on the other, is indicative of wide areal disparities in industrial development. Again, the same five districts referred to in the preceding paragraph together claim 68.23 per cent of the factories, 73.91 per cent of the workers and 71.42 per cent of the NDDP from registered manufacturing, and the rest is thinly spread over the other 14 districts in the State.

The data for 1980-81 also lend adequate evidence to inter-district inequalities in industrial activity. In this year too, at the top there is Bangalore with 44.86 per cent of the factories, 41.94 per cent of the workers and 63.36 per cent of the NDDP from registered manufacturing. At the bottom there are districts like Bidar and Kodagu with meagre industrial activity; Bidar claims only 0.52 per cent of the factories, 0.44 per cent of the workers and 0.32 per cent of the NDDP from registered manufacturing; and Kodagu claims only 0.58 per cent of the factories, 0.59 per cent of the workers and 0.08 per cent of the NDDP from registered manufacturing.

A close scrutiny of the data furnished in Table 4.2 leads us to the inevitable conclusion that inter-district disparities in industrial development exist in all the three points of time considered here.

The values of all the measures of dispersion cited in Table 4.2 are indicative of the existence of regional disparities. The value of coefficient of variation also suggests something about the extent of disparities among the different characteristics. In 1960-61 and 1970-71 the disparities in workers are more pronounced than the disparities in factories and the NDDP from registered manufacturing. And in 1980-81, the disparities in the NDDP from registered manufacturing are more pronounced than the disparities in factories and workers.

4.5 Registered Manufacturing and Inter-District Disparities: An Inter-Temporal Analysis

A cross-section analysis has shown that registered manufacturing activity is distributed very unevenly among the districts. And this section proceeds to examine the trends in those disparities. The convergence-divergence trends are examined with reference to three characteristics, namely, factories, workers and the NDDP from registered manufacturing.

TABLE 4.2: Range Ratio, Standard Deviation and Coefficient of Variation of Registered Manufacturing in Karnataka: 1960-61, 1970-71, and 1980-81

Particulars	Number of Factories			Number of Workers			NDDP from Registered Manufacturing		
	1960-61	1970-71	1980-81	1960-61	1970-71	1980-81	1960-61	1970-71	1980-81
1	2	3	4	5	6	7	8	9	10
Range Ratio	0.976	0.959	0.977	0.997	0.987	0.979	0.980	0.984	0.997
Standard Deviation	134.08	293.05	970.22	15669.73	29538.16	50610.43	217.69	757.60	2180.47
Coefficient of Variation	115.75	145.98	185.42	175.21	203.44	174.58	128.97	181.50	261.94

Source: Derived from Appendix Table 4.1.

The districtwise data in respect of factories are furnished in Table 4.3. From the data in columns 4, 6 and 8, it becomes obvious that there is no significant change in the positions of the districts between 1960-61 and 1980-81. The rank correlation coefficients turn out to be 0.95, 0.94 and 0.93 for the periods 1960-61 to 1970-71, 1970-71 to 1980-81 and 1960-61 to 1980-81 respectively. These values indicate that the ranks of the districts have not undergone any material change over the period considered. Though there are a few marginal changes, they are not significant enough to affect the overall pattern of stability. From these values we can only infer that the disparities have been perpetuating.

TABLE 4.3: **Registered Manufacturing in Karnataka by Districts: 1960-61, 1970-71 and 1980-81 (in terms of Number of Factories)**

Sl No.	Districts	1960-61		1970-71		1980-81	
		No. of Factories	Rank	No. of Factories	Rank	No. of Factories	Rank
1	2	3	4	5	6	7	8
1.	Bangalore	575	1	1350	1	4460	1
2.	Dharwad	255	2	373	2.5	588	4
3.	Dakshina Kannada	248	3	373	2.5	737	3
4.	Belgaum	231	4	310	4	1210	2
5.	Mysore	171	5	196	6	481	5
6.	Raichur	137	6	271	5	334	7
7.	Bijapur	120	7	141	8	432	6
8.	Bellary	75	8	155	7	258	9
9.	Gulbarga	69	9	101	10	215	11
10.	Chitradurga	65	10	102	9	226	10
11.	Shimoga	60	11	69	12	278	8
12.	Kolar	36	12	75	11	105	14
13.	Tumkur	33	13	51	15	60	17
14.	Chikmagalur	30	14	36	17	86	16
15.	Uttara Kannada	29	15	48	16	133	12
16.	Hassan	22	16	54	13	125	13
17.	Kodagu	20	17	28	19	58	18
18.	Mandya	18	18	52	14	104	15
19.	Bidar	7	19	29	18	52	19
	Karnataka	2201	—	3814	—	9942	—

Note: 1. The districts are arranged in the descending order of number of factory units in 1960-61.
2. The 1980-81 figures pertain to 1979-80.

Source: Derived from Appendix Table 4.1.

To get a better grasp of the disparity trend, let us examine the values of standard deviation and coefficient of variation already presented in Table 4.2. There is a consistent increase in the absolute dispersion around the arithmetic mean, as measured by standard deviation; the value of standard deviation increases from 134.08 in 1960-61 to 293.05 in 1970-71, and on to 970.22 in 1980-81. It is also the case with relative dispersion; the value of coefficient of variation increases from 115.75 in 1960-61 to 145.98 in 1970-71, and on to 185.42 in 1980-81. Thus both the measures of dispersion show that inter-district disparities in factories have been consistently increasing. This finding lends empirical support to the "self-perpetuation" hypothesis, with specific reference to the areal dualism in industrial activity.[10]

Another indicator of the spread of industrial activity in the State is the inter-district spread of factory workers. Such districtwise data are presented in Table 4.4.

TABLE 4.4: Registered Manufacturing in Karnataka by Districts: 1960-61, 1970-71 and 1980-81 (in terms of Number of Workers)

Sl. No.	Districts	1960-61		1970-71		1980-81	
		No. of Workers	Rank	No. of Workers	Rank	No. of Workers	Rank
1	2	3	4	5	6	7	8
1.	Bangalore	72040	1	137430	1	230991	1
2.	Dakshina Kannada	17635	2	19392	2	46203	3
3.	Dharwad	12305	3	17421	3	36314	4
4.	Mysore	12040	4	14729	5	27260	5
5.	Belgaum	11764	5	14897	4	72544	2
6.	Chitradurga	10783	6	13252	7	12807	10
7.	Shimoga	6741	7	13272	6	14476	9
8.	Bellary	4419	8	7147	8	17832	7
9.	Raichur	4114	9	6162	10	22660	6
10.	Gulbarga	3741	10	6209	9	11101	11
11.	Bijapur	3727	11	4302	13	15380	8
12.	Uttara Kannada	3631	12	5128	11	7366	12
13.	Mandya	2492	13	4119	14	6193	15
14.	Hassan	1018	14	2441	15	6464	14
15.	Tumkur	974	15	1529	17	5369	17
16.	Kolar	959	16	4879	12	6491	13
17.	Chikmagalur	913	17	1540	16	5638	16
18.	Kodagu	528	18	882	19	3272	18
19.	Bidar	102	19	1141	18	2445	19
	Karnataka	169926	–	275872	–	550806	–

Note: 1. The districts are arranged in the descending order of number of Workers in 1960-61.
2. The 1980-81 figures pertain to 1979-80.

Source: Derived from Appendix Table 4.1.

The general impression that one gets by reading columns 4, 6 and 8 is that there are no significant changes in the position of the districts between 1960-61 and 1980-81. There appears to be reasonable stability in the rank-order of the districts over time. The rank correlation coefficient for the periods 1960-61 to 1970-71, 1970-71 to 1980-81, and 1960-61 to 1980-81 turns out to be 0.97, 0.93, and 0.94 respectively. From these values we can infer that inter-district disparities exist in all the three points of time.

The disparity trend becomes clear when we measure the disparities with standard deviation and coefficient of variation. Their values are already presented in Table 4.2. Here, it is interesting to note that the measure of absolute dispersion and of relative dispersion do not represent the same trend. The value of standard deviation records a consistent increase; it increases from 15,669.73 in 1960-61 to 29,538.16 in 1970-71, and on to 50,610.43 in 1980-81. This is not so with coefficient of variation. Initially it increases and then declines; it increases from 175.21 in 1960-61 to 203.44 in 1970-71, and then records a fall to 174.58. Thus in this case the measure of absolute dispersion lends empirical support to the "self-perpetuation" hypothesis[11], whereas the measure of relative dispersion lends empirical support to the "concentration cycle" hypothesis[12]. However, of the two, statistically, the latter measure is preferable to the former. From the values of the coefficient of variation we can infer that the first decade (1960-61 to 1970-71) is characterised by increasing disparities or the trend of divergence, whereas the second decade (1970-71 to 1980-81) is characterised by decreasing disparities or the trend of convergence. The trend appears to be heading towards the reduction of inter-district inequalities, and the disparity behaviour during the period under study resembles J.G. Williamson's inverted "U".[13] In this context it is useful to note that the disparity behaviour measured in terms of "workers" differs from that measured in terms of factories.

Yet another indicator of regional spread of industrial activity is the share of registered manufacturing in the NDDP. Such districtwise data for 1960-61, 1970-71 and 1980-81 are presented in Table 4.5.

The data in columns 4, 6 and 8 indicate no significant changes in the rank-order of the districts during the period under review. There is reasonable inter-temporal stability in the ranks of the districts. Though there are a few shifts, they seem to have little effect on the relative positions of the districts. The rank correlation coefficient turns out to be 0.94 for the period between 1960-61 and 1970-71, 0.87 for the period between 1970-71 and 1980-81, and 0.81 for the period between 1960-61 and 1980-81. From these values, we can infer that inter-district disparities in the share of registered manufacturing continue to persist.

TABLE 4.5: Registered Manufacturing in Karnataka by Districts: 1960-61, 1970-71 and 1980-81 (in terms of NDDP)

(In Rs. Lakhs)

Sl. No.	Districts	1960-61		1970-71		1980-81	
		NDDP	Rank	NDDP	Rank	NDDP	Rank
1	2	3	4	5	6	7	8
1.	Bangalore	1003	1	3535	1	10021	1
2.	Dakshina Kannada	422	2	635	2	665	5
3.	Dharwad	224	3	597	3	701	3
4.	Mysore	219	4	458	4	574	6
5.	Belgaum	205	5	439	5	515	7
6.	Shimoga	186	6	430	6	749	2
7.	Chitradurga	124	7	378	7	675	4
8.	Bijapur	118	8	179	10	90	14
9.	Gulbarga	108	9	199	9	426	8
10.	Uttara Kannada	101	10	165	12	131	13
11.	Bellary	81	11	223	8	364	9
12.	Kolar	75	12	145	13	29	18
13.	Mandya	72	13.5	135	14	190	11
14.	Tumkur	72	13.5	47	17	343	10
15.	Hassan	57	15	84	15	58	15
16.	Chikmagalur	53	16	50	16	40	17
17.	Raichur	40	17	167	11	182	12
18.	Kodagu	37	18	29	19	12	19
19.	Bidar	10	19	36	18	51	16
	Karnataka	3207	--	7931	--	15816	—

Note: The districts are arranged in the descending order of NDDP in 1960-61.
Source: Derived from Appendix Table 4.1.

To get a better insight into the inter-temporal trends in disparities in the share of registered manufacturing in the NDDP, standard deviation and coefficient of variation are used. Their values are already presented in Table 4.2. In this case, unlike the previous one, the values of both the measures of dispersion move in the same direction. Both of them record a consistent increase between 1960-61 and 1980-81. The value of standard deviation increases from 217.69 in 1960-61 to 757.60 in 1970-71, and on to 2,180.47 in 1980-81. Similarly, the value of coefficient of variation increases from 128.97 in 1960-61 to 181.50 in 1970-71, and on to 261.94 in 1980-81. These results provide conclusive evidence to the trend of widening disparities, and they lend empirical support to the "self-perpetuation" hypothesis.

Thus, we notice divergent trends in inter-district disparities in industrial activity when the trends are viewed from different criteria of the areal spread of industrialisation. The inter-district disparities in "factories" and "NDDP from registered manufacturing" have been consistently widening, whereas, the inter-district disparities in "workers" have been getting narrowed down.

4.6 Small-Scale Industry and Inter-District Disparities: A Cross-Section Analysis

The small-scale industrial activity, like the general economic activity, also has a tendency to concentrate itself in only certain regions of a nation or a State, unless its growth is consciously monitored by the Government in such a way as to ensure spatial parity. In Karnataka, despite the Government's "carrot and stick" policy, the small-scale industrial activity has come to concentrate itself only in a couple of districts. Of course, the recent trend in Karnataka seems to be in favour of equitable dispersal of small-scale industrial activity. The principal purpose of this section is to identify whether there is maldistribution of small-scale industrial activity among the districts of Karnataka. The regional disparities are analysed by considering three characteristics of small-scale industry, namely, "units", "employment", and "investment" as the indicators of the spread of small-scale industrial activity.

The districtwise data for all the three selected characteristics of small-scale industrial activity for 1970-71 and 1980-81 are given in Table 4.6.

The data in columns 3 and 4 show that small-scale industrial activity, as indicated by the number of factories, is found in all the 19 districts, but there are wide variations in their distribution. Columns 5 and 6 show a similar maldistribution of small-scale industrial activity as indicated by employment. And the data in columns 7 and 8 also indicate the existence of inter-district disparities in investment in small-scale industries. On the whole, Table 4.6 reveals the existence of inter-district disparities in the small-scale industrial activity in 1970-71 and 1980-81.

TABLE 4.6: Selected Characteristics of Small-Scale Industries in Karnataka: 1970-71 and 1980-81

Sl. No.	Districts	No. of Factories		No. of Employees		Investment (in Rs Lakhs)	
		1970-71	1980-81	1970-71	1980-81	1970-71	1980-81
1	2	3	4	5	6	7	8
1.	Bangalore	2332 (40.22)	9537 (34.53)	60889 (66.00)	137635 (39.94)	3174.75 (55.23)	10105.43 (38.26)
2.	Belgaum	256 (4.42)	1236 (4.48)	2069 (2.24)	8739 (2.54)	222.39 (3.87)	998.43 (3.78)
3.	Bellary	304 (5.24)	1304 (4.72)	2039 (2.21)	6034 (1.75)	146.22 (2.54)	407.10 (1.54)
4.	Bidar	75 (1.29)	381 (1.38)	797 (0.86)	3883 (1.13)	73.60 (1.28)	239.42 (0.91)
5.	Bijapur	241 (4.15)	875 (3.17)	1817 (1.97)	10177 (2.95)	187.12 (3.26)	442.14 (1.68)
6.	Chikmagalur	122 (2.10)	443 (1.60)	1120 (1.22)	3262 (0.95)	99.11 (1.72)	270.35 (1.02)
7.	Chitradurga	180 (3.10)	1292 (4.68)	1829 (1.98)	9139 (2.65)	120.05 (2.09)	714.29 (2.70)
8.	Dakshina Kannada	268 (4.62)	1800 (6.52)	3874 (4.20)	48656 (14.12)	236.80 (4.12)	3281.69 (12.42)
9.	Dharwad	304 (5.24)	1811 (6.55)	3640 (3.95)	18134 (5.26)	226.71 (3.94)	1465.79 (5.55)
10.	Gulbarga	77 (1.33)	497 (1.80)	1394 (1.51)	5329 (1.55)	103.97 (1.81)	403.99 (1.53)
11.	Hassan	136 (2.34)	625 (2.26)	1191 (1.29)	4742 (1.37)	100.91 (1.76)	467.13 (1.77)
12.	Kodagu	60 (1.03)	366 (1.32)	588 (0.64)	10163 (2.95)	60.91 (1.06)	887.82 (3.36)
13.	Kolar	369 (6.36)	1113 (4.03)	1196 (1.30)	6652 (1.93)	229.46 (3.99)	615.96 (2.33)
14.	Mandya	258 (4.45)	959 (3.47)	930 (1.00)	5476 (1.59)	93.74 (1.63)	495.09 (1.88)
15.	Mysore	290 (5.00)	1873 (6.78)	4080 (4.42)	16867 (4.89)	225.41 (3.92)	1635.96 (6.19)
16.	Raichur	69 (1.19)	645 (2.34)	754 (0.82)	18133 (5.26)	53.59 (0.93)	1357.28 (5.14)
17.	Shimoga	184 (3.17)	1253 (4.54)	1520 (1.65)	9752 (2.83)	165.10 (2.87)	1445.85 (5.48)
18.	Tumkur	189 (3.26)	949 (3.44)	1678 (1.82)	13730 (3.98)	144.59 (2.52)	811.17 (3.07)
19.	Uttara Kannada	84 (1.49)	660 (2.39)	850 (0.92)	8138 (2.36)	84.00 (1.46)	367.23 (1.39)
	Karnataka	5798 (100)	27619 (100)	92255 (100)	344641 (100)	5748.43 (100)	26412.12 (100)
	State Average	305	1454	4856	18139	303	1390

Source: Derived from Appendix Table 4.2.

In 1970-71, a sizeable proportion of the small-scale industrial activity of the State is found in Bangalore, and the remaining 18 districts claim very little industrial activity. Bangalore alone claims 40.22 per cent of the factories, 66 per cent of the employees and 55.23 per cent of the total investment. Thus, Bangalore has excessive concentration of small-scale industrial activity. On the other extreme, there is Kodagu with only 1.03 per cent of the factories, 0.64 per cent of the employees and 1.06 per cent of the investment. Furthermore, the claims of the other 18 districts in all the three characteristics do not exceed single digit. These statistical facts express the wide spread that exists among the districts. This disparity situation can be viewed from another angle also, i.e, by considering the State average as an indicator of equitable spread of industrial activity. The State average in terms of factories comes to 305. Of the 5,798 factories, Bangalore alone claims 2,332 factories and the one more district whose claim exceeds the State average of 305 factories is Kolar which has 369 factories. The other two districts which come nearer to the State average are Bellary and Dharwad with 304 factories each. The State average in terms of employees comes to 4,856. In this case Bangalore with 60,889 employees is the lone district which far exceeds the State average, and all the districts lag far behind the State average. The same situation holds good in the case of investment also. The State average comes to Rs. 303 lakhs. In this case also, Bangalore with Rs. 3,174.75 lakhs is the lone district to exceed nearly 10 times the State average. Thus, all these figures show one thing in unequivocal terms: that there is acute maldistribution of small-scale industrial activity in the State; Bangalore suffers from an excessive concentration of small-scale industrial activity, whereas many other districts suffer from the paucity of such activity.

The disparity situation in 1980-81 is not qualitatively different from the situation in 1970-71. Inter-district disparities do exist, though in a relatively lesser magnitude. Again, Bangalore dominates the scene by claiming for itself 34.53 per cent of the factories, 39.94 per cent of the employees and 38.26 per cent of the investment, and the remaining portion is thinly spread over the remaining 18 districts. On the other hand, at the bottom of the ladder, there are some districts like Bidar, Chikmagalur and Gulburga, whose share in the State total of factories, workers and investment is less than two per cent; in districts like Bellary, Hassan, Mandya, their share in the State total of workers and investment is less than two per cent; in districts like Bijapur and Uttara

Kannada, their share in the State total of investment is less than two per cent, and in Kolar its share in the State total of workers is less than two per cent. Gladys Sumitra reports a similar situation in her recent study.[14]

Almost the same result emerges, if we judge the disparity situation by taking the State average as the basis. The State average of factories works out to 1,454. Besides Bangalore which claims 9,537 factories, only three districts, namely, Dakshina Kannada with 1,800, Dharwad with 1,811 and Mysore with 1,873 factories to their credit, exceed the State average and all the other 15 districts lag behind the State average. The State average of employees works out to 18,139. In addition to Bangalore which claims 137,635 employees, only Dakshina Kannada with 48,656 employees exceeds the State average. And two more districts, namely, Dharwad with 18,134 and Raichur with 18,133, employees, come nearer the State average; all other districts remain far from the State average. The situation appears to be somewhat encouraging in the case of investment. The State average of investment comes to Rs. 1,390 lakhs. Besides Bangalore which claims Rs. 10,105.43 lakhs, four districts, namely, Dakshina Kannada with Rs. 3,281.69 lakhs, Dharwad with Rs. 1,465.79 lakhs, Mysore with Rs. 1,635.96 lakhs and Shimoga with Rs. 1,445.85 lakhs, exceed the State average. All these figures about factories, workers and investment, indicate one fundamental fact: that there is maldistribution of small-scale industrial activity in Karnataka.

To identify the extent of disparities, some of the measures of dispersion such as range ratio, standard deviation and coefficient of variation are used. Their values for factories, employees and investment are presented in Table 4.7.

TABLE 4.7: Range Ratio, Standard Deviation and Coefficient of Variation of Small-Scale Industries Units in Karnataka: 1970-71 and 1980-81

Particulars	No. of Units		No. of Employees		Investment	
	1970-71	1980-81	1970-71	1980-81	1970-71	1980-81
1	2	3	4	5	6	7
Range Ratio	0.95	0.93	0.98	0.95	0.97	0.95
Standard Deviation	486.57	1961.35	13246.30	29828.76	679.70	2170.58
Coefficient of Variation	159.45	134.93	272.81	164.45	224.66	156.14

Source: Derived from Table 4.6.

The values of all the measures of dispersion cited in Table 4.7 are indicative of the existence of inter-district disparities in small-scale industrial activity in 1970-71 and 1980-81. Among these measures, the coefficient of variation suggests something about the extent of relative disparities among the different characteristics of small-scale industrial activity. Both in 1970-71 and 1980-81, the disparities seem to be more pronounced in employees than those in investment and units, because, the value of coefficient of variation for employees is higher than the corresponding values for investment and units in both the points of time.

4.7 Small-Scale Industry and Inter-District Disparities: An Inter-Temporal analysis

The cross-section analysis has shown that the small-scale industrial activity is spread very inequitably among the districts of Karnataka in both the points of time 1970-71 and 1980-81. The study, to be of some use in policy-making, need also throw some light on the trends in regional disparities; it has to find out whether the trend is towards convergence or divergence. And the present section is designed to meet such a need. Here also, as in the previous sections, the trend study is conducted with reference to three characteristics of small-scale industrial activity, namely, units, employees and investment, for two points of time – 1970-71 and 1980-81.

The data pertaining to the distribution of small-scale industrial activity among the districts of Karnataka in 1970-71 and 1980-81, in terms of number of units, are furnished in Table 4.8. Columns 4 and 6 indicate no significant changes in the positions of the districts between 1970-71 and 1980-81. The rank correlation coefficient turns out to be 0.85, which indicates relative stability in the rank-order inter-temporally. No doubt, there are a few significant shifts; Kolar which held the 2nd rank in 1970-71 scaled down to the 9th rank in 1980-81, whereas Mysore which held the 5th rank in 1970-71 acquired the 2nd rank in 1980-81, Shimoga and Chitradurga which held the 11th and 12th ranks in 1970-71 attracted the 7th and 6th ranks respectively in 1980-81. This analysis of ranks does not throw any light on the trends in disparities, but, from it, we can infer that regional disparities persist over the time considered.

TABLE 4.8: Small-Scale Industrial Units in Karnataka by Districts (in Terms of factories): 1970-71 and 1980-81

Sl. No.	District	1970-71		1980-81	
		No of Factories	Rank	No of Factories	Rank
1	2	3	4	5	6
1.	Bangalore	2,332	1	9537	1
2.	Kolar	369	2	1113	9
3.	Bellary	304	3.5	1304	5
4.	Dharwad	304	3.5	1811	3
5.	Mysore	290	5	1873	2
6.	Dakshina Kannada	268	6	1800	4
7.	Mandya	258	7	959	10
8.	Belgaum	256	8	1236	8
9.	Bijapur	241	9	875	12
10.	Tumkur	189	10	949	11
11.	Shimoga	184	11	1253	7
12.	Chitradurga	180	12	1292	6
13.	Hassan	136	13	625	15
14.	Chikmagalur	122	14	443	17
15.	Uttara Kannada	84	15	660	13
16.	Gulbarga	77	16	497	16
17.	Bidar	75	17	381	18
18.	Raichur	69	18	645	14
19.	Kodagu	60	19	366	19
	Karnataka	5798	—	27619	—

Note: The districts are arranged in the descending order of rank in 1970-71.
Source: Derived from Table 4.6.

The values of the measures of dispersion like range ratio, standard deviation and coefficient of variation already presented in Table 4.7 would be able to identify whether the disparities are tending towards convergence or further divergence. The range ratio indicates a reduction of disparities, but it is a crude method of measuring dispersion, and hence, not dependable. The value of standard deviation increases from 486.57 in 1970-71 to 1961.35 in 1980-81 and as such it indicates an inter-temporal trend of divergence. Whereas, the value of coefficient of variation which records a decline from 159.45 in 1970-71 to 134.93 in 1980-81 indicates a trend of convergence. Of the two, the trend-behaviour indicated by the latter is more dependable.

That means inter-district disparities in small-scale industrial units have been converging.

Table 4.9 gives the data in respect of the districtwise spread of small-scale industrial activity in terms of employees for 1970-71 and 1980-81. Columns 4 and 6 indicate some significant changes in the positions of the districts. Tumkur, Raichur and Kodagu, which hold the 9th, 18th and 19th ranks respectively in 1970-71, claim the 6th, 4th and 8th ranks respectively in 1980-81. On the other hand, Mysore, Bellary, Chitradurga, Gulbarga, Hassan and Chikmagalur, which hold the 2nd, 6th, 7th, 11th, 13th and 14th ranks respectively in 1970-71, slide back to the 5th, 14th, 10th, 16th, 17th and 19th ranks respectively in 1980-81. And the rank correlation coefficient turns out to be only 0.53. This pattern of change in ranks of the districts indicates a trend towards reduction of regional disparities.

TABLE 4.9: Small-scale Industrial Units in Karnataka by Districts (in Terms of Employees): 1970-71 and 1980-81

Sl. No.	District	1970-71		1880-81	
		No of Employees	Rank	No of Employees	Rank
1	2	3	4	5	6
1.	Bangalore	60889	1	137635	1
2.	Mysore	4080	2	16867	5
3.	Dakshina Kannada	3874	3	48656	2
4.	Dharwad	3640	4	18134	3
5.	Belgaum	2069	5	8739	11
6.	Bellary	2039	6	6034	14
7.	Chitradurga	1829	7	9139	10
8.	Bijapur	1817	8	10177	7
9.	Tumkur	1678	9	13730	6
10.	Shimoga	1520	10	9752	9
11.	Gulbarga	1394	11	5329	16
12.	Kolar	1196	12	6652	13
13.	Hassan	1191	13	4742	17
14.	Chikmagalur	1120	14	3262	19
15.	Mandya	930	15	5476	15
16.	Uttar Kannada	850	16	8138	12
17.	Bidar	797	17	3883	18
18.	Raichur	754	18	18133	4
19.	Kodagu	588	19	10163	8
	Karnataka	92255	—	344641	—

Note: The districts are arranged in the descending order of rank in 1970-71.
Source: Derived from Table 4.6.

Of course, the values of certain measures of dispersion presented in Table 4.7 indicate different trends. The range ratio and coefficient of variation indicate a narrowing down tendency, whereas standard deviation indicates a widening trend. The value of range ratio registers a marginal decline; it declines from 0.98 in 1970-71 to 0.95 in 1980-81. The value of standard deviation increases from 13,246.30 in 1970-71 to 29,828.76 in 1980-81, and thereby indicates a trend of divergence. Whereas, the value of coefficient of variation records a fall from 272.81 in 1970-71 to 164.45 in 1980-81, and thereby indicates a trend of convergence. Since the values of the latter are more reliable than the values of the former, we can safely say that inter-district disparities in employment have been moving towards convergence.

The inter-temporal trends in inter-district disparities in investment in small-scale industries seem to resemble the trends in employment. The districtwise details of investment and ranks, which the various districts claim on the strength of their share in the State total of investment in small-scale industries, are given in Table 4.10.

The data reveal significant changes in the ranks of the districts between 1970-71 and 1980-81, and the rank correlation coefficient turns out to be 0.58. Some districts which hold relatively higher ranks in 1970-71 lose their ranks in 1980-81, while some other districts which hold relatively lower ranks in 1970-71 better their ranks in 1980-81. Kolar, Bijapur, Bellary, Gulbarga, Chikmagalur and Bidar, which hold the 3rd, 7th 9th, 12th, 14th, and 17th ranks respectively in 1970-71 move down to the 11th, 14th, 15th, 16th, 18th, and 19th ranks in 1980-81. On the contrary, Mysore, Shimoga, Mandya, Kodagu and Raichur, which hold the 5th, 8th, 15th, 18th, and 19th ranks respectively in 1970-71, acquire the 3rd, 5th, 12th, 8th, and 6th ranks respectively in 1980-81. From these changes, one can safely infer that the trend has been in favour of convergence.

The values of some of the measures of dispersion given in Table 4.7 also confirm the converging trend. The value of range ratio and the value of coefficient of variation do indicate a clear trend towards reduction of spatial disparities. The value of range ratio declines from 0.97 in 1970-71 to 0.95 in 1980-81. Similarly, the value of coefficient of variation declines from 224.66 in 1970-71 to 156.14 in 1980-81. But the value of standard deviation increases from 679.70 in 1970-71 to 2,170.58 in 1980-81. Since the value of coefficient of variation is more reliable than the value of standard deviation, one can safely say that inter-district disparities in investment have been declining.

TABLE 4.10: Small-Scale Industrial Units in Karnataka by Districts (in Terms of Investment): 1970-71 and 1980-81

(in Rs. lakhs)

Sl. No.	District	1970-71		1980-81	
		Investment	Rank	Investment	Rank
1	2	3	4	5	6
1.	Bangalore	3174.75	1	10105.43	1
2.	Dakshina Kannada	236.80	2	3281.69	2
3.	Kolar	229.46	3	615.96	11
4.	Dharwad	226.71	4	1465.79	4
5.	Mysore	225.41	5	1635.96	3
6.	Belgaum	222.39	6	998.43	7
7.	Bijapur	187.12	7	442.14	14
8.	Shimoga	165.10	8	1445.85	5
9.	Bellary	146.22	9	407.10	15
10.	Tumkur	144.59	10	811.17	9
11.	Chitradurga	120.05	11	714.29	10
12.	Gulbarga	103.97	12	403.99	16
13.	Hassan	100.91	13	467.13	13
14.	Chikmagalur	99.11	14	270.35	18
15.	Mandya	93.74	15	495.09	12
16.	Uttar Kannada	84.00	16	367.23	17
17.	Bidar	73.60	17	239.42	19
18.	Kodagu	60.91	18	887.82	8
19.	Raichur	53.59	19	1357.28	6
	Karnataka	5748.43	—	26412.12	—

Note: The districts are arranged in the descending order of rank in 1970-71.
Source: Derived from Table 4.6.

4.8 Main Findings

(i) The areal maldistribution of industrial activity in Karnataka is not a recent development. The roots of inter-district disparities are to be found in the reorganisation of the State in 1956, when the two halves – Old Mysore and New Mysore – which, were at different levels of industrial development, were brought together. And not only the two halves were at variance, but also the districts within them.

(ii) The cross-section analysis of the district-wise distribution of the registered manufacturing activity, judged from three criteria, namely, factories, workers and the NDDP from registered manufacturing, reveals the existence of glaring regional disparities in 1960-61, 1970-71 and 1980-81. Excessive concentration of industrial activity is found in Bangalore. It also shows that in 1960-61 and 1970-71, the disparities in workers were more pronounced than the disparities in factories and the NDDP from registered manufacturing, but in 1980-81, the disparities in the NDDP from registered manufacturing were more pronounced than the disparities in factories and workers.

(iii) The inter-temporal analysis of regional disparities in registered manufacturing shows the differential behaviour of the three indicators of industrial activity used in the study. The value of coefficient of variation for factories and the NDDP from registered manufacturing registers a consistent increase indicative of divergence, whereas its value for workers registers a rise between 1960-61 and 1970-71 and a fall between 1970-71 and 1980-81, indicating initial divergence followed by convergence.

(iv) Inter-district disparities in small-scale industrial activity are also found in 1970-71 and 1980-81. A cross-section analysis provides adequate empirical evidence to the existence of maldistribution of industrial activity among the districts of Karnataka. Here also, Bangalore dominates the scene by claiming for itself a sizeable proportion of the small-scale industrial activity in the State. The analysis also shows that the inter-district disparities in employees are more pronounced than the disparities in units and investment in both the points of time considered.

(v) But it is heartening to note that the inter-temporal trend has been in favour of convergence. The value of coefficient of variation for all the three indicators of industrial activity used in the analysis records a fall between 1970-71 and 1980-81. That means the disparities have been converging over time.

NOTES

1. National Committee on the Development of Backward Areas, *Report on Industrial Dispersal*, Planning Commission, Government of India, Oct. 1980, p. 3.
2. For details, see Chapter II.
3. For details, see Bureau of Economics and Statistics, *Economic Development of*

Mysore 1956-69, Government of Mysore, Bangalore, 1970.

4. Munshi, M.C., *location of Industries in Mysore State*, Indian Statistical Institute Calcutta, 1962, pp.34-35 and p.95.
5. National Council of Applied Economic Research, *Techno-Economic Survey of Mysore*, NCAER, New Delhi, 1965, p.126.
6. Angadi, V.B., "Structure and Prospects of Industries in Mysore", in T.K. Meti (ed.), *Economic Development and Social Change in Mysore State*, Karnataka University, Dharwad 1971, p.87.
7. Hiremath, N.S., "Industrial Development of Mysore" in T.K. Meti (ed.) *Economic Development and Social Change in Mysore* State, Karnataka University, Dharwad, 1971, p.130.
8. Nanjundappa, D.M., *Some Aspects of Karnataka's Economy*, Bharat Prakashan, Dharwad, 1971, pp. 248-249.
9. Naidu, K Munirathna, "Industrial Progress in Karnataka — A Critical Review", *Southern Economist*, Vol. 17, No. 13, November 1, 1978, p.15.
10. For details, see Hughes, R.B., "Interregional Income Differences: Self-Perpetuation", *Southern Economic Journal*, Vol. 28, No. 1. July 1961, pp. 41-45.
11. *Ibid.*, pp. 41-45.
12. For details, See Chapter II of the Present work.
13. For details, See Williamson, J.G., "Regional Inequality and the Process of National Development", *Economic Development and Cultural Change*, Vol. 13, No. 4, Part II, July 1965.
14. Sumithra, Gladys, *Some Aspects of Regional Development in Karnataka — An Inter-district Analysis* (a Paper presented at the Seminar on Regional Dispersal of Industries in Karnataka, held at B.R. Project, P.G. Centre, in January 1984), pp. 12-13.

APPENDIX TABLE 4.1: Registered Manufacturing in Karnataka by Districts: 1960-61, 1970-71 and 1980-81

(In Rs. lakhs)

Sl. No.	District	Number of Units/ factories			Number of Workers			NDDP from Registered Manufacturing		
		1960-61	1970-71	1980-81	1960-61	1970-71	1980-81	1960-61	1970-71	1980-81
1	2	3	4	5	6	7	8	9	10	11
1.	Bangalore	575	1350	4460	72040	137430	230991	1003	3535	10021
2.	Belgaum	231	310	1210	11764	14897	72544	205	439	515
3.	Bellary	75	155	258	4419	7147	17832	81	223	364
4.	Bidar	7	29	52	102	1141	2445	10	36	51
5.	Bijapur	120	141	432	3727	4302	15380	118	179	90
6.	Chikmagalur	30	36	86	913	1540	5638	53	50	40
7.	Chitradurga	65	102	226	10783	13252	12807	124	378	675
8.	Dakshina Kannada	248	373	737	17635	19392	46203	422	635	665
9.	Dharwad	255	373	588	12305	17421	36314	224	597	701
10.	Gulbarga	69	101	215	3741	6209	11101	108	199	426
11.	Hassan	22	54	125	1018	2441	6464	57	84	58
12.	Kodagu	20	28	58	528	882	3272	37	29	12
13.	Kolar	36	75	105	959	4879	6491	75	145	29
14.	Mandya	18	52	104	2492	4119	6193	72	135	190
15.	Mysore	171	196	481	12040	14729	27260	219	458	574
16.	Raichur	137	271	334	4114	6162	22660	40	167	182
17.	Shimoga	60	69	278	6741	13272	14476	180	430	749
18.	Tumkur	33	51	60	974	1529	5369	72	47	343
19.	Uttara Kannada	29	48	133	3631	5128	7366	101	165	131
	Karnataka	2201	3814	9942	169926	275872	550806	3207	7931	15816

Note: 1980-81 figures pertain to 1979-80.

Sources: 1. The Chief Inspector of Factories and Boilers, Government of Karnataka, Bangalore.
2. The Directorate of Economics and Statistics, Government of Karnataka, Bangalore.

APPENDIX TABLE 4.2: Small-Scale Industrial Units in Karnataka by Districts: 1970-71 and 1980-81

Sl. No.	District	No. of Factories		No. of Employees		Investment (in Rs Lakhs)	
		1970-71	1980-81	1970-71	1980-81	1970-71	1980-81
1	2	3	4	5	6	7	8
1.	Bangalore	2332	9537	60889	137635	3174.75	10105.43
2.	Belgaum	256	1236	2069	8739	222.39	998.43
3.	Bellary	304	1304	2039	6034	146.22	407.10
4.	Bidar	75	381	797	3883	73.60	239.42
5.	Bijapur	241	875	1817	10177	187.12	442.14
6.	Chikmagalur	122	443	1120	3262	99.11	270.35
7.	Chitradurga	180	1292	1829	9139	120.05	714.29
8.	Dakshina Kannada	268	1800	3874	48656	236.80	3281.69
9.	Dharwad	304	1811	3640	18134	226.71	1465.79
10.	Gulbarga	77	497	1394	5329	103.97	403.99
11.	Hassan	136	625	1191	4742	100.91	467.13
12.	Kodagu	60	366	588	10163	60.91	887.82
13.	Kolar	369	1113	1196	6652	229.46	615.96
14.	Mandya	258	959	930	5476	93.74	495.09
15.	Mysore	290	1873	4080	16867	225.41	1635.96
16.	Raichur	69	645	754	18133	53.59	1357.28
17.	Shimoga	184	1253	1520	9752	165.10	1445.85
18.	Tumkur	189	949	1678	13730	144.59	811.17
19.	Uttara Kannada	84	660	850	8138	84.00	367.23
	Karnataka	5798	27619	92255	344641	5748.43	26412.12

Source: Directorate of Industries and Commerce (Statistical Section) Government of Karnataka, Bangalore.

5

INDUSTRIALISATION AND STRUCTURAL TRANSFORMATION IN KARNATAKA

5.1 Introduction

INDUSTRIALISATION, whether spontaneous or deliberately induced, being an integral part of the dynamic process of economic development, is said to engender certain fundamental changes in the economic structure of the economy. Whatever may be the terminology employed to define and describe the quantitative and qualitative changes that go with industrialisation, one thing is found to be certain that, *inter alia*, a structural change in terms of the sectoral composition of income and workforce is an inseparable concomitant of industrialisation. While writing about the structural transformation that accompanies industrialisation, R.B. Sutcliffe says that industrialisation is a concept which in essence is dynamic, and which in practice involves a radical transformation of society in all its aspects – economic, social, political and cultural.[1] As far as the economic structure is concerned, industrialisation causes a sort of creative disequilibrium in the hitherto stagnant or semi-stagnant economies by injecting an element of dynamism into them, and with it, it initiates a new process of development based on the changing sectoral behaviour. The significance of structural change lies in the mutually reinforcing relationship that exists between it and the level of economic development. It is particularly so in economies like India where significant per capita labour productivity differences exist among different sectors. In this regard, K.R.G. Nair opines: "The level of NDP of an economy depends, by definition, upon the number of workers and on the product per worker. The product per worker differs also among the different sectors of an economy, such variation being more marked, the less developed the economy. The distribution of workers among the various sectors of an economy has, hence, an important bearing on product per worker, and therefore on NDP".[2]

The exponents and advocates of the sectoral theory identify a definite functional relationship between the levels of development and the relative importance of the three sectors – primary, secondary and tertiary – in output and employment.[3] The sectoral theorists view industrialisation as that part of the process of development which involves a sure structural shift in production and employment patterns away from the primary sector and towards the secondary and tertiary sectors. "It has been observed", says T.Y. Srinivas, "that economic development involves an inevitable shift away from agriculture in favour of manufacturing, and transport and communications. This structural shift away from agriculture, which is the essence of the process of economic development, is termed as industrialisation. This structural shift is found to have taken place in the present industrially advanced countries and also recently in the developing countries as well. The structural shift which results in a reduction in the share of agriculture in national income and employment, and a corresponding improvement in the shares of manufacturing and service sectors is a historically observed fact of development".[4]

A few empirical studies have already been conducted at various spatial levels – International, National and State – to test the sectoral hypothesis. Some have found empirical support in respect of the relationship between per capita NDP and industrial structure at the national level, and some others have found such relationship between per capita NDP and the sectoral composition of output at the national level. A few initial attempts have also been made to study the dynamics of structural transformation in Karnataka; some of them lend empirical support, and some of them do not, for the relationship between the level of development and sectoral shares envisaged in the sectoral thesis.[5]

At this stage, as a sort of preface to the present chapter, it is necessary to say that the principal aim of this chapter is not to develop and test any new hypothesis related to the nature and extent of the functional relationship that exists between industrialisation and structural transformation, but, the principal aim is to analyse and comprehend the nature and extent of structural transformation that has been taking place in the State and district economies of Karnataka since 1960-61. The main focus would be on the changes in the sectoral shares of output and employment. At the same time an attempt is also made to examine the relationship between the levels of the NDP and the relative importance of the sectors. And in that process, we also test the sectoral hypothesis. This chapter, including this introductory section, consists of five sections. The second section narrates the nature and limitations of the data used. The sectoral shares of the net State Domestic Product (NSDP) and workforce and their changing behaviour between 1960-61 and 1980-81 are examined in detail in the third section. A similar exercise in respect of the district economies is undertaken in the fourth section. And the fifth section concludes the discussion by bringing together all the principal findings.

5.2 The Data Used

The entire study of structural transformation, as viewed in the present study, needs data on only two aspects of the State and district economies, namely, sectoral origin of the NDP and workforce. As far as the Net State Domestic Product (NSDP) and the Net District Domestic Product (NDDP) are concerned, the data are collected mainly from the publications and the unpublished records of the State Incomes Division of the Directorate of Economics and Statistics (DES), Bangalore. And the data pertaining to the sectoral origin of workforce are collected from the Census publications of the Government of India.

5.2.1 NDP Data

In India, the NSDP is estimated by two agencies, namely, the Central Statistical Organisation (CSO) at the national level, and the DES at the State level. Both the estimates are based on the same methodology prepared by the CSO. In this connection, it is to be said that the DES estimates of the NSDP by industry origin differ considerably from those of the CSO for Karnataka. A recent study finds that the incomes of some sectors are overestimated, and of some others are underestimated by the DES when compared to the estimates of the CSO.[6] However, in view of the fact that the DES estimates are used for evaluating the annual economic performance of the State and district economies by the Government of Karnataka, the present study, to be relevant to Karnataka, uses the estimates made by the DES, Bangalore. It is indeed a limitation that governs the present analysis.

The NSDP and NDDP estimates of the DES are by industry origin. Initially, the estimates are made for 16 sub-sectors, which can be brought under three major sectors, namely, primary sector, secondary sector and tertiary sector. Generally the estimates are done both at current and constant prices. In Karnataka, the estimates for 1960-61 are available at 1960-61 prices which incidentally happens to be the base year of the present study. Whereas, similar estimates for 1970-71 and onwards are available in 1970-71 and current prices, but not in 1960-61 prices. By and large, in an inflationary economy, the income estimates at current prices, particularly when the time-spread between the base year and the current year is considerably long, do not reflect the real growth of the economy. So, to get a relatively realistic account of the inter-temporal changes in economic performance, the income estimates have been reduced to the base year prices, i,e., 1960-61 in the present study. In this connection the deflator implicit in the deflated estimates of the NSDP done by the DES is used.[7]

5.2.2 Workforce Data

The Government of Karnataka does not have any agency of its own which collects and publishes comprehensive data on workforce for the State and district economies. Of course, the data on the workforce engaged in the organised sectors of the economy are being compiled and published by the DES. Such estimates exclude more workers than they include; vast multitudes who are engaged in agricultural operations in different capacities in rural areas, and those sucked into the informal sectors of urban areas, find no place in the estimates. In these circumstances, we have to depend upon the Census data – the basic source of data on workforce in India.

But there are some problems in using the Census data for inter-temporal studies like the one in hand. The present study, workforcewise, spreads over three Censuses – 1961, 1971 and 1981. Any inter-temporal study needs comparable data. But the workforce data of 1961 Census are not straightaway comparable with those of 1971 and 1981. There exist quite a few differences in concepts and industrial classification of workers used in 1961 and the subsequent censuses. A few attempts have already been made by researchers to make the data of 1961 comparable with that of 1971.[8] However, the present study does not intend to go into the methodological details involved in making 1961 Census figures comparable with those of 1971. In respect of Karnataka, a recent doctoral study[9] has adjusted the 1961 workforce estimates to suit the industrial category of workers of the 1971 Census. And those adjusted estimates of workforce for 1961 are used in the present work. However, there is no such problem with regard to the workforce estimates of the 1971 and 1981 Censuses. As per 1981 Census the total workforce is made up of "main workers" plus "marginal workers", and it is comparable with the aggregate of "main workers" plus "non-workers with secondary work" of 1971 Census. This is what the Census authorities also say.[10]

Thus, the discussion of structural transformation of the State and district economies of Karnataka that follows is done within the frame-work of limitations set by the available data on NDP and workforce.

5.3 The Changing Structure of the State Economy

The standard tri-sectoral classification of the economy is adopted in this chapter and also in all other chapters of this work wherever sectoral analysis is involved. An attempt is first made to identify the relative importance of primary, secondary and tertiary sectors in the State total of income and workforce at three points of time, namely, 1960-61, 1970-71 and 1980-81.[11] Secondly, the inter-temporal changes in their relative importance in the State economy are examined. And thirdly, the sectoral analysis is extended to know the nature of relationship that obtains between the level of the NSDP and the economic structure of the State. Such a study of the structure of the State economy, among other things, is expected to provide a very useful backdrop for the district-level inquiry that follows.

5.3.1 Sectoral Composition of NSDP and Workforce

The data pertaining to the sectoral composition of NSDP and workforce for 1960-61, 1970-71 and 1980-81 are given in Table 5.1.

A close scrutiny of the data reveals some vital facts about the sectoral aspects of the structure of the State economy. A horizontal reading of the columns across the sectors for all the three points of time shows that the share of the primary sector in the State total of NSDP and workforce in decidedly far larger than that of the secondary and tertiary sectors in all the three points of time considered here. In 1960-61, the primary sector claims 61.25 per cent of the NSDP which is more than four times the share of the secondary sector, and a little over two and a half times the share of the tertiary sector. In the same year, a similar situation with some quantitative difference is found in the sectoral shares of workforce; the primary sector's share of workforce exceeds 75 per cent which is more than seven times the share of the secondary sector, and more than five times the share of the tertiary sector. That is to say, in 1960-61, the economic structure of the State is dominated by the primary sector. A similar inter-sectoral situation is obtained in 1970-71 and 1980-81 also. In 1970-71, the primary sector dominates the economic structure of the State by claiming more than 58 per cent of the NSDP and more than 71 per cent of the workforce for itself. And in 1980-81 also it dominates the economic structure of the State by claiming more than 49 per cent of the NSDP and more than 71 per cent of the workforce.

TABLE 5.1: Sectoral Origin of NSDP and Workforce in Karnataka: 1960-61, 1970-71 and 1980-81

Year	NSDP (in Rs. lakhs) from			No. of Workers in			
	Primary Sector	Secondary Sector	Tertiary Sector	Primary Sector	Secondary Sector	Tertiary Sector	Per Capita NSDP (in Rs.)
1	2	3	4	5	6	7	8
1960-61	42366 (61.25)	10486 (15.16)	16312 (23.59)	6198651 (75.14)	885040 (10.73)	1165788 (14.13)	293
1970-71	61416 (58.70)	18596 (17.77)	24619 (23.53)	7262124 (71.34)	1220626 (11.99)	1696364 (16.67)	357
1980-81	68167 (49.04)	31740 (22.84)	39078 (28.12)	10626404 (71.08)	2020875 (13.52)	2301440 (15.40)	374

Notes: 1. The workforce data pertain to 1961, 1971 and 1981.
2. The figures placed are in brackets are the percentages of the respective sectoral shares.

Sources: 1. NSDP figures are derived from Appendix Tables 3.1, 3.2 and 3.3.
2. Workforce figures are derived from Appendix Table 5.1, 5.2 and 5.3.

Table 5.1 enables us to look at the inter-sectoral issue from the point of view of the non-primary sectors also. So far as the non-primary sectors are concerned, the data show that at all the three points of time, the tertiary sector has higher NSDP and workforce compared to the secondary sector. The tertiary sector claimed 23.59, 23.53 and 28.12 per cent of the NSDP in 1960-61, 1970-71 and

1980-81 respectively, as against the secondary sector's claim of 15.16, 17.77 and 22.84 per cent respectively for the same reference years. In the case of workforce, it claims 14.13, 16.67 and 15.40 per cent of the total workforce in 1960-61, 1970-71 and 1980-81 respectively as against the claim of the secondary sector of 10.73, 11.99 and 13.52 per cent respectively for the same reference years.

Furthermore, Table 5.1 exhibits the presence of only one order of sectoral dominance in all the three points of time. The primary sector is the lead sector, and it is followed by the tertiary and secondary sectors.

5.3.2 Sectoral Composition of NSDP and Workforce: An Inter-Temporal Analysis

The inter-temporal analysis is designed to find out the inter-temporal changes in the sectoral shares of the NSDP and workforce. If we read the data in columns 2 and 3, 5 and 6 of Table 5.1 vertically, it becomes clear that the primary sector records a consistent fall in its share of both NSDP and workforce, whereas, on the contrary, the secondary sector records a consistent increase in its share of both NSDP and workforce from one point of time to the other. The tertiary sector, in keeping with the expected pattern, does not exhibit any consistency. Column 4 shows that its share of NSDP records a fall from 23.59 per cent in 1960-61 to 23.53 in 1970-71, but again moves up to 28.12 per cent in 1980-81. And column 7 shows that its share of workforce records an increase from 14.13 per cent in 1960-61 to 16.67 per cent in 1970-71, but again moves down to 15.40 per cent in 1980-81. A similar trend is found in the international long-term trend study of Simon Kuznets.[12]

The table also reveals some interesting facts about the way the decline in the share of the primary sector is compensated by the non-primary sectors. Generally, a major proportion of the decline in the primary sector's share of income is compensated by the secondary sector, whereas a major proportion of the decline in the primary sector's share of workforce is compensated by the tertiary sector. In Karnataka between 1960-61 and 1970-71, the entire decline in the primary sector's share of NSDP is absorbed by the secondary sector, but between 1970-71 and 1980-81, a relatively higher proportion is absorbed by the secondary sector. In the case of workforce, between 1960-61 and 1970-71, the reduction in the primary sector's share is more compensated by the tertiary sector than by the secondary sector, but between 1970-71 and 1980-81, the entire decline in the primary sector's share of workforce is absorbed by the secondary sector.

Another simple exercise is done to identify the sectoral differences in growth rates amongst themselves as well as between them and the overall growth rates of the State economy. For this purpose, annual compound growth rates of all the three sectors in the NSDP and workforce are calculated and presented in Table 5.2.

TABLE 5.2: Annual Compound Growth Rates of NSDP and Workforce by Sectors: 1960-61 to 1970-71, 1970-71 to 1980-81 and 1960-61 to 1980-81

(in percentages)

Period	Annual Compound Growth Rates in NSDP of the			Annual Compound Growth Rates in workforce of the			Annual Compound Growth Rates in	
	Primary Sector	Secondary Sector	Tertiary Sector	Primary Sector	Secondary Sector	Tertiary Sector	Total NSDP	Total Workforce
1	2	3	4	5	6	7	8	9
1960-61 to 1970-71	3.78	5.90	4.20	1.60	3.27	3.82	4.23	2.12
1970-71 to 1980-81	1.05	5.49	4.73	3.88	5.17	3.10	2.88	3.92
1960-61 to 1980-81	2.41	5.69	4.47	2.73	4.21	3.46	3.55	3.02

Note: The Annual Compound Growth Rates of Workforce refer to 1961 to 1971, 1971 to 1981, and 1961 to 1981.

Sources: 1. Growth Rates of NSDP are derived from Appendix Tables 3.1, 3.2 and 3.3.
2. Growth Rates of Workforce are derived from Appendix Tables 5.1, 5.2, and 5.3.

From the data it is evident that not only are there inter-temporal variations in the growth of every sector, but also in the inter-sectoral growth rates. As far as the overall growth rates are concerned, columns 8 and 9 show that in the first decade, the NSDP records a higher growth rate than the workforce; in the second decade, the latter records a higher growth rate than the former; and for the two decades taken together, the NSDP's performance is slightly better than that of the workforce. Sectorally speaking, for all the three periods, the highest growth in the NSDP is registered by the secondary sector, and the second and third positions go to the tertiary and primary sectors respectively. The situation is different as far as the growth of workforce is concerned. During the first decade, the highest growth rate is recorded by the tertiary sector, and the second and third positions go to the secondary and primary sectors respectively; in the second decade, the first place goes to the secondary sector, and the second and third positions go to the primary and tertiary sectors respectively; and for the two decades taken together, the secondary sector occupies the first place and the second and third places go to the tertiary and primary sectors respectively.

Thus, regarding the relative growth rates of the sectors in the NSDP and workforce one can infer that the secondary sector has been growing at a faster rate than the tertiary sector, which gets the second place, and the primary sector which gets the third place. So far as the overall growth rates are concerned, the NSDP has been growing at a slightly higher rate than the workforce.

5.3.3. Level of Per Capita NSDP and Sectoral Composition of Income and Workforce

The data in Table 5.1 help us to identify the dynamics of the relationship between the level of economic development, as measured by per capita NSDP, and the sectoral composition of income and workforce. The data show the expected pattern of association between the two variables. The increase in per capita NSDP is accompanied by a reduction in the share of the primary sector in the NSDP and workforce and an increase in the shares of the non-primary sectors. Between 1960-61 and 1970-71, 1970-71 and 1980-81 and between 1960-61 and 1980-81, a common trend is visible in the sectoral behaviour in response to the changes in the per capita NSDP. As the per capita NSDP increases from Rs. 293 in 1960-61 to Rs. 357 in 1970-71, and to Rs. 374 in 1980-81, there is a clear shift away from the primary sector to the non-primary sectors. But here it is pertinent to note that the shift is relatively more pronounced in the case of the NSDP than in the case of the workforce. And it is equally important to note that the behaviour of the tertiary sector is inconsistent. That is to say, every increase in the per capita NSDP is accompanied by a consistent decline in the share of the primary sector and an equally consistent increase in the share of the secondary sector. But in the case of the tertiary sector, no clear pattern of change is found. A study[13] conducted for the entire nation for the same reference years reports consistent decline in the share of the primary sector in the GDP, and also equally consistent increase in the shares of both the secondary and tertiary sectors. And two State-level studies[14] for Karnataka report not only a decline in the share of the primary sector in output and employment but also a matching increase in the shares of the non-primary sectors.

To better comprehend the nature of association between the level of per capita NSDP and sectoral shares of income and employment, the inter-temporal changes in both the variables are worked out in terms of percentages, and are presented in Table 5.3.

Table 5.3 shows that in all the three spells of time considered, positive changes in the per capita NSDP are accompanied by negative changes in the share of the primary sector indicating the expected declining trend, and a positive change in the share of the secondary sector indicating the expected increasing trend, in terms of the sectoral composition of income and workforce. And, it also shows the expected inconsistency of the tertiary sector; it acquires negative and positive signs for its share of the NSDP and workforce respectively, in the first decade, and positive and negative signs respectively for them in the second decade, but, for both the decades put together, it acquires positive signs for both NSDP and workforce.

TABLE 5.3: Changes in the Economic Structure of Karnataka: 1960-61 to 1970-71, 1970-71 to 1980-81, and 1960-61 to 1980-81

Period	Percentage Change in the Share in NSDP of the			Percentage Change in the Share in the Workforce of the			Percentage change in per capita NSDP
	Primary Sector	Secondary Sector	Tertiary Sector	Primary Sector	Secondary Sector	Tertiary Sector	
1	2	3	4	5	6	7	8
1960-61 to 1970-71	-4.16	+17.22	-0.25	-5.06	+11.74	+17.98	+21.84
1970-71 to 1980-81	-16.46	+28.53	+19.51	-0.36	+12.76	-7.62	+4.76
1960-61 to 1980-81	-19.94	+50.66	+19.20	-5.40	+26.00	+8.99	+27.65

Note: The reference period for the changes in workforce are: 1961 to 1971, 1971 to 1981 and 1961 to 1981.

Source: Derived from Table 5.1.

5.4 Changing Structure of District Economies

The preceding section *inter alia* has shown that the structure of the State economy has been 'undergoing a change indicative of a slow but sure shift away from the primary sector to the secondary and tertiary sectors. When it is so, the structure of the district economies must also have been experiencing changes, because the changes in the structure of the State economy are nothing but a manifestation of the aggregate of changes of the district economies. Chapters III and IV have shown that there are inter-district disparities in the economic and industrial development in Karnataka. And the present section by analysing the changes in the structure of the district economies in terms of the changes in the sectoral shares of income and employment over a span of two decades acquires all the three essential dimensions of development analysis, namely, inter-regional, inter-sectoral and inter-temporal, involving space, sector and time respectively. In this section, first of all, an attempt is made to understand the differential nature of the structure of the district economies at three points of time – 1960-61, 1970-71 and 1980-81. Secondly, the inter-temporal changes in the sectoral shares of income and employment are examined. And in doing so, an effort is also made to identify the nature of association between the levels of the per capita NDDP and the sectoral shares.

5.4.1 Structure of District Economies: A Cross-Section Analysis

The data pertaining to the economic structure of all the districts of Karnataka for 1960-61 are presented in Table 5.4.

A broken line is drawn in the table to separate the districts whose per capita NDDP is higher than the per capita NSDP from those whose per capita NDDP is lower than the per capita NSDP. The districts which lie above the line belong to the first category, and those below the line belong to the second category. For the sake of brevity, in the discussion that follows, the former are called Group I and the latter Group II districts. The table reveals some vital facts about the structure of the district economies.

Columns 3 and 6 very clearly show that with the exception of Bangalore, all other districts of Karnataka, irrespective of their levels of development, are basically primary economic-activity-oriented districts. The primary sector in these districts claims a substantial proportion of the NDDP and workforce. But its dominance is not uniform in both NDDP and workforce. In majority of the districts, dominance of the primary sector is found to be more pronounced in workforce than in NDDP. It is so, because, 16 out of the 19 districts have more than 70 per cent of their workforce engaged in the primary sector, whereas only five out of the 19 districts claim more than 70 per cent of their NDDP from the primary sector.

TABLE 5.4: Economic Structure of the Districts of Karnataka: 1960-61

Sl. No.	District	% NDDP from			% Workers in		
		Primary Sector	Secondary Sector	Tertiary Sector	Primary Sector	Secondary Sector	Tertiary Sector
1	2	3	4	5	6	7	8
1.	Kodagu	84.32	5.84	9.84	74.40	7.69	17.91
2.	Shimoga	66.27	22.00	11.73	65.78	18.62	15.60
3.	Uttara Kannada	77.26	9.03	13.71	71.61	11.13	17.26
4.	Chikmagalur	76.71	10.71	12.58	78.73	8.26	13.01
5.	Dakshina Kannada	64.53	14.47	21.00	68.80	15.20	16.00
6.	Bellary	60.58	14.79	24.63	74.26	9.09	16.65
7.	Hassan	73.54	7.50	18.96	86.23	5.29	8.48
8.	Tumkur	71.64	10.61	17.75	85.82	6.13	8.05
9.	Chitradurga	58.56	18.08	23.36	79.31	10.13	10.56
10.	Belgaum	65.70	11.55	22.75	79.19	10.10	10.71
11.	Mysore	56.04	16.55	27.41	75.21	9.47	15.32
12.	Mandya	69.55	11.90	18.55	86.11	6.16	7.73
13.	Dharwad	53.52	14.13	32.35	74.22	11.41	14.37
14.	Bangalore	30.21	29.22	40.57	53.80	19.59	26.61
15.	Kolar	64.39	10.55	25.06	85.14	4.66	10.20
16.	Raichur	59.90	12.80	27.30	78.93	7.06	14.01
17.	Gulbarga	55.19	14.97	29.84	75.39	9.23	15.38
18.	Bijapur	51.44	18.83	29.73	77.83	12.57	9.60
19.	Bidar	54.09	12.99	32.92	78.20	6.73	15.07
	Karnataka	61.25	15.16	23.59	75.14	10.73	14.13

Note: The districts are arranged in the descending order of per capita NDDP in 1960-61.

Source: Derived from Appendix Tables 3.1, 3.2, 3.3, 5.1, 5.2 and 5.3.

It is quite interesting and surprising to note that the highest share of the primary sector in both NDDP and workforce is found not in the districts of Group II as expected, but in the Group I districts of Kodagu and Hassan respectively, and its lowest share of the NDDP and workforce is found not in the districts of Group I, but in the Group II district of Bangalore. This appears to be a departure from the expected pattern of sectoral behaviour.

The excessive dominance of the primary sector has affected the shares of the non-primary sectors in the NDDP and workforce. The shares of the secondary and tertiary sectors are so small that even if their shares are put together they cannot equal the share of the primary sector both in NDDP and workforce. However, the smallness of their shares is more pronounced in workforce than in NDDP. From columns 4 and 5 we know that, with the exception of Shimoga whose secondary sector's share of the NDDP is larger than that of its tertiary sector's, in all other districts of both Group I and Group II, the tertiary sector's share is decidedly larger than the share of the secondary sector. A perusal of columns 7 and 8 reveals that in the case of workforce also, with the exception of Shimoga in Group I and Bijapur in Group II in which the secondary sector's share is larger than the share of the tertiary sector, in all other districts, the tertiary sector's share is larger than the share of the secondary sector.

In order to get a graphic picture of the diversified economic structure of the district economies, an attempt is made to derive a sort of typology of districts taking the shares of the non-primary sectors in NDDP and workforce as the basis. Keeping in view the minimum and maximum performance recorded by the non-primary sectors in 1960-61, the districts are classified into three orders: First Order, Second Order and Third Order. All those districts whose share of the non-primary sectors is above 50 per cent come under the First Order; those whose share lies between 25 and 50 per cent come under the Second Order; and those whose share is less than 25 per cent come under the Third Order. The differential ordering of the districts is given in Table 5.5.

It is interesting to note that in terms of the share in the NDDP, all the three districts of the Third Order and four districts of the Second Order belong to group I, and all the districts of group II, with the exception of Bangalore which is found in the First Order, are found in the Second Order. The ordering of the districts is slightly different when viewed from the workforce angle. Here, no district is found in the First Order. The first two districts of the Third Order, and the first five districts of the Second Order belong to Group I, and the last two districts of the Second Order and all the districts of the Third Order from serial number 3 to 12 belong to Group II. This classification of districts into different orders, besides giving a rough picture of the types, shows that neither all the high per capita NDDP districts have attained a higher degree of industrialisation, nor do all the low per capita income districts suffer from total absence of industrial activity. The fact that all the Second Order districts under NDDP classification belonging to Group II, with the exception of Dharwad, are found in the Third Order under workforce classification, may be a reflection of the relatively higher per capita productivity of workers in the non-primary sectors.

TABLE 5.5: Classification of Districts according to the Share of the Non-Primary Sectors in NDDP and Workforce 1960-61.

% Share of Non-Primary Sectors in NDDP			% Share of Non-Primary Sectors in Total Workforce of Districts		
Above 50 %	25 to 50 %	Below 25 %	Above 50 %	25 to 50 %	Below 25 %
1	2	3	4	5	6
1. Bangalore	1. Shimoga	1. Kodagu	Nil	1. Kodagu	1. Chikmagalur
	2. Dakshina Kannada	2. Uttara Kannada		2. Shimoga	2. Hassan
	3. Bellary	3. Chikmagalur		3. Uttara Kannada	3. Tumkur
	4. Hassan			4. Dakshina Kannada	4. Chitradurga
	5. Tumkur			5. Bellary	5. Belgaum
	6. Chitradurga			6. Dharwad	6. Mysore
	7. Belgaum			7. Bangalore	7. Mandya
	8. Mysore				8. Kolar
	9. Mandya				9. Raichur
	10. Dharwad				10. Gulbarga
	11. Kolar				11. Bijapur
	12. Raichur				12. Bidar
	13. Gulbarga				
	14. Bijapur				
	15. Bidar				

Source: Derived from Table 5.4.

The cross-section data presented in Table 5.6 give the tri-sectoral situation that prevailed in 1970-71 in terms of the sectoral shares of output and employment. A cursory glance at the table is enough to know that in 1970-71 the economic structure of all the districts, except Bangalore, is predominantly primary-economic activity-oriented. The primary sector dominates the economic scene of almost every district by claiming for itself two to three times the share of the non-primary sectors in both output and employment. However, the primary sector's dominance is more pronounced in its share of workforce than in its share of the NDDP. All the districts of both Group I and Group II, with the exception of Bangalore and Dakshina Kannada which have relatively lower shares, have more than 70 per cent of their workforce engaged in the primary sector. On the other hand, in the case of the NDDP, only five districts claim more than 70 per cent of the NDDP from the primary sector. In this year, Bangalore claims the distinction for having the least share of the primary sector and the highest share of the secondary and tertiary sectors. On the other hand, Kodagu has the distinction of claiming the highest share of the primary sector and the lowest share of the secondary and tertiary sectors in the NDDP, and Mandya claims a similar position in respect of workforce in the primary and secondary sectors.

TABLE 5.6: Economic Structure of the Districts of Karnataka: 1970-71

Sl. No.	District	% NDDP from			% Workers in		
		Primary Sector	Secondary Sector	Tertiary Sector	Primary Sector	Secondary Sector	Tertiary Sector
1	2	3	4	5	6	7	8
1.	Kodagu	85.61	5.80	8.59	72.55	8.10	19.35
2.	Chikmagalur	79.41	7.00	13.59	76.30	6.88	16.82
3.	Bellary	68.54	12.18	19.28	76.49	8.68	14.83
4.	Shimoga	66.44	15.94	17.62	74.07	11.15	14.78
5.	Raichur	74.09	8.99	16.92	79.78	7.06	13.16
6.	Uttara Kannada	63.14	13.90	22.96	70.75	10.13	19.12
7.	Bangalore	20.72	42.75	36.53	42.85	24.56	32.59
8.	Chitradurga	63.39	17.31	19.30	77.08	10.31	12.61
9.	Hassan	71.22	12.04	16.74	80.64	7.03	12.33
10.	Dakshina Kannada	49.82	23.55	26.63	59.14	22.22	18.64
11.	Mysore	56.85	19.68	23.47	71.09	11.08	17.83
12.	Gulbarga	64.65	13.38	21.97	74.32	10.18	15.50
13.	Dharwad	52.15	17.50	30.35	70.80	10.97	18.23
14.	Mandya	72.30	9.61	18.09	82.71	6.12	11.17
15.	Belgaum	59.65	17.01	23.34	75.23	11.72	13.05
16.	Bidar	63.69	9.29	27.02	74.70	8.01	17.29
17.	Kolar	61.03	12.78	26.19	82.34	6.34	11.32
18.	Tumkur	66.05	10.67	23.28	81.75	7.45	10.80
19.	Bijapur	56.68	14.43	28.89	75.37	12.00	12.63
	Karnataka	58.70	17.77	23.53	71.34	11.99	16.67

Note: The districts are arranged in the descending order of per capita NDDP in 1970-71.

Source: Derived from Appendix Tables 3.1, 3.2, 3.3, 5.1, 5.2 and 5.3.

It is interesting to observe that in the case of the NDDP, the highest share of the primary sector and the highest shares of the secondary and tertiary sectors are found in Group I. And in the case of workforce, the highest share of the primary sector is found in Group II, and the highest shares of the secondary and tertiary sectors are found in Group I.

In majority of the districts, the non-primary sectors have smaller shares in both NDDP and workforce. But the smallness of their share is more pronounced in the workforce than in the NDDP. And among the non-primary sectors, the tertiary sector is more predominant than the secondary sector both in its share of NDDP and workforce. With the exception of Bangalore in the NDDP and Dakshina Kannada in the workforce in which the shares of their secondary sectors are larger than those of their tertiary sectors, in all others districts, irrespective of the groups to which they belong, the share of the tertiary sector is larger than the share of the secondary sector. This situation shows that in majority of the districts in the State, the tertiary sector has a relatively broader base than the secondary sector.

To get a better comprehension of the diversified structure of the district economies and also to identify the similarities among the districts, the districts are classified into three orders : First Order, Second Order and Third Order. This analysis is intended to derive some operationally meaningful typology of the districts. Table 5.7 shows the classification of districts.

The table indicates some distinct types. As far as the classification based on the NDDP is concerned, all the districts of Group II constitute a type by claiming the Second Order. Three types of districts are found in Group I : Kodagu and Chikmagalur, with greater predominance of their primary sectors, constitute a type by attracting the Third Order; Bangalore and Dakshina Kannada together constitute another type by attracting the First Order; and the remaining six districts constitute yet another type by attracting the Second Order. So far as the classification based on workforce is concerned the districts of Group I lend themselves to three types and those of Group II lend themselves to two types. In Group I, Bangalore is the only district which attracts the First Order. Of the remaining nine districts, five districts, namely, Kodagu, Shimoga, Uttara Kannada, Chitradurga and Dakshina Kannada constitute a type by attracting the Second Order, and four districts, namely, Chikmagalur, Bellary, Raichur and Hassan, constitute yet another type by attracting the Third Order. In Group II, of the nine districts, four districts, namely, Mysore, Gulbarga, Dharwad and Bidar form a type by attracting the Second Order, and the remaining five districts, namely, Mandya, Belgaum, Kolar, Tumkur and Bijapur, form yet another type by attracting the Third Order.

TABLE 5.7: Classification of Districts according to the Share of the Non-Primary Sectors in NDDP and Workforce: 1970-71.

% Share of Non-Primary Sectors in NDDP			% Share of Non-Primary Sectors in Total Workforce of Districts		
Above 50 %	25 to 50 %	Below 25 %	Above 50 %	25 to 50 %	Below 25 %
1	2	3	4	5	6
1. Bangalore	1. Bellary	1. Kodagu	1. Bangalore	1. Kodagu	1. Chikmagalur
2. Dakshina Kannada	2. Shimoga	2. Chikmagalur		2. Shimoga	2. Bellary
	3. Raichur			3. Uttara Kannada	3. Raichur
	4. Uttara Kannada			4. Chitradurga	4. Hassan
	5. Chitradurga			5. Dakshina Kannada	5. Mandya
	6. Hassan			6. Mysore	6. Belgaum
	7. Mysore			7. Gulbarga	7. Kolar
	8. Gulbarga			8. Dharwad	8. Tumkur
	9. Dharwad			9. Bidar	9. Bijapur
	10. Mandya				
	11. Belgaum				
	12. Bidar				
	13. Kolar				
	14. Tumkur				
	15. Bijapur				

Source: Derived from Table 5.6

The NDDP and workforce data pertaining to 1980-81 are presented in Table 5.8.

Among other things, the table reveals the important fact that sectorwise, the structure of most of the district economies is dominated by the primary sector which leads the district economies by claiming for itself a relatively higher proportion of income and employment. However, its predominance is more pronounced in workforce than in the NDDP. It is so because, in the case of workforce, 16 out of 19 districts have more than 70 per cent of the workforce in their primary sectors, whereas, in the case of the NDDP, in only two districts the primary sector's share of the NDDP exceeds 70 per cent. Bangalore records the all-time high of 88.11 per cent for its non-primary sectors in its NDDP, and the lowest share for the same sectors is recorded by Kodagu. Strangely enough both these districts belong to Group I. In all other districts, with the exception of Bangalore, the share of the tertiary sector is larger than the share of the secondary sector. But Kolar, last-ranked in the State in per capita NDDP, claims 37.73 per cent of the NDDP for its tertiary sector, which is the highest amongst the districts. In the case of workforce also among the non-primary sectors, the tertiary sector's performance in all the districts, with the exception of Dakshina Kannada, Belgaum and Bijapur, is superior to the performance of the secondary sector. This aspect of the relative claims of the secondary and tertiary sectors in the NDDP and workforce is indicative of the greater importance that the tertiary sector has come to acquire in the district economies of Karnataka.

TABLE 5.8: Economic Structure of the Districts of Karnataka: 1980-81

Sl. No.	District	% NDDP from			% Workers in		
		Primary Sector	Secondary Sector	Tertiary Sector	Primary Sector	Secondary Sector	Tertiary Sector
1	2	3	4	5	6	7	8
1.	Kodagu	81.66	6.70	11.64	76.00	7.75	16.25
2.	Chikmagalur	73.92	7.38	18.70	82.32	5.90	11.78
3.	Bangalore	11.89	51.08	37.03	36.82	29.55	33.63
4.	Shimoga	59.67	19.93	20.40	75.63	11.31	13.06
5.	Dakshina Kannada	44.17	25.18	30.65	50.33	32.28	17.39
6.	Chitradurga	58.88	19.71	21.41	76.55	10.89	12.56
7.	Hassan	66.56	11.34	22.10	82.44	6.34	11.22
8.	Bellary	57.68	15.42	26.90	76.73	9.34	13.93
9.	Mandya	65.94	9.75	24.31	82.75	6.80	10.45
10.	Raichur	67.45	11.14	21.41	81.89	7.79	10.32
11.	Mysore	48.63	24.27	27.10	72.43	11.63	15.94
12.	Belgaum	56.73	17.66	25.61	75.66	12.18	12.16
13.	Uttara Kannada	56.19	13.69	30.12	67.43	12.68	19.89
14.	Dharwad	49.59	18.45	31.96	72.96	11.28	15.76
15.	Gulbarga	52.74	19.00	28.26	78.43	9.96	11.61
16.	Tumkur	56.10	16.37	27.53	82.35	7.75	9.90
17.	Bidar	59.58	11.38	29.04	79.30	7.79	12.91
18.	Bijapur	47.50	17.43	35.07	77.02	11.93	11.05
19.	Kolar	48.50	13.77	37.73	81.58	7.36	11.06
	Karnataka	49.04	22.84	28.12	71.08	13.52	15.40

Note: The districts are arranged in the descending order of the per capita NDDP in 1980-81.

Source: Derived from Appendix Tables 3.1, 3.2, 3.3, 5.1, 5.2 and 5.3.

To lend some order to the diversified economic structure of the district economies, the districts are classified into different orders based on the performance of their non-primary sectors. Table 5.9, furnishes the classification of districts.

TABLE 5.9: Classification of Districts according to the Share of the Non-Primary Sectors in NDDP and Workforce: 1980-81

% Share of Non-Primary Sectors in NDDP			% Share of Non-Primary Sectors in Total Workforce of Districts		
Above 50 %	25 to 50 %	Below 25 %	Above 50 %	25 to 50 %	Below 25 %
1	2	3	4	5	6
1. Bangalore	1. Chikmaga-lur	1. Kodagu	1. Banga-lore	1. Dakshina Kannada	1. Kodagu
2. Dakshina Kannada	2. Shimoga			2. Mysore	2. Chikmagalur
3. Mysore	3. Chitradurga			3. Uttara Kannada	3. Shimoga
4. Dharwad	4. Hassan			4. Dharwad	4. Chitradurga
5. Bijapur	5. Bellary				5. Hassan
6. Kolar	6. Mandya				6. Bellary
	7. Raichur				7. Mandya
	8. Belgaum				8. Raichur
	9. Uttara Kannada				9. Belgaum
	10. Gulbarga				10. Gulbarga
	11. Tumkar				11. Tumkur
	12. Bidar				12. Bidar
					13. Bijapur
					14. Kolar

Source: Derived from Table 5.8.

The classification based on the NDDP shows that Group I districts fall into three types: Two districts, namely, Bangalore and Dakshina Kannada claim the First Order; only Kodagu claims the Third Order; and the remaining five districts of the group claim the Second Order. The Group II districts come under only two types: four districts, namely, Mysore, Dharwad, Bijapur and Kolar, attract the First Order; the remaining seven districts of the group attract the Second Order. So far as the workforce-based classification is concerned, Group I lends itself to three types: Bangalore attracts the First Order; Dakshina Kannada attracts the Second Order; and the remaining six districts of the group attract the Third Order. Group II districts form only two types: three districts, namely, Mysore, Uttara Kannada and Dharwad, attract the Second Order; the remaining eight districts of the group attract the Third Order.

5.4.2 Structure of District Economies: An Inter-Temporal Analysis

The changes in the sectoral shares of the NDDP and workforce in the different districts of Karnataka between 1960-61 and 1980-81 are presented in Table 5.10. The table also gives the changes in the per capita NDDP for the same reference period.

TABLE 5.10: The Changing Economic Structure of the District Economies of Karnataka: 1960-61 to 1980-81

Sl. No.	District	% Change in the Share in NDDP of the			% Change in the share in the number of Workers of the			% Change in the Per Capita NDDP
		Primary Sector	Secondary Sector	Tertiary Sector	Primary Sector	Secondary Sector	Tertiary Sector	
1	2	3	4	5	6	7	8	9
1.	Kodagu	-3.16	+14.73	+18.29	+2.15	+0.78	-9.27	+35.78
2.	Shimoga	-9.96	-9.41	+73.91	+14.97	-39.26	-16.28	-22.73
3.	Uttara Kannada	-27.27	+51.61	+119.69	-5.84	+13.92	+15.24	-40.91
4.	Chikmagalur	-3.64	-31.09	+48.65	+4.56	-28.57	-9.45	+19.79
5.	Dakshina Kannada	-31.55	+73.98	+45.95	-26.85	+112.37	+8.69	+12.99
6.	Bellary	-4.79	+4.26	+9.22	+3.33	+2.75	-16.33	+27.06
7.	Hassan	-9.49	+51.20	+16.56	-4.40	+19.85	+32.31	+30.10
8.	Tumkur	-21.69	+54.29	+55.10	-4.04	+26.43	+22.98	+7.12
9.	Chitradurga	+0.55	+9.02	-8.35	-3.48	+7.50	+18.94	+47.06
10.	Belgaum	-13.65	+52.90	+12.57	-4.46	+20.59	+13.54	+28.79
11.	Mysore	-13.22	+46.65	-1.13	-3.70	+22.81	+4.05	+41.63
12.	Mandya	-5.19	-18.07	+31.05	-3.90	+10.39	+35.19	+45.70
13.	Dharwad	-7.34	+30.57	-1.81	-1.70	-1.14	+9.67	+30.59
14.	Bangalore	-60.64	+71.81	-8.73	-31.56	+50.84	+26.38	+97.24
15.	Kolar	-24.68	+30.52	+50.56	-4.18	+57.94	+8.43	-15.68
16.	Raichur	+12.60	-12.97	-21.58	+3.75	+10.34	-26.34	+64.64
17.	Gulbarga	-4.44	+26.92	-5.30	+4.03	+7.91	-24.51	+38.01
18.	Bijapur	-7.66	-7.44	+17.96	-1.04	-5.09	+15.10	+16.42
19.	Bidar	+10.15	-12.39	-11.79	+1.41	+15.75	-14.33	+50.25
	Karnataka	-19.94	+50.66	+19.20	-5.39	+26.00	+8.92	+27.65

Note: The districts are arranged in the descending order of Per Capita NDDP in 1960-61.

Source: Derived from Table 5.4 and 5.8 and Appendix Tables 3.1, 3.2, and 3.3.

The inter-temporal changes in the sectoral shares and the changes in the NDDP are presented in percentages and they carry the positive and negative signs depending upon the nature of change they represent. This table, by itself, cannot tell anything certain about the nature of relationship between the levels of the per capita NDDP and the economic structure of the districts in terms of the sectoral shares. And unless we identify this relationship, we will not be in a position to say whether the structural change that has been taking place in the districts has been in accordance with the expected pattern or not. So, based on the data available in Table 5.10, Table 5.11 is derived which provides the required information.

TABLE 5.11: Changes in the Economic Structure of the Districts: 1960-61 to 1980-81.

	No of Districts with signs of Change	
	Positive	Negative
(i) *Changes in the share of the NDDP of the:*		
(a) Primary Sector	03	16
(b) Secondary Sector	13	06
(c) Tertiary Sector	12	07
(ii) *Changes in the share of the Workforce in the*:		
(a) Primary Sector	07	12
(b) Secondary Sector	15	04
(c) Tertiary Sector	12	07
(iii) Changes in Per Capita NDDP	16	03

Source: Derived from Table 5.10.

If we compare the signs of change assigned to each sector in terms of the NDDP and workforce with those of the changes assigned to the per capita NDDP, it appears that the majority of the districts have the expected signs of change both in the sectoral composition of the NDDP and workforce. Table 5.11 shows that 16 out of 19 districts have positive signs in respect of the changes in the per capita NDDP, which indicates improvement in the levels of development. As far as the sectoral composition of the NDDP is concerned, majority of the districts have the expected signs in all the three sectors: in the primary sector, 16 out of 19 districts have negative signs indicating a declining trend; in the secondary sector, 13 out of 19 districts have positive signs indicating an increasing trend; and similarly in the tertiary sector, 12 out of 19 districts have positive signs indicating an increasing trend.

With some minor differences, almost the same trend is observed in the sectoral composition of workforce. The majority of the districts have the expected signs in all the sectors: in the primary sector, 12 out of 19 districts have negative signs indicating a declining trend; in the secondary sector, 15 out of 19 districts have positive signs indicating an increasing trend; and in the tertiary sector, 12 out of 19 districts have positive signs indicating an increasing trend.

All these facts roughly indicate that between 1960-61 and 1980-81 the structural change in the district economies is in accordance with the views of the sectoral theories; in the majority of the districts, the increase in the per capita NDDP is accompanied by changes in the sectoral shares of output and employment along the expected lines.

5.5 Main Findings

The principal findings of the empirical analysis of the changing structure of the State economy and of the district economies are presented below:

(i) The economic structure of the State is such that in all the three points of time considered — 1960-61, 1970-71 and 1980-81 — the primary sector is found to be the most dominant sector in the economy both in terms of its share in the NSDP and workforce. However, its dominance is not uniform in its share of the NSDP and workforce; its dominance is more pronounced in the latter than in the former. The structural situation prevailing in the district economies is not different from the one which is found at the State level. The cross-section analysis shows that, with the exception of Bangalore, all the districts of Karnataka, irrespective of their levels of per capita NDDP, are basically primary-economic-activity-oriented districts. In majority of the districts, the primary sector claims a substantial proportion of the NDDP and workforce. Here also, as at the State level, its predominance is more pronounced in the latter than in the former.

(ii) The State economy, despite significant changes in the sectoral shares of income and employment, presents a consistent order of sectoral dominance. In all the three points of time, the primary sector is the lead sector, and is followed by the tertiary and secondary sectors. This order of dominance is found both in terms of the NSDP and workforce. With a few exceptions, majority of the districts reveal a similar order of sectoral dominance.

(iii) As expected by the pattern finders, with the increase in the per capita NSDP, a consistent decline in its share of income and employment is registered by the primary sector, and an equally consistent increase is registered by the secondary sector; but the tertiary sector has not exhibited any consistent pattern of change. And, as expected, the decline in the share of the primary sector is duly compensated by the increase in the share of the non-primary sectors. In the case of district economies, neither all the high per capita income districts are associated with relatively lower shares of their primary sectors in the total output and employment, nor are all the low per capita income districts associated with relatively higher shares of their primary sectors. But, inter-temporally, by and large, the changes in the per capita NDDP are accompanied by changes in the sectoral composition of output and employment along the expected lines.

(iv) The ordering of the districts based on the share of the secondary sector shows that neither all the high per capita NDDP districts have attained a higher degree of industrialisation, nor all the low per capita income districts suffer from total absence of industrial activity.

(v) The structural change in Karnataka, not merely shows a slow and steady shift away from the primary sector towards the secondary and tertiary sectors, but also the progress in terms of the NSDP and total workforce. In the first decade (1960-61 to 1970-71), the NSDP records a higher growth rate than workforce; in the second decade (1970-71 to 1980-81), the latter records a higher growth rate than the former; and for the two decades (1960-61 to 1980-81) put together, the NSDP improves upon the workforce by a slender margin of 0.53 per cent. So far as inter-sectoral growth rates are concerned, the highest growth rates are recorded by the secondary sector both in terms of the NSDP and workforce; the second place goes to the tertiary sector; and the third to the primary sector.

(vi) An inter-temporal analysis of the relationship between the levels of the per capita NDDP and the sectoral shares of output and employment reveals that the changes in the two variables between 1960-61 and 1980-81 are in accordance with the views of the sectoral theorists. In the majority of the districts, the increase in the per capita NDDP is accompanied by changes in the sectoral shares of output and employment along the expected lines.

NOTES

1. Sutcliffe, R.B., *Industry and Underdevelopment*, Addison-Wesley Publishing Company, London, 1971, p. ix.
2. Nair, K.R.G., *Regional Experience in a Developing Economy*, Wiley Eastern Ltd., New Delhi, 1982, p. 81.
3. For a detailed discussion of the sectoral theory, see Chapter II of the present work.
4. Thakur, Y., Srinivas, *Industrialisation and Economic Development*, Ph.D. Thesis, Bombay University, 1975, p. 22.
5. For details, see Chapter II of the present work.
6. Special Studies Division State Income Estimates of India: With particular reference to Karnataka, Planning Department, Government of Karnataka, Bangalore, March 1985, pp 4-7.
7. The details of sectoral disaggregation of the NSDP and NDDP, and of the deflator employed by the DES, are available in the unpublished official records of the DES.
8. For the details of various studies, see Dadibhavi, R.V., *Inter-district Variations in Income, Productivity and Industrial Structure in Karnataka State*, Ph.D. Thesis, M.S. University, Baroda, 1983, pp. 67-87.
9. *Ibid*, pp. 104-114.
10. Director of Census Operations, *Census of India 1981*, Series 9, Karnataka, Part II; Special Report and Tables based on five per cent sample data, p. 49.
11. *Note:* In the case of workforce, the data belong to 1961, 1971 and 1981, since the workforce data are obtained from the Censuses of 1961, 1971 and 1981. However, to avoid confusion, in the present analysis, the years 1960-61, 1970-71 and 1980-81 are used in the place of 1961, 1971 and 1981 respectively.
12. Kuznets, Simon, "Quantitative Aspects of the Economic Growth of Nations: II, Industrial Distribution of National Product and Labour Force", *Economic Development and Cultural Change*, Supplement to Vol. 4, July 1957, pp. 3-111.
13. Saxena, Pradeep Kumar, "Interrelationship between Socio-Economic Development and Economic Structure: Indian Experience", *Margin, Quarterly Journal*, Vol. 18, No. 4, July 1986, pp. 84-85.
14. (i) Venkataraman, L.S., Prahladachar, and Deshpande, R.S., *Dynamics of Rural Transformation in Karnataka*, 1956-76, ISEC, Bangalore, 1985, pp. 18-28.
    (ii) Project Formation Division, Background paper on Planning in Karnataka, Performance and Strategy, Planning Department, Government of Karnataka, Bangalore, January, 1984, pp. 163-165.

APPENDIX TABLE 5.1: Distribution of Workforce by Industrial Categories, Karnataka, 1961 (Reclassified as per the 1971 Census Classification of Workers)

Sl.No.	District	Total Workers	Culti-vators	Agricul-tural labour	Live-stock, fishing, forestry & logging	Mining and quarrying	House-hold	Non-household	Construc-tion	Trade & Comm-erce	Transport, storage & communi-cation	Other services
1	2	3	4	5	6	7	8	9	10	11	12	13
			I	II	III	IV	V(a)	V(b)	VI	VII	VIII	IX
1.	Kodagu	128180	40979	16176	37967	244	2269	4140	3448	4307	1205	17445
2.	Shimoga	343919	172063	39723	11590	2855	9320	18709	36008	11693	3439	38519
3.	Uttara Kannada	237470	110067	25101	28425	6460	10330	10187	5913	9261	3467	28259
4.	Chikmagalur	214671	107228	21682	39328	773	5109	5281	7342	5689	1696	20543
5.	Dakshina Kannada	593627	278708	106081	23270	356	38942	45116	6174	26832	9498	58650
6.	Bellary	354920	176147	79609	4827	2981	15013	8908	8341	13061	4046	41987
7.	Hassan	287157	212353	15966	19153	144	7552	5111	2527	5600	1522	17229
8.	Tumkur	464760	329980	41642	25748	1487	18172	6414	3904	10225	1627	25561

Contd.

APPENDIX TABLE 5.1 *Contd.*

1	2	3	4	5	6	7	8	9	10	11	12	13
			I	II	III	IV	V(a)	V(b)	VI	VII	VIII	IX
9.	Chitradurga	410845	248315	58710	17749	1068	21200	11997	8422	13147	2301	27936
10.	Belgaum	700072	422353	116982	13511	1540	43474	21912	5321	23802	5391	45786
11.	Mysore	558199	312089	73124	34385	223	22495	22216	8150	21546	6587	57384
12.	Mandya	296907	216861	32155	6592	59	8402	6592	3296	5344	1009	16597
13.	Dharwad	693271	310447	193631	9498	970	45548	24819	8735	33069	10954	55600
14.	Bangalore	770334	339794	49070	25190	385	28502	102454	19952	50072	17024	137891
15.	Kolar	452455	317442	38640	16153	12985	10135	7330	3620	13483	2805	29862
16.	Raichur	419753	235607	86133	7640	1931	20106	4323	5205	12677	2854	43277
17.	Gulbarga	498505	227068	131805	14806	2144	32004	10618	3390	16450	3340	56880
18.	Bijapur	601152	283684	170186	13646	361	58312	11843	5410	19537	3366	34807
19.	Bidar	223282	90898	75648	8038	22	12772	915	1340	8306	1183	24160
	Karnataka	8249479	4432083	1372064	357516	36988	409657	328885	146498	304101	83314	778373

Sources: 1. *Census of India*, 1961, Vol. XI, Mysore, Part II-B(i), General Economic Tables, Table B-I.
2. *Census of India*, 1961, Vol. XI, Mysore, Part II-B(i), General Economic Tables, Table B-IV, Part C.
3. Dadibhavi, R.V., Inter-district Variations in Income Productivity and Industrial Structure in Karnataka State, Ph.D. Thesis, M.S. University, Baroda, 1983, pp. 123-125.

APPENDIX TABLE 5.2: Distribution of Workforce by Industrial Categories, Karnataka, 1971

Sl.No.	District	Total Workers	Culti-vators	Agricul-tural labour	Live-stock, fishing, forestry & logging	Mining and quarrying	House-hold	Non-household	Construc-tion	Trade & Comm-erce	Transport, storage & communi-cation	Other services
1.	2	3	4	5	6	7	8	9	10	11	12	13
			I	II	III	IV	V(a)	V(b)	VI	VII	VIII	IX
1.	Kodagu	152838	35996	30053	44292	539	2484	4925	4963	8689	2824	18073
2.	Shimoga	416663	160788	132519	14719	590	11720	25574	9162	25346	10031	26214
3.	Uttara Kannada	285939	107105	49995	40394	4795	7678	16247	5039	16497	10746	27442
4.	Chikmagalur	254921	96628	47832	48536	1515	4866	7867	4789	11906	4796	26186
5.	Dakshina Kannada	748744	219945	185591	35157	2104	86506	66383	13503	56562	20727	62266
6.	Bellary	426462	138999	171188	6208	9787	13342	16654	6931	20679	13110	29474

(Contd.)

APPENDIX TABLE 5.2 *Contd.*

1	2	3	4	5	6	7	8	9	10	11	12	13
7.	Hassan	349976	216496	40549	24404	760	7141	8925	8548	13826	6646	22681
8.	Tumkur	553723	320832	109990	20332	1520	21172	13317	6759	22133	7760	29908
9.	Chitradurga	519379	223162	156528	19362	1300	17703	26519	9321	26050	9327	30107
10.	Belgaum	859783	403814	222812	19334	854	45227	41235	14292	42182	14652	55381
11.	Mysore	698214	336566	141138	17412	1260	20631	37433	19275	39151	19887	65461
12.	Mandya	375845	223143	81274	5491	489	8637	11078	3303	13930	4570	23480
13.	Dharwad	831478	249756	320187	16575	2156	39639	39559	12057	60968	29618	60963
14.	Bangalore	1062757	312926	120988	20730	759	31390	199814	29776	111329	69041	166004
15.	Kolar	529432	289899	112554	20007	13490	9881	18080	5574	24035	7801	28111
16.	Raichur	527001	208235	193736	15115	3363	17905	12396	6925	24179	9894	35353
17.	Gulbarga	607762	207589	222107	18284	3698	26547	24653	10677	30867	12700	50640
18.	Bijapur	706099	231309	275507	23291	2072	54914	21891	7907	35229	13055	40924
19.	Bidar	272098	89691	102539	10177	837	11082	7359	3361	15024	5735	26293
	Karnataka	10179114	4072879	2717537	419820	51888	438555	599909	182162	598582	272920	824862

Source: *Census of India*, 1971, Series No. 14, Mysore, Part I-A, Vol. II, General Report Statement No., 10.15.

APPENDIX TABLE 5.3: Workers Classified by Industrial Category, Karnataka: 1981 Census

Sl.No.	District	Total Workers	Cultivators	Agricultural labour	Live-stock, forestry, forestry, fishing, hunting, plantation, overheads & other allid activities	Mining and quarrying	Manufacturing, processing and servicing: Household	Manufacturing, processing and servicing: Other than household	Construction	Trade & Commerce	Transport, storage & communication	Other services
1	2	3	4	5	6	7	8	9	10	11	12	13
			I	II	III	IV	V(a)	V(b)	VI	VII	VIII	IX
1.	Bangalore	1673319	399466	181128	33119	2343	50584	378247	65656	197180	95861	269735
2.	Belgaum	1231571	555119	351104	24526	978	54909	73564	21469	66046	21631	62125
3.	Bellary	636101	219269	245415	7521	15839	20435	29763	9233	34007	14901	39718
4.	Bidar	402136	127840	180021	10671	347	10851	15494	4969	20991	7778	23174
5.	Bijapur	999111	336763	409284	22892	552	59305	44644	15264	48606	14055	47746
6.	Chikmagalur	407012	170198	88423	74401	2032	7605	10843	5582	19393	6082	22453
7.	Chitradurga	763474	311374	248967	22007	2113	27050	44690	11378	43566	12536	39793
8.	Dakshina Kannada	998937	251499	201150	48817	1346	158547	148565	15308	73169	35498	65038

Contd.

APPENDIX TABLE 5.3 *Contd.*

1	2	3	4	5	6	7	8	9	10	11	12	13
			I	II	III	IV	V(a)	V(b)	VI	VII	VIII	IX
9.	Dharwad	1228966	379677	495382	18648	2905	52105	70241	16253	82820	36569	74366
10.	Gulbarga	941592	295980	394279	33986	14207	29077	42353	22409	44928	15492	48881
11.	Hassan	549920	336065	81321	34324	1658	10082	16295	8468	24338	9909	27460
12.	Kodagu	218349	53115	35581	77158	105	2240	9304	5368	12677	5336	17465
13.	Kolar	752550	391875	184781	23308	13997	13563	34653	7159	34559	11749	36906
14.	Mandya	522107	306442	118778	6777	31	10244	19747	5527	22158	5037	27366
15.	Mysore	980372	449721	230130	29381	875	21597	71162	21223	58868	24028	73387
16.	Raichur	782967	276511	346529	12495	5646	22187	26393	12439	35927	10605	34235
17.	Shimoga	630196	247656	213366	13176	2413	14805	41944	14507	36701	10363	35265
18.	Tumkur	818093	459157	198690	14836	1025	29435	26477	7447	31850	9550	39626
19.	Uttara Kannada	411946	153654	72913	45422	5804	11769	29749	10698	33413	14739	33785
	Karnataka	14948719	5721381	4277342	553465	74216	606390	1134128	280357	921197	361719	1018524

Source: *Census of India*, 1981, Series No. 9, Karnataka, Part III A and B(i) General Economic Tables (Tables B-1 to B-6) 1986.

6

STRUCTURE OF LARGE-SCALE INDUSTRIES IN KARNATAKA

6.1 Introduction

THE STRUCTURAL transformation that has been accompanying industrialisation and development in Karnataka, as in any other industrialising region, is a multi-dimensional phenomenon. As already stated in the introductory chapter, the present study has addressed itself to only inter-sectoral and inter-industry aspects of the structural transformation. Since the inter-sectoral aspect has been discussed in the preceding chapter, the present chapter takes up the study of the inter-industry aspect of structural transformation, that, too, with reference to only the large-scale industries in Karnataka. As a prominent part of the industrial sector, the segment of large-scale industries has been continuously growing and in that process, it has been undergoing changes in its basic structure.

There are at least two broad views on the structural change that involves alteration in the inter-industry importance. The first view is concerned with the input-based classification of large-scale industries into agro-based and non-agro-based industries. It is generally said, of course based on the historical patterns of industrialisation, that the initial stages of industrialisation are characterised by the relative dominance of agro-based, industries, whereas the mature stages of industrialisation are characterised by the relative dominance of non-agro-based industries. And over a period of time, there is a tendency for the agro-based industries to decline in importance, and for the non-agro-based industries to increase in importance. The second view is concerned with the output-based classification of large-scale industries into consumer goods and capital goods industries. It is generally held that the initial stages of industrialisation are characterised by the predominance of consumer goods industries, whereas the mature stages of industrialisation are characterised by the predominance of capital-goods industries. And over a period of time, there is a tendency for the former to decline in importance, and for the latter to increase in importance, as industrialisation proceeds, and ultimately the latter excels the former.[1]

Any dispassionate survey of research literature on the industrialisation of Karnataka would give the impression that no in-depth inquiry worth the name has been made into these inter-industry aspects of structural transformation. With the express intention to contribute something meaningful to the existing understanding of the growth trends and the structural changes in the large-scale industrial activity in the State, an attempt is made in this chapter to examine the growth of large-scale industries between 1960 and 1980-81. And at the same time the inter-temporal trends in inter-industry behaviour are also assessed. With such ends in view, the chapter is divided into eight sections. The sources, the nature and the limitations of the data used in this chapter are detailed in the second section. The third section identifies the changing status of Karnataka in the large-scale industrial activity of the country. It also throws some light on the nature of industrial activity located in the State. The changes in the industrial structure of the State by the major industry groups between 1960 and 1980-81 are examined in the fourth section; in this section, the view relating to the relative importance of agro-based and non-agro-based industries in the process of industrialisation is empirically verified with reference to Karnataka. The fifth section continues the discussion of the fourth section with special emphasis on the growth of large-scale industries in Karnataka. Some of the important economic ratios of the major industry groups are analysed and discussed in the sixth section. The seventh section examines the view pertaining to the comparative importance of consumer goods and capital goods industries in the changing industrial structure of Karnataka. Incidentally, in this section an attempt is also made to test Hoffmann's hypothesis.[2] The eighth section concludes the discussion by presenting all the principal findings.

6.2 The Data Used

The CSO which brings out periodically the Annual Survey of Industries (ASI) is the basic source of data for the present chapter. Neither the Directorate of Economics and Statistics nor the Directorate of Industries and Commerce at the State level has any comparable data on the large-scale industries for the period under consideration. In view of such source limitation, the ASI data on the Census Sector is used in this chapter to analyse the growth, etc., of the large-scale industrial sector in Karnataka. The Census Sector covers all those factories which employ 50 or more workers with the aid of power, or 100 or more workers without the aid of power. In fact, this is the definition of large-scale industry which is adopted by the ASI in order to cover all the factories coming under the purview of the Industrial Development and Regulation Act of 1951.[3] And all other factories come under the Sample Sector. It covers all those factories which employ 10 to 49 workers with the aid of power, or 20 to 99 workers without the aid of power. In the present analysis, the Census Sector data alone are used.

Here it is pertinent to point out that in view of the dominance that the Census Sector industries enjoy in the overall industrial activity of the State, the analysis based on the Census Sector data not only throws light on the structure and growth of the large-scale industries, but also indicates the general trends in the overall industrial activity of the State. To identify the commanding position of the Census Sector industries in the State, the data representing the relative positions of the Census and Sample Sectors are presented in Table 6.1.

TABLE 6.1: The Relative Positions of the Census and Sample Sectors in Karnataka: 1970

Sl. No.	Selected Characteristics	Unit	Census Sector	Sample Sector	Total of Census & Sample Sectors	Percentage share of	
						Census Sector	Sample Sector
1	2	3	4	5	6	7	8
1.	Factories Reporting	Number	596	2904	3500	17.03	82.97
2.	Workers	Number	152088	43248	195336	77.86	22.14
3.	Employees	Number	195407	52428	247835	78.85	21.15
4.	Fixed Capital	Rs crores	392.84	21.80	414.64	94.74	5.26
5.	Working Capital	Rs crores	158.03	12.59	170.62	92.62	7.38
6.	Productive Capital	Rs crores	550.87	34.39	585.26	94.12	5.88
7.	Value Added	Rs crores	167.15	14.03	181.18	92.26	7.74

Source: *Statistical Abstract of Karnataka*, 1976-77, Bureau of Economics and Statistics, Bangalore, 1978, p. 143.

The data are indicative of the indisputable dominance of the Census Sector industries in the State. It claims 77.86 per cent of the workers, 78.85 per cent of the employees, 94.74 per cent of the fixed capital, 92.62 per cent of the working capital, 94.12 per cent of the productive capital and 92.26 per cent of the value added. It is only in terms of "factories reporting" that the Sample Sector claims a higher share of 82.97 per cent. This higher share in factories and very low share in other characteristics speaks of the smallness of the factories covered under the Sample Sector.

The ASI data on the Census Sector industries of Karnataka suffer from some limitations. Since the entire analysis in this chapter is based on the ASI data, by and large, the limitations of the analysis of this chapter are essentially a reflection of the data limitations. The limitations include:

(i) The ASI data on time-series basis are not available for the period under study, i.e., from 1960-61 to 1980-81. As such, an inter-temporal analysis is undertaken in the present chapter.

(ii) Areally, all the vital statistics provided by the ASI are available for two spatial units, namely, Country and State. This limitation has virtually prevented us from undertaking an inter-district analysis of large-scale industries; the inquiry is confined to the State-level analysis only.

(iii) There is no year-to-year uniformity in the industrial classification adopted by the ASI. For instance, many industries which assumed separate classification in 1960 did not find their place in the survey of the subsequent years.[4] So, to ensure reasonable uniformity in the industrial classification, the present analysis adopts the National Industrial Classification (NIC) – 70, which is being currently used by the ASI.[5]

(iv) Regarding the data-accounting year, it is necessary to know that calendar years are considered up to 1970, and financial years thereafter. And to suit our requirements, we have taken the ASI data for 1960, 1970 and 1980-81 to represent the financial years 1960-61, 1970-71 and 1980-81 respectively. Such adaptation slightly affects the period analysis; the period between 1960 and 1970 works out to 10 years, but the period between 1970 and 1980-81 works out to 10 years and 3 months. So, this limitation need be borne in mind while evaluating the inter-temporal industrial change.

(v) Another important limitation which has very much affected the empirical analysis in the present chapter is the absence of uniformity in data available on the selected characteristics by major industry groups. The 1980-81 survey of the State provides industrywise data on selected characteristics such as fixed capital, working capital, productive capital, workers, employees, value added by manufacturing, etc. But it is not so in the case of 1960 and 1970. In these surveys, as found in the Statistical Abstracts of the State, the aggregate values of all such characteristics are available, but not the industrywise break-up. For 1960 and 1970, industrywise break-up of "fixed capital" and "working capital" is not readily available; in its place, we have data on "employees" and "productive capital". In view of the fact that the data on "workers" and "fixed capital" are more relevant in the study of "industrial employment" and "industrial investment" respectively, they are used wherever the inquiry proceeds on the aggregate levels, of course without materially affecting the analysis; and wherever the industrywise break-up is involved in the analysis, the data on "employees" and "productive capital" are used.[6]

6.3 Karnataka's Place in the All-India Perspective

The main objective of this section is to provide a broad and comprehensive background of the dynamics of the large-scale industrial activity of the State in the all-India perspective, so as to facilitate a meaningful analysis, interpretation and evaluation of the inter-industry structural variations in the subsequent sections. And to realise such an objective, efforts are made here to locate the place of Karnataka in the all-India context from three angles: first, by assessing Karnataka's position in terms of some selected characteristics like factories, workers, fixed capital and value added; second, by examining the inter-temporal trends in the growth rate of large-scale industries; and third, by identifying the nature of industrial localisation in the State.

The first two exercises consider three points of time – 1960, 1970 and 1980-81 – spread over two decades, whereas the third exercise takes into account only 1980-81. The data related to the State in the all-India industrial aggregates are given in the Table 6.2.

TABLE 6.2: Karnataka's Share in the All-India Industrial Aggregates (Census Sector): 1960, 1970 and 1980-81

Sl. No.	Selected Characteristics	Unit	1960			1970			1980-81		
			All India Total	Karnataka	% Share of the State	All India Total	Karnataka	% Share of the State	All India Total	Karnataka	% Share of the State
1	2	3	4	5	6	7	8	9	10	11	12
1.	Factories Reporting	Number	8391	433	5.16	13280	596	4.49	19115	970	5.07
2.	Workers	Number	2580599	92616	3.59	3465000	152000	4.39	4814816	241014	5.01
3.	Fixed Capital	Rs Crores	1286.50	44.00	3.42	8367.00	392.80	4.70	28301.95	1216.07	4.30
4.	Value Added	Rs Crores	864.30	26.30	3.04	2811.30	167.10	5.94	10511.18	503.21	4.79

Note: The data for 1960 and 1970 are for the respective calendar years, and the data for 1980-81 are for the financial year.

Source: Derived from Appendix Table 6.1.

The table shows that Karnataka's share in the country in all the characteristic considered for all the three points of the time, varies between three and six per cent. If these data are viewed along with the State-wise data presented in Appendix Table 6.1, we come to know that Karnataka has been consistently holding the middle order ranks ranging between 6th and 11th. That is to say Karnataka's position in the all-India perspective is relatively stable over time.

In this regard, the annual compound growth rates of large-scale industries in terms of factories, workers, fixed capital, and value added are worked out to know whether the large-scale industrial sector of the State has been growing at a faster or a slower rate than the national average growth rate. The related data are given in Table 6.3.

TABLE 6.3: Compound Growth Rates of Large-scale Industrial Sector in Karnataka and India : 1960-1980-81

Sl. No.	Selected Character-istics	1960 to 1970		1970 to 1980-81		1960 to 1980-81	
		All India	Karna-taka	All India	Karna-taka	All India	Karna-taka
1	2	3	4	5	6	7	8
1.	Factories Reporting	4.70	3.25	3.71	4.99	4.20	4.12
2.	Workers	2.99	5.08	3.34	4.72	3.17	4.90
3.	Fixed Capital	20.59	24.47	12.96	11.96	16.71	18.05
4.	Value Added	12.52	20.31	14.10	11.66	13.30	15.90

Note: For the purpose of calculating the annual compound growth rates, the period between the calendar year 1970 and the financial year 1980-81 is taken to be 10 years, and the period between the calendar year 1960 and the financial year 1980-81 is taken to be 20 years.

Source: Derived from Table 6.2.

The overall impression that one gets from the perusal of the data cited in Table 6.3 is that except in terms of "factories" the growth performance of the State in the all other characteristics is better than the all-India performance. The situation becomes more clear when we examine the figures in column 7 and 8 which express the 20-year annual performance of the country and the State respectively.

The study of localisation of large-scale industries in the State helps in identifying the differential importance of different industry groups in the State's industrial economy, and also in locating the State's position at the national level. The percentage share of the State in the country's total of factories, workers, fixed capital and value added in each industry group, and their corresponding location quotients[7] are given in Table 6.4. The last row in the Table gives the percentage share of the State in the national aggregates.

The State claims 5.07 per cent of the total factories in the country. Of the 23 major industry groups, in nine industry groups bearing code Nos. 23, 26, 27, 28, 32, 36, 38, 42 and 97, the State claims more than five per cent of the factory units in the country; all these industry groups with location quotients greater than 1 are said to be localised in the State. Of all the industry groups considered, the group which manufactures Wood and Wood Products, Furniture and Fixtures (Code No. 27) tops the list; based on its share and location quotient – the highest in the State – it claims the highest degree of localisation. On the other extreme, the industry groups which manufactures Leather and Fur Products (Code No. 29) with lowest share and location quotient claims the lowest degree of localisation.

When the localisation issue is examined with reference to "workers", a slightly different picture emerges. The State's share in the total industrial workers of the country is 5.01 per cent. Looked from this angle, 10 out of the 23 industry groups, bearing Code Nos. 20-21, 22, 26, 27, 28, 32, 35, 36, 38 and 97 with their shares higher than five per cent and location quotients greater than 1 are said to be localised in the State. In this case also the industry group which manufactures Wood and Wood Products, Furniture and Fixtures (Code No. 27), with the highest share and location quotient, claims the highest degree of localisation; the least degree of localisation is found in the industry group which manufactures Leather and Fur Products (Code No. 29).

"Fixed capital" as a value-based criterion of localisation confers a relatively higher degree of localisation to industry groups other than those considered to be important from the other two characteristics – "factories" and "workers". Karnataka claims 4.3 per cent of the country's fixed capital invested in the large-scale industries. In this case, 11 industry groups baring code Nos. 20-21, 22, 27, 28, 30, 32, 34, 35, 36, 38 and 42, with their shares exceeding five per cent and location quotients exceeding 1, are found to be localised in the State. Surprisingly enough the industry groups named "Other Manufacturing Industries" enjoys the highest degree of localisation by claiming the highest share (31.96 per cent) and the highest location quotient (7.43 per cent). And the lowest degree of localisation is found in the industry group which manufactures Wool, Silk and Synthetic Fibre Textiles (Code No. 24).

TABLE 6.4: Localisation of Industries in Karnataka by Selected Characteristics: 1980-81

Sl. No.	NIC two-digit code	Description of Industries	Factories		Workers		Fixed Capital		Value Added	
			% Share of the State in the total No. of Factories in the Industry in the country	Location Quotient	% Share of the State in the total No. of Workers in the Industry in the country	Location quotient	% Share of the State in the total Fixed Capital of the Industry in the country	Location Quotient	% Share of the State in the total Value Added in the Industry in the country	Location Quotient
1	2	3	4	5	6	7	8	9	10	11
1.	20-21	Manufacture of Food Products	3.95	0.78	6.33	1.26	8.13	1.89	4.14	0.86
2.	22	Manufacture of Beverages, Tobacco & Tobacco Products	4.08	0.81	5.73	1.14	13.72	3.19	13.56	2.83
3.	23	Manufacture of Cotton Textiles	5.91	1.17	3.99	0.80	3.17	0.74	3.78	0.79
4.	24	Manufacture of Wool, Silk and Synthetic Fibre Textiles	2.60	0.51	2.34	0.47	0.40	0.09	0.65	0.14
5.	25	Manufacture of Jute, Hemp and Mesta Textiles	—	—	—	—		—	—	—
6.	26	Manufacture of Textile Products (including Wearing Apparel other than Footwear)	7.98	1.57	9.60	1.92	2.38	0.55	4.57	0.95
7.	27	Manufacture of Wood and Wood Products, Furniture and Fixtures	11.02	2.17	15.65	3.12	13.43	3.12	13.37	2.79

Contd.

TABLE 6.4 *Contd.*

1	2	3	4	5	6	7	8	9	10	11
8.	28	Manufacture of Paper and Paper Products, Printing Publishing and allied industries	5.79	1.14	7.23	1.44	25.04	5.82	5.28	1.10
9.	29	Manufacture of Leather and Fur Products (except repairs)	1.39	0.27	0.68	0.14	1.04	0.24	0.33	0.07
10.	30	Manufacture of Rubber, Plastic, Petroleum and Coal Products	4.02	0.79	2.30	0.46	5.93	1.38	0.39	0.08
11.	31	Manufacture of Chemicals and Chemical Products (except products of Petroleum and Coal)	4.39	0.87	2.90	0.58	2.88	0.67	2.91	0.61
12.	32	Manufacture of Non-Metallic Mineral Products	7.44	1.47	7.71	1.54	9.86	2.29	8.34	1.74
13.	33	Basic Metal and Alloys Industries	4.78	0.94	4.21	0.84	2.42	0.56	4.57	0.95
14.	34	Manufacture of Metal Products and Parts except Machinery & Transport Equipment	3.65	0.72	2.77	0.55	6.23	1.45	4.38	0.91
15.	35	Manufacture of Machinery, Machine Tools and Parts except Electrical Machinery	4.79	0.94	5.79	1.16	7.02	1.63	4.52	0.94

Contd.

TABLE 6.4 *Contd.*

1	2	3	4	5	6	7	8	9	10	11
16.	36	Manufacture of Electrical Machinery, Apparatus, Appliances and supplies and Parts	8.48	1.67	13.14	2.62	9.78	2.27	10.41	2.17
17.	37	Manufacture of Transport Equipment and Parts	4.28	0.84	3.95	0.79	2.33	0.54	4.80	1.00
18.	38	Other Manufacturing Industries	8.00	1.58	8.11	1.62	31.96	7.43	8.19	1.71
19.	39	Electricity	3.86	0.76	4.78	0.95	3.23	0.75	5.25	1.10
20.	41	Gas and Steam	N.A.	N.A.	N.A.	N.A.	N.A.	N.A.	N.A.	N.A.
21.	42	Water Works and Supply	6.78	1.34	4.88	0.97	9.80	2.28	1.80	0.38
22.	74	Storage and Warehousing (Cold Storage)	N.A.	N.A.	N.A.	N.A.	N.A.	N.A.	N.A.	N.A.
23.	97	Repair Services	6.51	1.28	5.53	1.10	3.96	0.92	8.23	1.72
		Percentage share of the State in the Country's total	5.07		5.01		4.30		4.79	

Note: N.A. indicates the absence of such industrial units in the State.
Source: Derived from Appendix Table 6.2.

The extent of localisation of the different industry groups can also be gauged from another value-based criterion – "value added". The State's share in the total value added by the large-scale industries in the country is 4.79 per cent. Taking this figure as a measure of reasonable degree of localisation, we find nine industry groups bearing Code Nos. 22, 27, 28, 32, 36, 37, 38, 40 and 97 localised in the State. All these industry groups have location quotients greater than 1. As per this criterion, the industry group which manufactures Beverages, Tobacco and Tobacco Products (Code No. 22) with the highest share (13.56 per cent) and the highest location quotient (2.83) is said to be highly localised in the State. Whereas, the industry group which manufactures Leather and Fur Products (Code No. 29) with the lowest share (0.33 per cent) and the lowest location quotient (0.07) is said to be the least localised in the State.

On the whole, Table 6.4 gives us an idea as to the nature of large-scale industrial activity localised in the State. The data show that some industry groups qualify themselves to be localised in the State as per certain characteristics and do not as per certain other characteristics. There are also some industry groups which qualify themselves to be localised as per all the four characteristics considered here. The industry groups which manufacture Wood and Wood Products, Paper and Paper Products, Non-Metallic Mineral Products and Electrical Machinery and Apparatus may be adjudged as localised in terms of all the four characteristics. And if localisation is judged from the point of view of "workers" and "fixed capital" – the two important indicators of industrial concentration – three more industry groups get added to the above list of localised industries; they are the industry groups which manufacture Food Products, Beverages, Tobacco and Tobacco Products, and Machinery and Machine Tools.

6.4 Changing Structure of Large-Scale Industries in Karnataka

The principal aim of this section is to analyse the inter-temporal changes in the structure of large-scale industries in the State with the express intention to verify empirically the view that the initial stages of industrialisation are characterised by the predominance of agro-based industries, and the mature stages of industrialisation are characterised by the predominance of non-agro-based industries. Here in this section, an attempt is also made to verify empirically whether the inter-temporal trend is characterised by the declining importance of the agro-based industries and the increasing importance of the non-agro-based industries.

To facilitate such an analysis, all the industry groups originally classified as per the two-digit NIC Code Numbers are reclassified into six broad industry groups in the first instance. They are: Agro-based industries, Fertilisers, Chemicals and Chemical-based industries, Cement and Non-Metallic Mineral Products, Iron and Steel and Metal Products, Machinery Manufacturing, and Other Manufacturing Industries.[8] But in the present analysis, the major industry group entitled "Other Manufacturing Industries" is excluded for sound reasons. To avoid all possible confusion, Appendix Table 6.3 which carries the data of all the industry groups is divided into two parts – Part I and Part II. The industry groups falling under the first five major industry groups referred to above are placed under Part I, and all the other industry groups falling under the sixth major industry group, viz. "Other Manufacturing Industries" are placed under Part II. The industry groups coming under Part II are deliberately excluded from the present analysis to prevent the possible distortion they would cause in the proportions of agro-based and non-agro-based industries, since they are not amenable to proper classification. Thus in the present and the subsequent sections of this chapter, the term "All Industry" means only the industry groups covered under Part I of Appendix Table 6.3. The data on "Employees" "Productive Capital" and "Value Added" in respect of all the five major industry groups constituting "All Industry" total for three points of time spread over two decades of planned development are given in Table 6.5.

The data in the table, besides throwing light on the relative importance of the different major industry groups in the large-scale industrial sector of the State, help in examining the structural change that has been occurring in terms of the changing significance of the agro-based and non-agro-based industries.

Columns, 3, 4 and 5 show the changing importance of the different major industry groups in terms of "employees" over time. In all the three points of time – 1960, 1970 and 1980-81 – the Agro-based Industries group dominates the industrial activity by claiming for itself the highest share of employees. The second, third, fourth and fifth places go to the major industry groups entitled "Machinery Manufacturing", "Iron and Steel and Metal Products", "Cement and Non-Metallic Mineral Products", and "Fertilisers, Chemicals and Chemical-based Industries" respectively. Inter-temporally, Agro-based

TABLE 6.5: Selected Characteristics of Major Industry Groups (Census Sector) of Karnataka: 1960, 1970 & 1980-81

Sl. No.	Major Industry Group	No. of Employees			Productive Capital (in Rs. Crores)			Value Added (in Rs. crores)		
		1960	1970	1980-81	1960	1970	1980-81	1960	1970	1980-81
1	2	3	4	5	6	7	8	9	10	11
1.	Agro-based Industries	59131 (58.54)	78990 (49.10)	148429 (54.52)	21.50 (41.17)	78.36 (24.76)	394.60 (33.62)	10.91 (47.81)	59.94 (47.43)	120.32 (30.08)
2.	Fertilisers, Chemicals & Chemical-based Industries	2577 (2.55)	2949 (1.84)	14368 (5.28)	1.81 (3.47)	14.33 (4.53)	180.59 (15.39)	0.99 (4.34)	1.91 (1.51)	39.21 (9.80)
3.	Cement and Non-Metallic Mineral Products	8501 (8.41)	11169 (6.94)	18545 (6.81)	2.78 (5.32)	26.62 (8.41)	69.89 (5.95)	1.14 (5.00)	6.13 (4.85)	28.66 (7.17)
4.	Iron and Steel and Metal Products	10330 (10.23)	16503 (10.26)	23727 (8.71)	5.64 (10.80)	95.73 (30.24)	196.38 (16.73)	1.87 (8.19)	15.26 (12.08)	61.44 (15.36)
5.	Machinery Manufacturing	20472 (20.27)	51255 (31.86)	67194 (24.68)	20.49 (39.24)	101.49 (32.06)	332.27 (28.31)	7.91 (34.66)	43.13 (34.13)	150.37 (37.59)
	All Industry Total	101011 (100)	160866 (100)	272263 (100)	52.22 (100)	316.53 (100)	1173.73 (100)	22.82 (100)	126.37 (100)	400.00 (100)

Notes: 1. The figures in parentheses are the percentages to the total.

2. Composition of Major Industry Groups: (a) The industry groups bearing the two-digit code Nos. 20-21, 22, 23, 24, 26, 27, 28 & 29 are grouped under "Agro-based Industries"; (b) The industry groups bearing the two-digit code Nos. 30 & 31 are grouped under "Fertilisers, Chemicals and Chemical-based Industries"; (c) The industry group bearing the two-digit code No. 32 is brought under "Cement and Non-metallic Mineral Products"; (d) The industry groups bearing the two-digit code Nos. 33 & 34 are grouped under "Iron & Steel & Metal Products"; (e) The industry groups bearing the two-digit code Nos. 35, 36 & 37 are grouped under "Machinery Manufacturing"; (f) The industry groups bearing the two-digit code Nos. 38, 40, 42 & 97 are grouped under "Other Manufacturing Industries".

3. For the detailed description of code numbers see Appendix Table 6.3, and ASI 1980-81, *Summary Results for the Census Sector*, Vol. 1, CSO, May 1984, pp. 154-163.

4. "All Industry Total" refers to the total of Part I of Appendix Table 6.3.

Source: Derived from Appendix Table 6.3.

industries and the Fertiliser and Chemical Industries record a decline in 1970 and again an increase in 1980-81; the Cement and Non-Metallic Mineral Products industries record a consistent fall; the Iron and Steel and Metal Products industries record a marginal increase in 1970, and then a substantial fall in 1980-81; and the Machinery Manufacturing industries record a substantial increase in 1970, and an equally substantial decline in 1980-81. And if the structural change is viewed in terms of the agro-based and non-agro-based industries for the overall period of two decades, the data indicate a decline in the importance of the former and an increase in the importance of the latter. But it is important to note that neither the magnitude of decline nor the magnitude of increase is indicative of any significant trend away from the former and towards the latter as per the expected pattern. Thus, viewed from "Employees" criterion, it is intriguing to note that despite two decade of deliberate industrialisation, the large-scale industrial sector of the State continues to exhibit the predominance of the agro-based industries. A similar trend in the structural change of large-scale industries is also found in the neighbouring State of Andhra Pradesh.[9]

A slightly different picture emerges when the relative importance of the major industry groups is judged on the basis of "Productive Capital". The Agro-based Industries group, which occupies the first place in 1960, moves down to the third place in 1970, and again gets back to the first place in 1980-81. The Machinery Manufacturing Industries group which occupies the second place in 1960, gains the first place in 1970, and again slips back to the second place in 1980-81. The Iron and Steel Industries group which holds the third place in 1960, moves up to the second place in 1970, and again moves down to the third place in 1980-81. The Cement and Non-Metallic Mineral Industries group, which holds the fourth place in 1960 and 1970, further moves down to the fifth place in 1980-81. And the Fertiliser, Chemicals and Chemical-based Industries group, which holds the fifth place in 1960 and 1970, gains the fourth place in 1980-81. If the entire situation is viewed by classifying industry groups into agro-based and non-agro-based industries, over a span of two decades, the expected pattern of structural change becomes obvious – the former showing a tendency to decline, and the latter a tendency to increase. Among other things, this trend indicates that more and more capital is being ploughed into the non-traditional and modern industries in the State. This type of structural change has also taken place in the large-scale industrial sector of Andhra Pradesh.[10]

Columns 9, 10 and 11 of Table 6.5 indicate the relative positions of the different industry groups in terms of "Value Added" in 1960, 1970 and 1980-81 respectively. The agro-based industries group, which holds the first place in 1960 and 1970, moves down to the second place in 1980-81. The Machinery Manufacturing Industries group which holds the second place in 1960 and 1970 moves up to the first place in 1980-81. The Iron and Steel Industries group occupies the third place in all the three points of time. The Cement and Non-Metallic Mineral Industries group, which holds the fourth place in 1960 and 1970, moves down to the fifth place in 1980-81. The Fertilisers Chemicals and Chemical-based Industries group, which holds the fifth place in 1960 and 1970, gains the fourth place in 1980-81. If the trend is viewed in terms of the agro-based and non-agro-based industries, for the entire period of two decades, we do notice a substantial decline in the importance of the agro-based industries, and a matching increase in the importance of the non-agro-based industries. A similar trend is also observed in the growth pattern of large-scale industries in Andhra Pradesh.[11]

6.5 Growth of Large-Scale Industries in Karnataka

The preceding section has shown that the industrial structure has been undergoing a change in terms of the relative importance of the five major industry groups. This section as a sequel to the earlier one attempts to examine the rates at which the five major industry groups have been growing from time-to-time. In this connection, the annual compound growth rates of "employees", "productive capital" and "value added" for all the five major industry groups are calculated and presented in Table 6.6.

Considerable variations in the inter-temporal growth rates of the different industry groups are revealed by the data presented in the Table. In the first decade, the highest and the lowest growth rates in "employees" are recorded by the "Machinery Manufacturing Industries" group and the "Fertilisers, Chemicals and Chemical-based Industries" group respectively, but in the Second decade, the latter group records the highest growth rate, and the former the lowest. And for the two decades put together, the highest and lowest growth rates are recorded by the "Fertilisers, Chemicals and Chemical-based Industries" and the "Cement and Non-Metallic Mineral Products Industries". If we compare the growth rates of these industry groups

TABLE 6.6: Compound Growth of Major Industry Groups (Census Sector) in Karnataka: 1960-1970, 1970-1980-81 and 1960-1980-81

Sl. No.	Name of the Industry Group	Employees			Productive Capital			Value Added		
		1960 to 1970	1970 to -1980-81	1960 to 1980-81	1960 to 1970	1970 to 1980-81	1960 to 1980-81	1960 to 1970	1970 to 1980-81	1960 to 1980-81
1	2	3	4	5	6	7	8	9	10	11
1.	Agro-based Industries	2.94	6.51	4.71	13.80	17.55	15.66	18.57	7.22	12.75
2.	Fertilisers, Chemicals and Chemical-based Industries	1.36	17.15	8.97	22.99	28.84	25.88	6.79	35.28	20.16
3.	Cement and Non-metallic Mineral Products	2.77	5.20	3.98	25.35	10.13	17.49	18.32	16.68	17.49
4.	Iron and Steel and Metal Products	4.80	3.69	4.25	32.73	7.45	19.42	23.36	14.94	19.08
5.	Machinery Manufacturing	9.61	2.74	6.12	17.35	12.59	14.95	18.48	13.30	15.86
	All Industry growth rate	4.76	5.40	5.08	19.75	14.00	16.84	18.67	12.21	15.40

Note: For the purpose of calculating the annual compound growth rates, the period between the calendar year 1960 and the financial year 1980-81 is taken to be 20 years.

Source: Derived from Table 6.5.

with those of the "All Industry" growth rates presented in the last row of Table 6.6, it becomes clear that not all the groups equal or excel the "All Industry" average growth rate.

Columns, 6, 7 and 8 of Table 6.6 show the relative growth rates of the major industry groups in terms of "Productive Capital". In the first decade, the highest and lowest growth rates are recorded by the "Iron and Steel and Metal Products Industries" and the "Agro-based Industries" respectively. Whereas in the second decade, the highest and lowest growth rates are recorded by the "Fertilisers, Chemicals and Chemical-based Industries", and the Iron and Steel and Metal Products Industries respectively. And for the period of two decades, the Fertilisers and Chemicals and Chemical-based Industries" record the highest growth rate, whereas the "Machinery Manufacturing Industries" record the lowest growth rate. In this case of "Productive Capital" also, not all the industry groups equal or excel the "All Industry" average growth performance.

Columns 9, 10 and 11 of Table 6.6 show the growth performance of all the five major industry groups in terms of "Value Added". In the first decade, the highest and lowest growth rates are recorded by the "Iron and Steel and Metal Products Industries", and the "Fertilisers, Chemicals and Chemical-based Industries" respectively; in the second decade and in the overall period of two decades, the highest and lowest growth rates are recorded by the "Fertilisers, Chemicals and Chemical-based Industries", and the "Agro-based Industries" respectively. Here also not all the groups equal or excel the "All Industry" average growth rate.

One important fact that emerges from an analysis of the overall growth rates of the five major industry groups in terms of Employees, Productive Capital and Value Added is that the Agro-based Industries group has not been keeping pace with the "All Industry" average growth rates. This trend in the growth performance of the Agro-based Industries group lends support to the view that emerged from the analysis of the changing shares of the major industry groups in the preceding section. And among the Non-Agro-based Industries, the highest growth performance is recorded by the Fertilisers and Chemicals and Chemical-based Industries.

6.6 Factor-Mix and Productivity in Large-Scale Industries

The factor-mix or the ratio in which the various factors of production are combined in the process of production, to a great extent, depends upon the technology employed. Considering the labour-capital mix to be very significant, economists often speak of labour-intensive and capital-intensive technologies. Technically, the higher the capital-labour ratio, the higher the output-labour ratio, and a higher output-labour ratio is a manifestation of higher labour productivity. And it is generally believed that the labour productivity or per capita output of labour is relatively low in the agro-based industries since the capital-labour ratio in them is relatively low; and, on the other hand, the labour productivity is relatively high in the non-agro-based industries since the capital-labour ratio in them is relatively high. To verify these views with regard to the large-scale industries in Karnataka, the three important economic ratios, namely, Output-Labour Ratio, Capital-Labour Ratio and Output-Capital Ratio, are worked out for all the five major industry groups, and are presented in Table 6.7.

The data in columns 3, 4 and 5 indicate that starting with a small output-labour ratio in the base year, all the industry groups record a consistent increase in the ratio between 1960 and 1980-81. But there are wide variations in which this ratio has been increasing among the different industry groups. As far as the annual compound growth rate is concerned, the lowest growth rate is recorded by the Agro-based Industries group, and relatively higher growth rates are recorded by the industry groups that constitute the non-agro-based Industries group. The data in these columns also show that the per capita productivity of labour in the non-agro-based Industries is higher than the per capita labour productivity in the agro-based Industries.

Columns 6, 7 and 8 of Table 6.7 present the data in respect of the capital-labour ratios which indicate the capital intensity of industries. The data show very conclusively that the agro-based industries are less capital-intensive than the non-agro-based industries. They also show that there is a consistent increase in the capital-labour ratio in all the industry groups. But the increase is less pronounced in the agro-based industries and more pronounced in the non-agro-based industries. As far as annual compound growth rates are concerned, the highest compound growth rate is recorded by the Fertilisers, Chemicals and Chemical-based Industries group which comes under the classification of Non-agro-based Industries. And if capital-intensity is viewed from the data for 1980-81, it becomes clear that disproportionately high capital intensity is found in the Fertilisers, Chemicals and Chemical-based Industries, and the lowest capital-intensity is found in the Agro-based Industries.

TABLE 6.7: Economic Ratios of Major Industry Groups (Census Sector) in Karnataka: 1960, 1970 and 1980-81

Sl. No.	Name of the Industry Group	Output-Labour Ratio (in Rs. thousands)			Capital-Labour Ratio (in Rs. thousands)			Output-Capital Ratio		
		1960	1970	1980-81	1960	1970	1980-81	1960	1970	1980-81
1	2	3	4	5	6	7	8	9	10	11
1.	Agro-based Industries	1.845	7.588	8.106 (7.68)	3.636	9.920	26.585 (10.46)	0.5074	0.7649	0.3049 (-2.51)
2.	Fertilisers, Chemicals and Chemical-based Industries	3.842	6.477	27.290 (10.30)	7.024	48.593	125.689 (15.51)	0.5470	0.1333	0.2171 (-4.50)
3.	Cement and Non-Metallic Mineral Products	1.341	5.488	15.454 (13.00)	3.270	23.834	37.687 (13.00)	0.4101	0.2303	0.4101 (0.00)
4.	Iron and Steel and Metal Products	1.810	9.247	25.895 (14.23)	5.460	58.008	82.766 (14.56)	0.3316	0.1594	0.3129 (-0.29)
5.	Machinery Manufacturing	3.864	8.415	22.378 (9.18)	10.009	19.801	49.449 (8.31)	0.3860	0.4250	0.4526 (0.80)
	All Industry Groups	2.259	7.856	14.692 (9.81)	5.170	19.677	43.110 (11.19)	0.437	0.399	0.341 (-1.233)

Note: The figures in parentheses are the annual compound growth rates of the respective ratios for the period from 1960 to 1980-81.
Source: Derived from Table 6.5.

The output-capital ratios presented in columns 9, 10 and 11 of Table 6.7 express the per-unit productivity of capital in the different industry groups. The highest ratios in 1960, 1970 and 1980-81 are recorded by the Fertilisers, Chemicals and Chemical-based Industries, the Agro-based Industries, and by the Machinery Manufacturing Industries respectively. And as far as annual compound growth rates are concerned, three out of the five industry groups record negative growth rates, one industry group records zero growth rate and one industry group records a growth rate of just 0.80 per cent.

The inter-relationship among these three ratios is such that the per capita productivity of labour as measured by the output-labour ratio becomes a direct function of the other two economic ratios, namely, the capital-labour ratio and the output-capital ratio. In the case of "All Industry" an annual compound growth of 11.19 per cent in the capital-labour ratio is accompanied by only 9.81 per cent in the output-labour ratio, for the reason that the output-capital ratio records a negative growth rate (-1.233 per cent). A similar situation is found in three industry groups. The growth rates of output-labour ratios of the Agro-based Industries, the Fertiliser, Chemicals and Chemical-based Industries, and the Iron and Steel and metal Products Industries are not commensurate with the growth rates of capital-labour ratios because of the negative growth rates recorded by them in output-capital ratios. The growth rate of the output-labour ratio of the Cement and Non-Metallic Mineral Industries is commensurate with the growth rate of its capital-labour ratio, since there is no inter-temporal change in its output-capital ratio. And the growth rate of the output-labour ratio of the Machinery Manufacturing Industries is higher than its growth rate of capital-labour ratio because its output-capital ratio records a positive growth rate. Thus, the lower productivity of labour is ascribable to the negative growth rates of the output-capital ratio.

6.7 Value Added in Consumer Goods and Capital Goods Industries: A Comparative Analysis

As already stated in Chapter II, W.G. Hoffmann[12] has attempted – theoretically and empirically – to explain the stages of industrialisation by using the ratios of consumer-goods output to capital-goods output. According to Hoffmann, consumer goods industries always develop first during the process of industrialisation, but the capital goods industries soon develop faster than the former. He also says that the ratio of the net output (value added) in the consumer goods industries continually declines as compared with the net output of capital-goods industries.[13] His analysis of the growth pattern of the ratio of consumer goods output to capital-goods output undergoes a change as under:

(i) Stage I has a ratio of 5 ($\pm$ 1) : 1
(ii) Stage II has a ratio of 2.5 ($\pm$ 1) : 1
(iii) Stage III has a ratio of 1 ($\pm$ 0.5) : 1
(iv) Stage IV represents a situation where the capital-goods output exceeds the consumer-goods output.[14]

In this section, by using Hoffmann's criteria, an attempt is made to identify the stages of industrialisation through which Karnataka has been passing since the 1960s. And in doing so, it attempts to test Hoffmann's hypothesis empirically with reference to Karnataka. For the purpose of the present analysis the large-scale sector is divided into two halves, namely, consumer goods industries and capital goods industries. The consumer goods industries include the industry groups manufacturing Food Products, Beverages, Tobacco and Tobacco Products, Cotton Textiles, Wool, Silk and Synthetic Fibre Textiles, Textile Products (including Wearing Apparels), Wood and Wood Products, Furniture and Fixtures, Paper and Paper Products (including Printing and Publishing), and Leather and Leather Products; and on the other hand the capital goods industries include the industry groups manufacturing Rubber, Plastic, Petroleum and Coal products, Chemicals and Chemical Products, Non-Metallic Mineral Products, Basic Metals and Alloys, Metal Products and Parts, Machinery, Machine Tools and Parts, Electrical Machinery, Apparatus, Appliances and Parts, and Transport Equipment and Parts. Incidentally, here it is to be pointed out that though this analysis is based on only large-scale industries (Census Sector) and excludes the small-scale industries (Sample Sector) the proportion of the former in the total manufacturing sector is large enough to represent the entire manufacturing sector.[15] The net value added in the consumer goods and capital goods industries at three points of time – 1960, 1970 and 1980-81 – and their ratios are given in Table 6.8.

The table reveals the relative predominance of capital goods industries in all the three points of time. The data show that there is a clear tendency towards decline in the net output of the consumer goods industries as compared with the net output of the capital goods industries. The ratios for 1960 (0.92:1) and 1970 (0.90:1) further indicate that Karnataka entered Hoffmann's Stage III in 1960 itself, and continued to be in it in 1970 also. The ratio for 1980-81 (0.43:1) shows that Karnataka has been passing through Stage IV, where the capital goods net output is decidedly higher than the net output of consumer goods. However, these empirical facts should not lead us to the hasty conclusion that Karnataka has attained the much coveted industrial maturity, and is a very rich State. It is so because, Karnataka with its primary sector claiming 49.04 per cent of the NSDP and 71.08 per cent of the total workforce, can neither claim the status of a highly industrialised State nor that of a rich State. The fact is that it is still in the process of transformation.[16]

TABLE 6.8: Net Value Added in Consumer-Goods Industries and Capital-Goods Industries (Census Sector) in Karnataka: 1960, 1970 and 1980-81

Sl. No.	Description of Industries	Unit	Reference Period		
			1960	1970	1980-81
1	2	3	4	5	6
1.	Value Added in Consumer-Goods Industries	Rs. Crores	10.91 (47.81)	59.94 (47.43)	120.32 (30.08)
2.	Value Added in Capital-Goods Industries	Rs. Crores	11.91 (52.19)	66.43 (52.57)	279.68 (69.92)
3.	Total Value Added in Manufacturing	Rs. Crores	22.82 (100)	126.37 (100)	400.00 (100)
4.	Net Output Ratio at the State Level	—	0.92:1	0.90:1	0.43:1

Note: All the Agro-based Industries are regarded as Consumer Goods Industries and all the Non-agro-based Industries are regarded as Capital Goods Industries.
Source: Derived from Table 6.5.

In order to see that Hoffmann's stage-analysis with reference to the industrialisation process of Karnataka does not mislead the policy-makers, some of its important limitations are considered here. First, Hoffmann's hypothesis of the time-pattern of stages is entirely based on his conception of "free economies". But, Karnataka, as an integral part of the Indian Union, has been consciously pursuing the policies of a mixed economy. Secondly, some of the industry groups which are included in the present analysis are not found in Hoffmann's analysis. For instance, the industry groups manufacturing Wood and

Wood Products, Paper and Paper Products are excluded from his classification of consumer goods industries, and the industry groups manufacturing Rubber and Plastics and Non-Metallic Mineral Products are excluded from the capital goods industries. Thirdly, Hoffmann's stages may not be relevant to the newly industrialising economies, i.e. late-comers to the field of industrialisation. It may not be necessary for these economies to pass through the early stages conceived by Hoffmann. The new technologies and new products, which were not there in the early phases of industrialisation of the present industrialised countries, are available in plenty to the late-comers. As such, it may become possible for them to industrialise with a much higher net output ratio of capital goods to consumer goods in the early phases itself.[17] And the low net output ratio of consumer goods to capital goods in Karnataka may be one such instance where a given economy has taken advantage of the new technologies available. Finally, Hoffmann's pattern does not tell planners whether it would be wise to leap over portions of this progression and take positive measures to establish capital goods industries in such a way as to deliberately reduce the net output ratio between the two sectors.[18]

6.8 Main Findings

(i) If industrial backwardness or advancement of a State is measured on the basis of the all-India average performance in industrial activity, Karnataka comes under the classification of the group of industrially advanced States in India. The annual compound growth rates recorded by Karnataka between 1960 and 1980-81 in respect of workers, fixed capital and value added are higher than the all-India average growth rates. And there has been relative stability in its rank order at the all-India level; it has been holding the ranks varying between 6th and 11th.

(ii) As far as the localisation of the nature of large-scale industries is concerned, the study shows that the major industry groups manufacturing Wood and Wood Products, Paper and Paper Products, Non-Metallic Mineral Products and Electrical Machinery are said to be localised in Karnataka.

(iii) The inquiry into the changing importance of the agro-based and non-agro-based industries in terms of "Employees", "Productive Capital" and "Value Added" shows that in keeping with the expected pattern, the agro-based industries have been registering a declining trend, and the non-agro-based industries an increasing trend.

(iv) The output-labour ratio shows that the lowest labour productivity is found in agro-based industries, and the per capita productivity of labour in the non-agro-based industries is higher than the per capita productivity of labour in the agro-based industries. Similarly, capital-labour ratio reveals that comparatively higher capital intensity is found in non-agro-based industries, and lower capital intensity is found in agro-based industries. And when these two ratios are interpreted in the context of the output-capital ratio for the entire period of two decades, it becomes evident that the growth rate of labour productivity in the agro-based industries is not commensurate with its growth rate of capital-labour ratio.

(v) The inter-industry analysis of the relative importance of consumer goods industries and capital goods industries in Karnataka does not lend support to Hoffmann's hypothesis. In 1960, instead of finding its place in State I or Stage II of Hoffmann, Karnataka is seen in Stage III, and it is seen in Stage IV – the final stage of industrialisation conceived by Hoffmann – in 1980-81. This finding, which goes against Hoffmann's hypothesis, is indicative of the fact that the late-comers to the industrialisation process can skip some of the initial stages of industrialisation.

NOTES

1. Hoffmann, W., *The Growth of Industrial Economies*, Oxford University Press, 1958, p. 2.
2. For details, see Chapter II of the present work.
3. Sharma Ramakrishna K., *Industrial Development of Andhra Pradesh — A Regional Analysis*, Himalaya Publishing House, Bombay, 1982, pp. 41-42.
4. *Ibid.*, p. 48.
5. For details of the Industrial Classification, see Annual Survey of Industries, 1980-81, Summary Results for Census Sector, Vol. I, C.S.O., 31-5-1984, pp. 154-163.
6. For details of the concepts and definitions used in the present study, see *Ibid.*, pp. 164-168.
7. The location quotients are obtained for each industry group for each characteristic by dividing the percentage share of the State in each industry group by the percentage share of the State in the national aggregates. For further details, see Sargent, Florence, P., *The Logic of British and American Industry*, Routledge and

Kegan Paul Ltd., London, 1961. p. 83.
See also Mehta, M.M., *Structure of Indian Industries*, Popular Book Depot, Bombay, 1961, p. 160.

8. For details of reclassification, see, Appendix Table 6.3 and Table 6.5.
9. Sharma Ramakrishna, K., *op. cit.*, pp. 59-61.
10. *Ibid.*, p. 61.
11. *Ibid.*, p. 62.
12. Hoffmann, W.G., *The Growth of the Industrial Economies*, Oxford University Press, 1958.
13. *Ibid.*, p. 2.
14. For further details, see Sutcliffe, R.B. *Industry and Underdevelopment*, Addison-Wesley Publishing Company, London, 1971, pp. 32-40.
15. For the relative shares of the Census and Sample Sectors in the value added, see Table 6.1.
16. For further particulars about sectoral shares in Karnataka, see Chapter V.
17. Sutcliffe, R.B., *op. cit.*, p. 38.
18. *Ibid.*, p. 40.

APPENDIX TABLE 6.1: **Annual Survey of Industries — Selected Characteristics of Census Sector Industries by States: 1960, 1970 and 1980-81**

Sl. No.	States/Union Territories	No. of Factories Reporting			Fixed Capital (in Rs. crores)			No. of Workers			Value Added by Manufacture (in Rs. crores)		
		1960	1970	1980-81	1960	1970	1980-81	1960	1970	1980-81	1960	1970	1980-81
1	2	3	4	5	6	7	8	9	10	11	12	13	14
1.	Andhra Pradesh	458 (8)	866 (5)	1507 (6)	51.20 (7)	461.60 (8)	1731.41 (8)	127824 (7)	214000 (6)	360686 (6)	23.30 (9)	107.60 (8)	500.07 (8)
2.	Assam	432 (10)	493 (10)	478 (14)	29.60 (11)	175.40 (15)	268.06 (16)	58212 (12)	61000 (15)	88809 (15)	25.60 (8)	39.10 (16)	101.40 (16)
3.	Bihar	241 (12)	464 (11)	766 (9)	198.00 (3)	665.20 (5)	3384.15 (2)	133096 (6)	178000 (7)	258110 (7)	60.50 (5)	166.80 (7)	473.10 (9)
4.	Gujarat	749 (3)	1166 (4)	2106 (3)	95.80 (4)	533.10 (6)	2480.64 (4)	254284 (3)	308000 (4)	444499 (5)	88.00 (3)	239.90 (4)	973.68 (4)
5.	Haryana	—	309 (14)	566 (12)	—	212.90 (13)	914.92 (12)	—	71000 (11)	106543 (13)	—	60.20 (11)	308.33 (11)
6.	Himachal Pradesh	10 (18)	61 (17)	66 (19)	0.40 (17)	17.60 (18)	185.81 (17)	1317 (17)	12000 (17)	13022 (19)	1.00 (16)	12.30 (17)	58.82 (17)
7.	Jammu & Kashmir	34 (16)	36 (18.5)	63 (20)	0.70 (16)	39.70 (17)	90.94 (19)	6891 (16)	10000 (18.5)	18654 (17)	0.80 (17)	1.60 (20)	12.94 (21)
8.	Karnataka	433 (9)	596 (9)	970 (8)	44.00 (8)	392.80 (10)	1216.07 (11)	92616 (9)	152000 (8)	241014 (8)	26.30 (7)	167.10 (6)	503.21 (7)
9.	Kerala	558 (5)	666 (8)	703 (11)	27.70 (13)	182.00 (14)	751.96 (13)	121083 (8)	138000 (9)	182039 (10)	21.10 (10)	80.00 (10)	339.77 (10)

Contd.

APPENDIX TABLE 6.1 *Contd.*

1	2	3	4	5	6	7	8	9	10	11	12	13	14
10.	Madhya Pradesh	525 (7)	670 (7)	715 (10)	41.30 (9)	517.70 (7)	2064.32 (5)	77827 (10)	133000 (10)	185926 (9)	20.90 (11)	100.20 (9)	565.58 (6)
11.	Maharashtra	1688 (1)	2941 (1)	3114 (1)	276.20 (1)	1300.9 (1)	4437.95 (1)	575802 (2)	660000 (1)	774985 (1)	238.30 (1)	771.60 (1)	2634.82 (1)
12.	Manipur	—	4 (24)	5 (25)	—	0.10 (24)	1.12 (25)	—	1000 (23.5)	1207 (25)	—	0.10 (24)	0.42 (25)
13.	Meghalaya	—	—	11 (24)	—	—	71.22 (20)	—	—	3508 (24)	—	—	13.28 (20)
14.	Orissa	92 (15)	213 (15)	219 (16)	34.90 (10)	408.1 (9)	726.78 (14)	22558 (15)	60000 (16)	91220 (14)	8.50 (15)	56.70 (12)	184.92 (14)
15.	Punjab	337 (11)	387 (12)	985 (7)	27.90 (12)	245.50 (12)	1276.47 (9)	60922 (11)	65000 (13)	114374 (12)	16.70 (12)	50.30 (14)	299.34 (12)
16.	Rajasthan	102 (14)	186 (16)	385 (15)	20.30 (14)	277.60 (11)	1275.60 (10)	37916 (13)	67000 (12)	116421 (11)	8.70 (14)	53.90 (13)	296.35 (13)
17.	Tamil Nadu	720 (4)	1268 (3)	1896 (4)	73.70 (6)	869.40 (4)	1804.78 (7)	187649 (5)	363000 (3)	480292 (4)	61.80 (4)	269.60 (3)	1056.86 (3)
18.	Tripura	15 (17)	25 (20)	104 (17)	0.30 (18)	0.20 (23)	8.82 (23)	755 (18)	1000 (23.5)	8696 (21)	0.20 (18)	0.30 (22.5)	2.23 (24)
19.	Uttar Pradesh	543 (6)	865 (6)	2235 (2)	83.70 (5)	939.40 (3)	2988.13 (3)	204383 (4)	266000 (5)	535014 (3)	55.70 (6)	187.90 (5)	672.56 (5)
20.	West Bengal	1312 (2)	1637 (2)	1600 (5)	270.00 (2)	1018.70 (2)	2033.65 (6)	582124 (1)	624000 (2)	685967 (2)	193.10 (2)	395.70 (2)	1287.85 (2)

Contd.

APPENDIX TABLE 6.1 *Contd.*

1	2	3	4	5	6	7	8	9	10	11	12	13	14
21.	Andaman and Nicobar Islands	—	6 (23)	12 (23)	—	0.80 (22)	4.29 (24)	—	2000 (22)	3696 (23)	—	0.30 (22.5)	3.54 (23)
22.	Chandigarh	—	16 (21)	45 (21)	—	3.50 (21)	10.75 (22)	—	3000 (20.5)	5657 (22)	—	4.30 (18)	12.08 (22)
23.	Delhi	142 (13)	359 (13)	500 (13)	10.80 (15)	93.40 (16)	400.58 (15)	35340 (14)	63000 (14)	72031 (16)	13.80 (13)	42.10 (15)	134.39 (15)
24.	Goa, Daman and Diu	—	36 (18.5)	75 (18)	—	3.80 (20)	152.79 (18)	—	3000 (20.5)	8960 (20)	—	0.60 (21)	56.87 (18)
25.	Pondicherry	—	13 (22)	19 (22)	—	7.60 (19)	20.74 (21)	—	10000 (18.5)	13486 (18)	—	3.10 (19)	18.77 (19)
	All India Total	8391	13280	19115	1286.5	8367.0	28301.95	2580599	3465000	4814816	864.3	2811.30	10511.18

Note:
1. The States/Union Territories are arranged in the order found in the ASI, 1980-81.
2. The data for 1960 and 1970 are for the respective calendar years, and the data for 1980-81 are for the financial year 1980-81.
3. The figures in parentheses show the ranks of the respective States.

Sources:
1. For 1961, *Statistical Abstract of the Indian Union*, 1963 and 1964, New Series. No. 12, CSO, 1965, pp. 122-125.
2. For 1970, *Statistical Abstract of India*, 1975, New Series No. 21, CSO, 1976, pp. 96-98.
3. For 1980-81, *Annual Survey of Industries*, 1980-81, *Summary Results for Census Sector*, Vol.1, Part II, CSO, May 1984, pp. 14-16.

APPENDIX TABLE 6.2: Annual Survey of Industries--Selected characteristics of Major Industry Groups (Census Sector) of India and Karnataka 1980-81.

Sl. No.	Two-digits NIC Codes	Description of Industries	No. of Factories Reporting			Fixed Capital (in Rs. Crores)			Workers (In Numbers)			Value Added by Manufacture (in Rs. Crore)		
			All India State	Karnataka	% Share of the State in the country	All India	Karnataka	% Share of the State in the country	All India	Karnataka	% Share of the State in the country	All India	Karnataka	% Share of the State in the country
1	2	3	4	5	6	7	8	9	10	11	12	13	14	15
	Manufacture of:													
1.	20-21	Food products	4329	171	3.95	985.54	80.09	8.13	806962	51073	6.33	548.99	22.71	4.14
2.	22	Beverages, Tobacco and Tobacco Products	907	37	4.08	105.61	14.49	13.72	150498	8627	5.73	151.58	20.56	13.56
3.	23	Cotton Textiles	2201	130	5.91	1038.87	32.89	3.17	855195	34078	3.99	1277.29	48.30	3.78
4.	24	Wool, Silk & Synthetic Fibre Textiles	732	19	2.60	439.27	1.75	0.40	147316	3447	2.34	336.37	2.20	0.65
5.	25	Jute, Hemp & Mesta Textiles	128	00	00	102.06	00	00	246434	-	-	297.70	00	00
6.	26	Textile Products (including Wearing Apparel other than footwear)	589	47	7.98	51.78	1.23	2.38	51569	4949	9.60	77.02	3.52	4.57
7.	27	Wood & Wood Products, Furniture and Fixtures	236	26	11.02	34.39	4.62	13.43	28995	4537	15.65	31.33	4.19	13.37
8.	28	Paper and Paper Products, Printing Publishing and Allied Industries	725	42	5.79	733.19	183.59	25.04	158407	11446	7.23	353.52	18.67	5.28
9.	29	Leather and Fur Products (Except Repair)	216	03	1.39	47.14	0.49	1.04	35105	237	0.68	51.28	0.17	0.33
10.	30	Rubber, Plastic, Petroleum & Coal Products	498	20	4.02	577.78	34.29	5.93	83458	1916	2.30	445.11	1.74	0.39
11.	31	Chemicals & Chemical Products (except Products of Petroleum and Coal)	1366	60	4.39	3511.47	101.20	2.88	262209	7607	2.90	1289.41	37.47	2.91
12.	32	Non-Metallic Minerals Products	1438	107	7.44	613.53	60.51	9.86	206063	15893	7.71	343.61	28.66	8.34
13.	33	Basic Metal & Alloys Industries	1339	64	4.78	4134.59	100.04	2.42	361161	15214	4.21	1111.57	50.81	4.57
14.	34	Metal Products and Parts except Machinery & Transport Equipments	630	23	3.65	155.65	9.70	6.23	81773	2264	2.77	242.43	10.63	4.38

Contd.

APPENDIX TABLE 6.2 *Contd.*

1	2	3	4	5	6	7	8	9	10	11	12	13	14	15
15.	35	Machinery, Machine Tools and Parts except Elec. Machinery	1064	51	4.79	654.57	45.96	7.02	205249	11873	5.79	728.90	32.98	4.52
16.	36	Elec. Machinery, Apparatus, Appliances & Supplies and Parts	719	61	8.48	631.92	61.79	9.78	174403	22918	13.14	755.16	78.62	10.41
17.	37	Transport Equipments and Parts	654	28	4.28	1317.14	30.64	2.33	339764	13422	3.95	808.38	38.77	4.80
18.	38	Other Manufacturing Industries	250	20	8.00	86.12	27.52	31.96	35806	2902	8.11	103.36	18.80	18.19
19.	40	Electricity	233	09	3.86	12959.28	418.74	3.23	486459	23263	4.78	1429.94	75.05	5.25
20.	41	Gas and Steam	06	00	00	5.33	00	0.00	860	-	-	1.00	0.00	0
21.	42	Water Works and Supply	59	04	6.78	40.81	4.00	9.80	6490	317	4.88	14.99	0.27	1.80
22.	74	Storage & Warehousing (Cold storage)	59	00	00	7.90	00	00	1630	-	-	1.68	0	0
23.	97	Repair Services	737	48	6.51	63.91	2.53	3.96	91048	5031	5.53	110.48	9.09	8.23
		Total for the Country and the State	19115	970	5.07	28301.85	1216.07	4.30	4814816	241014	5.01	10511.10	503.21	4.79

Source: *Annual Survey of Industries*, 1980-81, *Summary Results for the Census Sector*, Vol. 1, CSO, May 1984.

APPENDIX TABLE 6.3: Industry-wise Distribution of Factories, Employees, Productive Capital and Value Added in the Large-scale Industrial Sectior (Census Sector) in Karnataka: 1960, 1970 and 1980-81.

Sl. No.	Two-digits NIC Codes	Description of Industry Groups	Factories Reporting (Number)			Employees (Number)			Productive Capital (in Rs. lakhs)			Value Added (in Rs Lakhs)		
			1960	1970	1980-81	1960	1970	1980-81	1960	1970	1980-81	1960	1970	1980-81
1	2	3	4	5	6	7	8	9	10	11	:2	13	14	15
PART I														
		Manufacture of:												
1.	20-21	Food products	50	81	171	15226	19922	68264	696.56	2514.00	9132.00	344.47	909.35	2271.00
2.	22	Beverages, Tobacco and Tobacco Products	21	07	37	4537	3494	9987	325.75	778.72	2672.00	64.52	3125.51	2056.00
3.	23	Cotton Textiles	53	122	130	31680	39577	38479	922.02	2701.36	5056.00	569.20	1174.02	4830.00
4.	24	Wool, Silk & Synthetic Fibre Textiles	-	-	19	-	-	3949	-	-	1095.00	-	-	220.00
5.	26	Textile Products (including Wearing Apparel other than Footwear)	103	-	47	5165	-	5482	115.91	-	190.00	44.29	-	352.00
6.	27	Wood & Wood Products, Furniture and Fixtures	15	38	26	1674	5659	5766	66.16	313.04	709.00	42.97	123.50	419.00
7.	28	Paper and Paper Products, Printing Publishing and Allied Industries	08	28	42	849	10338	16217	23.64	1529.21	20564.00	25.72	662.03	1867.00
8.	29	Leather and Fur Products (Except Repair)	-	-	03	-	-	285	-	-	42.00	-	-	17.00
9.	30	Rubber Plastic, Petroleum & Coal Products	-	-	20	-	-	2605	-	-	3430.00	-	-	174.00
10.	31	Chemicals & Chemical Products (except Products of Petroleum and Coal)	15	32	60	2577	2949	11763	181.11	1432.83	14629.00	98.99	190.65	3747.00
11.	32	Non-Metallic Minerals Products	62	86	107	8501	11169	18545	278.37	2661.67	6989.00	113.99	613.00	2866.00
12.	33	Basic Metal & Alloys Industries	14	27	64	9908	14618	20557	544.37	9190.23	17954.00	177.59	1268.44	5081.00
13.	34	Metal Products and Parts (except Machinery & Transport Equipment)	05	15	23	422	1885	3170	19.48	382.67	1684.00	9.68	257.14	1063.00
14.	35	Machinery, Machine Tools and Parts (except Elec. Machinery)	15	32	51	7085	13109	17935	838.48	2693.84	10450.00	209.31	1129.99	3298.00

Contd.

APPENDIX TABLE 6.3 *Contd.*

1	2	3	4	5	6	7	8	9	10	11	12	13	14	15
15.	36	Elec. Machinery, Apparatus, Appliances & Supplies and Parts	08	23	61	11510	25384	32692	992.31	5807.96	17243.00	385.71	2347.00	7862.00
16.	37	Transport Equipments and Parts	02	08	28	1877	12762	16567	218.17	1647.35	5534.00	196.11	836.21	3877.00
		Part I Total	396	499	889	101011	160866	272263	5222.33	31652.88	117373.00	2282.55	12637.04	40000.00
PART II														
17.	38	Other Manufacturing Industries	04	11	20	242	2246	4097	1.79	322.36	4575.00	3.80	187.96	1880.00
18.	40	Electricity	-	15	09	-	19028	37154	-	21138.14	44875.00	-	3169.57	7505.00
19.	42	Water Works and Supplies	-	-	04	-	-	412	-	-	432.00	-	-	27.00
20.	97	Repair Services	11	40	48	1120	5038	6096	51.06	339.18	558.00	19.31	174.93	909.00
21.	-	Other Industry Group	22	31	-	7949	8229	-	1788.49	1633.96	-	327.71	545.80	-
		Part II Total	37	97	81	9311	34541	47759	1841.34	23433.64	50440.00	350.82	4078.26	10321.00
		Grand Total (Part I + II)	433	596	970	110322	195407	320022	7063.67	55086.52	167813.00	2633.37	16715.30	50321.00

Sources:
1. For 1960: *Statistical Abstract of Mysore* 1967-68, Economics and Statistics, Government of Mysore, Bangalore, 1969 (ASI Data).
2. For 1970: *Statistical Abstract of Karnataka* 1976-77, Economics and Statistics, Government of Karnataka, Bangalore, 1978 (ASI Data).
3. For 1980-81: *ASI, Summary Results for the Census Sector*, Vol. I, CSO, May 1984.

7

CONCLUSION

7.1 Introduction

THE PRINCIPAL objective of this concluding chapter is to give a succinct resume of the entire work. It is designed to give a brief summary of what was proposed to be done, how it was proposed to be done, and what has been done. It also presents the principal findings and their implications for theory and policy. Keeping these objectives in view, the chapter is split into five sections. The second section gives a summary of the dissertation design. The third section brings together all the important findings regarding the nature and extent of inter-district disparities and their inter-temporal behaviour during the period under study. A brief account of all the principal findings in respect of both the inter-sectoral and inter-industry aspects of structural transformation in the State is given in the fourth section. And the implications of all the important findings are briefly discussed in the fifth section.

7.2 Summary of The Dissertation Design

The present thesis, as the title suggests, is an inquiry into the regional and structural aspects of industrialisation and development in Karnataka. Industrialisation, being an integral and inseparable part of the dynamic process of development *inter alia* has been causing significant changes in the spatial and sectoral dimensions of development. Spatially, as the dialectics of development would have it, industrialisation has given birth to an economically unsound, socially disastrous, morally indefensible and politically dangerous phenomenon, viz. regional disparities. Industrialisation has been exhibiting a built-in tendency to concentrate itself in only certain regions of a country or State unless the tendency is consciously checked by effective Government intervention. India with its politico-economic federal structure has been faced with the problem of inter-State disparities. Only a few States show high industrial development, and others suffer lamentable deficiency of industrial activity. And Karnataka, as an integral part of the Indian Union, has been faced with the problem of inter-district disparities. Both the Centre and the State have been making concerted efforts to minimise regional disparities and to ensure inter-regional parity in industrialisation and development. Even then disparities persist.

And sectorally, as the dynamics of development would have it, the moment an economy begins to industrialise itself, its economic structure – inter-sectoral and inter-industry – starts undergoing a change. It has been observed that economic development involves an inevitable shift away from the primary to the secondary and tertiary sectors. In fact, such a structural change, which is the essence of economic development, is often referred to as industrialisation. India as a nation, and Karnataka as a State, have been experiencing inter-sectoral changes. There has been a definite shift away from the primary sector to the non-primary sectors, but amongst the non-primary sectors, much against the desirable pattern, the tertiary sector seems to have been more dominant than the secondary sector in the early phases of industrialisation. Such an aberration from the desirable pattern has been a cause of concern to planners at all spatial levels. And as a transitional economy, Karnataka has also been experiencing inter-industry changes involving variations in the relative importance of the agro-based and non-agro-based industries, and the consumer goods and capital goods industries.

Thus, in the present inquiry, the problem of industrialisation in Karnataka is viewed form two distinct, but related angles, viz. regional and structural.

The present study is directed towards certain definite objectives. Theoretically, it endeavours to identify the nature of the functional relationship that exists between industrialisation and economic development. Empirically, it attempts to understand the nature and extent of inter-district disparities, and also their inter-temporal trends; examine the inter-sectoral and inter-industry changes that have been accompanying the structural transformation that has been taking place in the State and district/economies of Karnataka; identify the place of Karnataka in the national perspective in terms of large-scale industries; and derive some policy guidelines which would be useful to the Government of Karnataka in formulating its regional development policy in general and industrial dispersal policy in particular.

The study is basically an empirical inquiry into the regional and structural aspects of industrialisation in Karnataka. Regionally, the analysis is generally done at two areal levels – State and district. And structurally, it embraces both the inter-sectoral and inter-industry aspects of structural transformation. So far as the time-cover is concerned, the inquiry is generally spread over two decades covering three points of time, viz. 1960-61, 1970-71 and 1980-81.

The entire work is based on the secondary sources of data, both published and unpublished. Mostly the data are obtained from the Directorate of Economics and Statistics, Government of Karnataka, the Chief Inspector of Factories and Boilers, Government of Karnataka, the Directorate of Industries and Commerce, Government of Karnataka, the Annual Survey of Industries of the Central Statistical Organisation, and the Census publications of the Government of India. To a great extent the study is constrained by the limitations of the data. And this, in turn, imposed limitations on a fuller analysis. Nevertheless, the inquiry has given us certain reliable indications regarding the inter-temporal behaviour of inter-district disparities during the period under review. It has also given us a reasonably reliable picture of the changing structure of the State and district economies during the process of industrialisation and development. Above all, a few useful policy guidelines have been derived from the findings of the study. To give a quantitative touch to the empirical analysis, a few simple statistical tools such as range ratio, rank correlation coefficient, correlation coefficient, coefficient of variation, location quotient, and district relatives are used.

7.3 Changes in Inter-District Disparities: Some Findings

The areal maldistribution of industrial activity in Karnataka is not a recent development. The enlarged State of Karnataka, as it exists today, had all the features of North-South regional mix on the eve of its birth on November 1, 1956. The two-halves – Old Mysore and New Mysore – which were brought together to form the enlarged State were at different levels of industrial development; the former was decidedly better placed in industrial activity than the latter. Furthermore, on the eve of the merger, both the halves were suffering from intra-regional disparities in industrialisation.

The cross-section analysis reveals the existence of inter-district disparities in the levels of development as measured by the per capita NDDP in all the three points of time – 1960-61, 1970-71 and 1980-81, whereas the inter-temporal analysis indicates variations in disparities. The value of coefficient of variation records an increase between 1960-61 and 1970-71 indicating a divergence trend, whereas it records a decline between 1970-71 and 1980-81 indicating a convergence trend. The district per capita income relatives worked out for 1960-61 and 1980-81 are also indicative of a convergence trend. This finding, thus, lends support to the "concentration cycle" hypothesis, according to which the regional disparities display an inverted U-shaped behaviour. However, it should be borne in mind that a 20-year period is too short either to say anything conclusively about the time pattern of divergence-convergence trends, or to test the validity of the various hypotheses about regional disparities, because, regional change is a matter of many decades, and patterns cannot be deciphered by a study of just two decades.

The disparity behaviour displayed by the primary and non-primary sectors is quite divergent. Inter-temporally, the inter-district disparities in the per capita primary income have been tending towards convergence, whereas the inter-district disparities in the per capita secondary and tertiary income have been tending towards divergence. These trends are exhibited by both the coefficient of variation and the district per capita income relatives. Thus, as far as the time pattern of disparity behaviour is concerned, the primary sector has come to display an inverted U-shaped or bell-shaped behaviour of regional disparities, whereas the secondary and tertiary sectors, by recording a consistent increase in disparities, have come to display the rising portion of the inverted U-shaped behaviour of regional disparities. Thus, the disparity behaviour of the primary sector lends support to the concentration cycle hypothesis, whereas, the secondary and tertiary sectors lend support to the "self-perpetuation" hypothesis.

Here it is pertinent to know that by virtue of the continued predominance of the primary sector in the economic structure of majority of the districts, its disparity behaviour had come to influence the aggregative disparity behaviour of the per capita NDDP.

Excessive concentration of registered manufacturing activity is found in Bangalore, and glaring inter-district disparities in registered manufacturing activity are found to exist in all the three points of time – 1960-61, 1970-71 and 1980-81. The inter-temporal analysis shows the differential behaviour of the three indicators of the spread of registered manufacturing, viz. factories, workers and NDDP from registered manufacturing. The inter-district disparities in factories and the NDDP from registered manufacturing register a consistent increase indicative of continuous divergence, and thereby lend support to the "self-perpetuation" hypothesis, whereas disparities in workers register an increase between 1960-61 and 1970-71 and a decline between 1970-71 and 1980-81, and thereby lend support to the well-known "concentration cycle" hypothesis. Since "workers" is a relatively better indicator of the spread of industrial activity, we can say that the disparities in registered manufacturing have been moving towards convergence.

The inter-district disparities in small-scale industrial activity are found to exist in 1970-71 and 1980-81, the two points of time considered in the study. The cross-section analysis provides ample evidence in support of the maldistribution of industrial activity among the districts of Karnataka. In this case also, Bangalore dominates the scene by claiming for itself a sizeable proportion of the small-scale industrial activity in the State. But, inter-temporally, it is heartening to note that the disparities have been heading towards convergence. The value of the coefficient of variation for all the three indicators of the spread of small-scale industrial activity, viz. units, employees and investment, has been showing a substantial decline between 1970-71 and 1980-81. However, a decade is too small a period either to test any hypothesis or to say anything conclusively about the time pattern of disparity behaviour.

7.4 Changes in the Economic Structure: Some Findings

Despite the structural transformation that has been taking place in Karnataka, the economic structure of the State exhibits the dominance of the primary sector in all the three points of time – 1960-61, 1970-71 and 1980-81. And its dominance is more pronounced in workforce than in the NSDP. The structural situation prevailing in the district economies is not materially different from the one which is found at the State level.

The structural change in the State has not been effective enough to alter the inter-sectoral dominance; the State economy has been presenting a consistent order of sectoral dominance. In all the three points of time considered, the primary sector is the lead sector, and is followed by the tertiary and secondary sectors. This order of dominance is found both in the NSDP and workforce. And with a few exceptions the majority of the districts reveal a similar order of sectoral dominance.

The inquiry shows that at the State level, economic development is accompanied by changes in the economic structure along the lines suggested by the sectoral theorists like Colin Clark and Simon Kuznets. With the increase in the per capita NSDP, a consistent decline in its share is registered by the primary sector, an equally consistent increase is registered by the secondary sector, and the tertiary sector does not exhibit any consistent pattern of change. In the case of the district economies, neither all the high per capita income districts are associated with relatively lower shares of their primary sectors in total output and employment, nor are all the low per capita income districts associated with relatively higher shares of their primary sectors. But, inter-temporally, by and large, the changes in the per capita NDDP are accompanied by changes in the sectoral composition of output and employment along the expected lines.

The State economy has been steadily growing. But its growth rate is not uniform in the NSDP and workforce. In the first decade (1960-61 to 1970-71) the growth rate of NSDP is more pronounced than the growth rate of workforce, whereas in the second decade (1970-71 to 1980-81), the growth rate of the latter is more pronounced than that of the former. Inter-sectorally, the highest growth rates are recorded by the secondary sector, and the second and third places go to the tertiary and primary sectors respectively.

Judged by the all-India average performance in industrial activity, Karnataka claims a place among the industrially advanced States of India. The growth rates recorded by Karnataka in "workers", "fixed capital" and "value added" – the three important indicators of the spread of industrial activity – are higher than the all-India average growth rates for the period 1960-61 to 1980-81. And relative stability is noticed in the rank-order of the State in the all-India context; it has been holding ranks ranging between 6th and 11th.

So far as the localisation of the nature of large-scale industrial activity is concerned, the study shows that the major industry groups manufacturing Wood and Wood Products, Paper and Paper Products, Non-Metallic Mineral Products, and Electrical Machinery are said to be localised in Karnataka.

The inquiry into the inter-industry importance reveals the declining importance of the agro-based industries, and increasing importance of the non-agro-based industries. The capital intensity and the per capita productivity of labour in the agro-based industries are lower than in the non-agro-based industries. Furthermore, the growth rate of labour productivity in the agro-based industries is not commensurate with its growth rate of capital-labour ratio.

The inter-industry analysis of the relative importance of the consumer goods and capital goods industries in Karnataka does not lend support to Hoffmann's hypothesis. In 1960 itself, instead of finding its place in Stage I or Stage II of Hoffmann, Karnataka is seen in Stage III and Stage IV, the final stage conceived by Hoffmann, in 1980-81.

7.5 Some Implications for Theory and Policy

Though it is not possible to prove empirically that there exists a direct and proportionate relationship between industrialisation and economic development, one cannot deny the theoretical possibility of making economic development a direct function of industrialisation, other things remaining constant. Despite the definite and determinant role that agriculture has in the process of economic development, it is to be borne in mind that industrialisation alone can cause the creative structural disequilibrium necessary for achieving the higher productivity of labour and higher level of output and employment. Economic development in the modern sense cannot be conceived without reference to industrialisation which involves an inevitable shift away from the primary sector to the secondary and tertiary sectors. So, sectorally, it is necessary to develop the secondary sector deliberately so as to initiate and accelerate the structural change necessary for attaining higher levels of development. And regionally, through controlled industrialisation, it may be possible to assess the divergence trend and promote the convergence trend. Thus, the space-biased controlled industrialisation may be effective in securing growth with spatial equity.

The empirical evidence indicates that regional disparities in the levels of development, as measured by the per capita NDDP, may show a declining trend even when the disparities in the secondary and tertiary sectors are widening. This type of disparity behaviour is owing to the fact that in regions where the primary sector is the dominant sector, the overall disparity in the levels of development becomes a direct function of the behaviour of the primary sector. In Karnataka, the inter-district disparities in the per capita NDDP and per capita primary income have come to display an inverted U-shaped behaviour though the secondary and tertiary sectors have been representing divergence trends. This kind of differential disparity behaviour, among other things, is indicative of the relatively higher degree of success achieved by the regional dispersal policies of the Government in the primary sector activities than in the non-primary sector activities. Assuming that the Government has been very sincere in implementing its industrial dispersal policy, the situation implies that the climate for industrial development in the relatively backward areas may not be as conducive as the climate for agricultural development.

It also implies that for growth with spatial equity, the non-primary sectors need be given higher accent in the State. Based on its past experience, the government may have to think of some innovative measures to spread the non-primary activities to under-industrialised areas.

The excessive concentration of industrial activity in Bangalore district implies that the internal and external economies that go with agglomeration are powerful enough to attract industrial activity to a given region. Policywise it implies that the Government has not been fully successful in dissuading entrepreneurs from establishing industries in Bangalore. Nor has it been fully successful in persuading entrepreneurs to establish industries in under-industrialised areas. In the given circumstances, if the Government is really keen on narrowing down the regional disparities in industrial development, it has to reconsider all its incentive and disincentive schemes.

The convergence trend which has been in operation in the case of inter-district disparities in small-scale industrial activity shows that small-scale industries are better suited for regional dispersal. The trend also implies that the Government's dispersal policy on small-scale industries is more effective than its policy on overall industrial dispersal. So, to minimise regional disparities in industrial activity, it may be desirable on the part of the Government to encourage the establishment of more and more small-scale industries in the backward regions.

The empirical fact that the primary sector, despite 30 years of economic planning, continues to claim a substantial proportion of the workforce, both in the State and district economies, indicates that there is vast scope for shifting the disguisedly unemployed from the primary sector to the non-primary sectors. And by doing so, the Government can increase the per capita productivity of labour, and thereby augment the per capita NDP. And deliberate measures to transfer the workforce from the relatively low-productivity primary activity to the relatively high-productivity non-primary activity would go a long way in accelerating the growth process.

In view of the significant differences that exist in the economic structure of the districts, the regional dispersal policies cannot afford to be uniform throughout the State; there is a need for formulating different policies for different districts, and also different policies for different sectors for one and the same district.

Not only the per capita productivity of labour in the agro-based industries is lower than the per capita productivity of labour in the non-agro-based industries, but also the growth rate of productivity in the former is lower than that in the latter. This shows that there is vast scope as well as urgent need to improve the technology in the agro-based industries so that its per capita labour productivity can be commensurate with the growth rate of capital-labour ratio in them.

The fact that the finding about the relative importance of consumer goods and capital goods industries goes against Hoffmann's hypothesis implies that in mixed economies the Government through deliberate industrialisation can skip some of the stages of industrialisation conceived by Hoffmann. The late entrants to industrialisation can maintain a higher ratio of capital goods to consumer goods from the beginning itself, and there can be no universal pattern as to the stages of industrialisation.

BIBLIOGRAPHY

A. Books and Dissertations

Agarwala, A.N. and Singh, S.P., (eds.), *The Economics of Underdevelopment*, Oxford University Press, New Delhi, 1976.

Alagh, Y.K., *Regional Aspects of Indian Industrialisation*, University of Bombay, 1972.

Ashton, T.S., *The Industrial Revolution*, Oxford University Press, 1948.

Balakrishna, R., *Industrial Development of Mysore*, Bangalore Press, 1940.

Baldwin, B. George, *Industrial Growth in South India*, The Free Press, Glencoe, Illinois, 1959.

Bauer, P.T., *Dissent on Development*, Weidenfeld and Nicolson, London, 1976.

Bhagavathi, J.N. and Eckaus, R.S., (eds.), *Development and Planning: Essays in Honour of Paul Rosenstein Rodan*, George Allen and Unwin Ltd., London, 1972.

Bognar, Josef, *Economic Policy and Planning in Developing Countries*, Akadomiai Kiado, Budapest, 1959.

Brookfield, Harold, *Interdependent Development*, Methuen and Company Ltd., London, 1975.

Bryce, D. Murray, *Industrial Development*, McGraw-Hill Book Company, New York, 1960.

Chaudhuri, M.R., *Indian Industries, Development and Location*, Oxford and IBH, Bombay, 1970.

Clark, Colin, *The Conditions of Economic Progress*, MacMillan and Company, London, 1957.

Colman, David and Nixson, Frederick, *Economics of Change in Less Developed Countries*, B.R. Publishing Corporation, Delhi, 1980.

Cukor, Gyorgy, *Strategies for Industrialisation in Developing Countries*, C. Hurst and Company, London, 1974.

Dadibhavi, R.V., *Inter-district Variations in Income Productivity and Industrial Structure in Karnataka State*, Ph.d. Thesis, M.S. University of Baroda, 1983.

Datta, Babatosh, *The Economics of Industrialisation*, The World Press Ltd., Calcutta, 1966.

Dennison, S.R., *The Location of Industry and the Depressed Areas*, Oxford University Press, London, 1939.

D'Souza, *Economic Development of Mysore*, Bangalore Press, 1937.

Friedman, John and Alonso, William, (eds), *Regional Development and Planning: A Reader*, The MIT Press, Cambridge, Massachussetts, 1972.

Gerald, A.P. Carrothers, (ed.), *Regional Science Association's Papers and Proceedings*, Sixth Annual Meeting, Washington D.C., 1959.

Garschenkron, Alexander, *Economic Backwardness in Historical Perspective*, Harvard University Press, 1966.

Gilbert, Alan, (ed.), *Development Planning and Spatial Structure*, John Wiley and Sons, London, 1976.

Godbole, M.D , *Industrial Dispersal Policies*, Himalaya Publishing House, Bombay.

Goswami, S.P., *Location of Factories in Maharashtra An Analysis of the Trends During 1960s*, Ph.D. Thesis, University of Bombay, 1981.

Gupta, L.C., *Growth Theory and Strategy: New Direction*, Oxford University Press, New Delhi, 1983.

Hanna, F.A., *State Income Differentials 1919-1954*, Duke University Press, Durban, 1959.

Hartwell, R.M., *Industrial Revolution and Economic Growth*, Methuen and Company Ltd., London, 1971.

Hicks, J.R., *Essays in World Economics*, Clarendon Press, Oxford, 1958.

Hiremath, N.S., *Economic Planning and Development in Karnataka*, Ph.D., Thesis, Karnataka University, 1978.

Hirschman, A.O., *The Strategy of Economic Development*, New Haven, Yale University Press, USA, 1958.

Hoffmann, Walter, *The Growth of Industrial Economies*, Manchester, 1958.

Holland, S., *Capital Versus Regions*, MacMillan, London, 1976.

Hoover, Edgar, M., *The Location of Economic Activity*, McGraw-Hill and Company, 1948.

Hoselitz, B. and Moore, W.E., (eds.), *Industrialisation and Society*, UNESCO, 1962.

John Cody., Helen Hughes, and Wall David, (eds.), *Policies for Industrial progress in Developing Countries*, (A Study jointly sponsored by UNIDO and the World Bank), Oxford University Press, New York, 1980.

Kamat, A.R., *Selected Writings and Speeches of Professor D.R. Gadgil on Planning and development (1967-1971)*, Gokhale Institute of Politics and Economics, Poona, 1973.

Kapoor, T.N., *Industrial Development in the States of India*, Sterling Publishers (P.) Ltd., Delhi, 1967.

Karl de Scheweinitz, Jr., *Industrialisation and Democracy*, The Free Press Glencoe, Collier-MacMillan Ltd., London, 1964.

Kemp, Tom, *Historical Patterns of Industrialisation*, Longman Group Ltd., London, 1978

Kulkarni, M.R., *Industrial Development*, National Book Trust, New Delhi, 1971.

Kuznets, Simon, *Modern Economic Growth — Rate Structure and Speed*, Yale University Press, London, 1969.

Kuznets, Simon, *Presidential Address Delivered to the American Economic Association*, December, 1954.

Lahari, T.B., (ed.), *Balanced Regional Development*, Oxford and IBH Publishing Company, Calcutta, 1970.

Livingstone, I., (ed.), *Economic Policy for Development (Selected Readings)*, Penguin Books, 1971.

Lutz, U., Italy: *A Study of Economic Development*, Oxford University Press, London, 1962.

Mandelbaum, K., *The Industrialisation of Backward Areas*, Basil Blackwell, Oxford, 1955.

Manganlal, K. Shah., *Industrial Planning in India*, M.Com. Thesis, Bombay Univeristy, 1944.

Mahajan, Y.S., *Industrialisation of Karnataka*, Karnätaka Chamber of Commerce, Hubli, 1950.

Mehta, M.M., *Structure of Indian Industries*, Popular Book Depot, Bombay, 1961.

Menon, K.S.V., *Development of Backward Areas Through Incentives: An Indian Experiment*, Vidya Vahini, New Delhi, 1979.

Meti, T.K., *The Economy of Karnataka: An Analysis of Development and Planning*, Oxford and IBH, Delhi, 1976.

Meti, T.K., (ed.), *Economic Development and Social Change in Mysore State*, Karnataka University, Dharwad, 1971.

Mezerik, A.G., *Industrialisation of Underdeveloped Countries*: UNIDO Symposium on Industrial Development, 1968.

Misra, R.P., Urs, D.V., and Nataraj, V.K., *Regional Planning and National Development*, Vikas Publishing House (P.) Ltd., New Delhi, 1978.

Mistry, P.P., *Aspects of Industrial Development in the Post-Independent India*, Ph.D. Thesis, University of Bombay, 1982.

Mount Joy. Alan B., *Industrialisation and Underdeveloped Countries*, Hutchinson University Library, London, 1963.

Munshi, M.C., *Location of Industries in Mysore State, Indian Statistical Institute*, Calcutta, 1962.

Myrdal, G., *An Approach to Asian Drama*, Vintage Books, New York, 1970.

Myrdal, G., *An International Economy*, Harper and Brothers, New York, 1956.

Myrdal, G., *Economic Theory and Underdeveloped Regions*, Garald Duckworth, 1957.

Naidu, Munirathna, K., *Industrial Development of Andhra Pradesh (A Study in Regional Planning)*, Sri Venkateswara University, Tirupati.

Nair, K.R.G., *Regional Experience in a Developing Economy*, Wiley Eastern Ltd., New Delhi, 1982.

Nanjundappa, D.M., *Some Aspects of Karnataka's Economy*, Bharat Prakashan, Dharwar, 1971.

Natarajan, K.A., *Industrial Economics: Industrial Development of Madras (With Special reference to Industrial Infrastructure, 1918-1939)*, M. Litt. Thesis Madras University, 1973.

Needleman, (ed.), *Regional Analysis*, Penguin Books, 1968.

Nehru Jawaharlal, *Speeches March 1953-August 1957*, New Delhi, 1958.

Nourse, Hough, O., *Regional Economics*, McGraw-Hill, 1968.

Pandit, S.A., *Regional Distribution of Industries in India*, Ph.D. Thesis University of Bombay, 1949.

Patnaik, S.C., *Economics of Regional Development and Planning in Third World Countries*, Associated Publishing House, New Delhi, 1981.

Paul Bairoch, *The Economic Development of the Third World Since 1900*, Methuen and Company Ltd., London, 1975.

Perloff, H.S. Dunn, Jr. E.S., Lampard, E.E. and Muth, Richard, F., *Regions, Resources and Economic Growth*, Resources for the Future, Johns Hopkins Press, Baltimore, 1960.

Puttaswamaiah, K., *Economic Development of Karnataka: A Treatise in Continuity and Change*, Oxford and IBH, 1980.

Rao, Hemalatha, *Regional Disparities and Development in India*, Ashish Publishing House, New Delhi, 1984.

Rangarajan, C., Rakesh, Kurana, Pathak, H., Wadhav, D., Chavan and Gupta, P. Anand, (eds.), *Strategy for Industrial Development in the 80s*, Oxford and IBH Publishing Company, New Delhi, 1981.

Richardson, H.W., *Elements of Regional Economics*, Penguin Books, 1969.

Robinson, Ronald, (ed.), *Developing the Third World: The Experience of the Nineteen-Sixties*, University Press, Cambridge, 1971.

Rosen, G., *Industrial Change in India: Industrial Growth, Capital Requirements and Technological Change, 1937-55*, Bombay, 1961.

Schumacher, E.F., *Small is Beautiful*, Radhakrishna Publishers, New Delhi, 1978.

Selvaraju, V., *Wage Differentials, Cost and Production Functions: A Cross-Section Study of Indian Census Sector Manufacturing Industries, 1974-75 — 1976-77*, M.Phil Thesis Bharatihar University, Coimbatore, 1986.

Seers, Dudley and Joy, Leonard, (eds.), *Development in a Divided World*, Penguin Books, 1970.

Sharma, Ramakrishna, K., *Industrial Development of Andhra Pradesh — A Regional Analysis*, Himalaya Publishing House, Bombay, 1982.

Shetty, H.V., *Industrial Problems of Mysore State (with special reference to Location and Regional Balance)*, Ph.D., Thesis, Karnataka University, Dharwad, 1964.

Shirokov, G.K., *Industrialisation of India*, Progressive Publishers, Moscow, 1973.

Singh, A.K., *Patterns of Regional Development: A Comparative Study*, Sterling Publishers (P.) Ltd., New Delhi, 1981.

Singh, Jiwitesh Kumar, *Regional Economics*, Bharathi Prakashan, Varanasi, 1978.

Sivaraman, B., *Key-Note Address to the Seminar on Industrial Development of Backward Areas*, IDBI, Bombay, 1980.

Somasekhara, N., *Planning and Development in Karnataka*, Geetha Book House, Mysore, 1978.

Srinivas, T.Y., *Industrialisation and Economic Development*, Ph.D., Thesis, Bombay University, 1975.

Staley, Eugene, *The Future of Underdeveloped Countries*, Harper and Brothers, New York, 1954.

Suteliffe, R.B., *Industry and Underdevelopment*, Addison-Wesley Publishing Company, London, 1971.

Tangamuthu, C., *Industrialisation of Tamil Nadu Since 1951: A Structural Analysis*, M.Litt. Thesis, Madras University, 1973.

Todaro, M.P., *Development Planning: Models and Methods*, Oxford University Press, Nairobi, 1971.

Vakil, C.N., (ed.), *Industrial Development of India: Policy and Problems*, Orient Longman, New Delhi, 1973.

Venkataraman, L.S., Prahladachar, M. and Deshpande, R.S., *Dynamics of Rural Transformation in Karnataka 1956-76*, Institute for Social and Economic Change, Bangalore, 1985.

Walker, F. David, (ed.), *Planning Industrial Development*, John Wiley and Sons, New York, 1980.

Wilson, R.K. and Wood, C.S., *Patterns of World Economic Development*, Longman Sorret, Melbourne, 1982.

Zacharia, T.C., *Role of Industrialisation in the Economic Development of a Country (With special reference to India)* Ph.D. Thesis, Bombay University, 1966.

B. Articles

Ahluwalia, S.S., "Regional Pattern of Industrial Development in India", *Regional Dimensions of India's Economic Development*, State Planning Commission, Government of U.P. Lucknow, 1983.

Alonso, William, "Urban and Regional Imbalances in Economic Development", *Economic Development and Cultural Change*, Vol. 17, No. 1, October, 1968.

Arndt. H.B., "The Trickledown Myth", *Economic Development and Cultural Change*, Vol. 32, No. 1, October, 1983.

Ashworth, William, "Backwardness, Discontinuity and Industrial Development, *Economic History Review*, Vol. 23, No. 1, April, 1970.

Aziz, Abdul, "Regional Dispersal of Industries Through Rural Industrialisation", *Paper Presented at the Seminar on Regional dispersal of Industries in Karnataka*, B.R. Project, P.G. Centre, Mysore University, January 1984.

Baer, Werner, "Regional Inequality and Economic Growth in Brazil", *Economic Development and Cultural Change*, Vol. XII, No. 1, October 1963.

Balogh, T., "Note on Deliberate Industrialisation for Higher Incomes", *Economic Journal*, June 1947.

Beckerman, W., and Bacon, R., "International Comparisons of Income Levels: A suggested New Measure" *Economic Journal*, 1960.

Belshaw, M., "Observations on Industrialisation for Higher Incomes", *Economic Journal*, September 1947.

Bennet, M.K., "International Disparities in Consumption Levels", *American Economic Review*, September, 1951.

Bhalla, S.S. and Glewwe, Paul, "Growth and Equity in Developing Countries: "A Reinterpretation of the Sri Lankan Experience", *The World Bank Economic Review*, Vol. 1, No. 1, September, 1986.

Bhattacharya, Manas, "Dynamics of Regional Transformation in West Bengal — A Quest for Hypothesis", *Indian Journal of Regional Science*, Vol. XIV, No. 1, 1982.

Booth, E.J.R., "Interregional Income Differences", *Southern Economic Journal*, Vol. 31, No. 1, July, 1964.

Boudeville, J.R., "A Survey of Recent Techniques for Regional Economic Analysis", *Regional Economic Planning*, 1960.

Boudhayan, Chattopadhya and Moonis Raza, "Regional Development: Analytical Framework and Indicators", *Indian Journal of Regional Science*, Vol. VII, No. 1, 1975.

Buchanan, N.S., "Deliberate Industrialisation for Higher Incomes", *The Economic Journal*, Vol. LVI, December, 1946.

Chachadi, N.G., "Regional Imbalances in Karnataka: An Analysis of a Decade's Progress", *Southern Economist*, Vol. 22, No. 13, November 1, 1983.

Chadha, V. and Johar, R.S., "Industrial Development of Punjab — Pattern, Problems and Perspective", *Economic Analyst, A Journal of the Punjab School of Economics*, December, 1980.

Chandrasekhar, C.P., "An Event in Economics", *Frontline*, December 13-26, 1986.

Channa, V.N., "Development of Backward Areas — Some Policy Implications", *A Paper Presented at the Seminar on Development of Backward Areas*, IDBI, Bombay, 1980.

Chaturvedi, B.K. and Tyagi, B.N., "Regional Disparities — A measure and an Explanation", *Indian Journal of Regional Science*, Vol. XV, No. 2, 1983.

Chebbi, K. Vijay, "Industrial Policies and Strategies for Backward Area Development", *A Paper Presented at the Seminar on Industrial Development of Backward Areas*, IDBI, Bombay, 1980.

Chenery, H.B., "The Role of Industrialisation in Development Programmes", in Agarwala, A.N. and singh, S.P., (eds.), *The Economics of Underdevelopment*, Oxford University Press, New Delhi, 1976.

Chenery, H.B. and L. Taylor, "Development Patterns: Among Countries and Over Time", *Review of Economics and Statistics*, November, 1968.

Chenery, H.B., "Patterns of Industrial Growth", *American Economic Review*, September, 1960.

Dadibhavi, R.V., "An Analysis of Inter-Taluka Disparity and Backwardness in Karnataka State, 1975-76", *Indian Journal of Regional Science*, Vol. XIV, No. 2, 1982.

David, A. Larson and Walton, T. Wilford, "The Physical Quality of Life Index: A New Measure of Welfare", *The Indian Economic Journal*, Vol. 27, No. 3, January-March, 1980.

Dharkar, B.C., *"A Plea for Regional Development in India" Industrial India*, Annual, 1971.

Dholakia, B.H., and Dholakia, R.H., "Inter-State Income Inequalities and Inter-State Variation in the Growth of real Capital Stock", *Economic and Political Weekly*, Vol. XV (38) September 20, 1980.

Elijah, M. James, "Some Determinants of Industrialisation in Small and Medium Size Economies: A Cross-Section Analysis", *The Indian Economic Journal*, Vol. 27, No. 2, October-December, 1979.

Gemmell, Norman, "Economic Development and Structural Change: The Role of the Service Sector" *The Journal of Development Studies*, Vol. 19, No. 1, October, 1982.

Gopalaswamy, R., "Regional Dimensions of Plan Development — Possible Approaches", *Regional Dimensions of India's Economic Development*, State Planning Commission, Government of U.P., Lucknow, 1983.

Gupta, K.L., "Development Patterns: An Interregional Study", *Quarterly Journal of Economics*, Vol. 85, No. 4, November, 1971.

Gupta, K. Surendra, "Perspective of New Policies and Strategy for Industrial Development of Backward Areas", *A Background Paper presented at the Seminar on Industrial Development of Backward Areas*, IDBI, Bombay, 1980.

Houchwald, W., "Conceptual Issues of Regional Income Estimates", *in NBER's Regional Income*, Princeton University Press, 1957.

Hughes, R.B. "Interregional Income Differences: Self-Perpetuation", *Southern Economic Journal*, Vol. 28, No. 1, July, 1961.

Iyengar, N.S. and Sudarshan, P., "On a Method of Classifying Regions from Multivariate Data", *Regional Dimensions of India's Economic Development, State Planning Commission*, Government of U.P., Lucknow, 1983.

Jacobs, Garry, "Comprehensive Measure of Total Development", *Regional Dimensions of India's Economic Development, State Planning Commission*, Government of U.P., Lucknow, 1983.

Jacques, Ledent, "Rural-Urban Migration, Urbanisation and Economic Development", *Economic Development and Cultural Change*, Vol. 30, No. 3, April, 1982.

Jha, D.N., "Regional Imbalances in India (1951-1971)", *Southern Economist*, Annual Number, May, 1978.

Joffery, B. Nugent, "An Alternative source of Measurement Error as an Explanation for the Inverted-U Hypothesis", *Economic Development and Cultural Change*, Vol. 31, No. 2, January, 1983.

Keshava Murthy, T.A., "Impediment to Faster Growth of Karnataka's Economy: An In-depth Study", *Southern Economist"*, Vol. 19, No. 13, November 1, 1980.

Khanna, C.D., "Regional Imbalances and their Rectification", *Industrial India*, Annual Number, 1971.

Khanna, J.S., "Lagging Industrial Development in Punjab: An Analysis", *Economic Analyst, A Journal of the Punjab School of Economics*, December, 1980.

Koropeckyj, I.S., "Equalisation of Regional Development in Socialist Countries", *Economic Development and Cultural Change*, Vol. 21, No. 1, October, 1972.

Kuznets, Simon, "Quantitative Aspects of the Economic Growth of Nations, II, Industrial Distribution of National Product and Labour Force", *Economic Development and Cultural Change*, Supplement to Vol. 4, July, 1957.

Little, I.M.D., "Small Manufacturing Enterprises in Developing Countries", *The World Bank Economic Review*, Vol. 1, No. 2, January, 1987.

Lurie, Samuel, "The International Symposium on Industrial Development", *U.N. Monthly Chronicle*, Vol. V, No. 1, January, 1968.

Manning, Nash, "Social prerequisites to Economic Growth in Latin America and South East Asia", *Economic Development and Cultural Change*, Vol. XII, No. 3, April, 1964.

Mathur, Ashok, "Regional Development and Income Disparities in India: A Sectoral Analysis", *Economic Development and Cultural Change*, Vol. 31, No. 3, April, 1983.

Mathur, K.B.L., "State-Wise Growth Pattern and Inter-State inequality in India", *Regional Dimensions of India's Economic Development*, State Planning Commission Government of U.P., Lucknow, 1983.

Mathur, O.P., "The Problem of Interregional Disparities: The Indian background:, *Indian Journal of Regional Science*, Vol. V, No. 1, 1973.

Mitra, A., "Levels of Regional Development in India", *Census of India*, 1961, Vol. I, Part I-A.

Naidu, Munirathna, K., "Industrial Progress in Karnataka — A Critical Review", *Southern Economist*, Karnataka Number, November 1, 1978.

Nair, K.R.G., "Regional Disparities in Kerala", in K.R.G. Nair (ed.), Regional Disparities in India, *(Papers presented at the All India Conference on Regional Disparities in India)*, New Delhi, April, 1979.

Nair, K.R.G., Inter-State Income Disparities in India", *Indian Journal of Regional Science*, Vol. III (2), 1971.

Nair, K.R.G., "A Note on Inter-State Differentials in India, 1950-51 to 1960-61", *Journal of Development Studies*, July, 1973.

Nair, N.P. and George, K.K., "Strategies for the Development of Backward Areas : Do they widen inter-state Disparities", *A Paper presented at the Seminar on Industrial Development of Backward Areas*, IDBI, Bombay, 1980.

Nanjundappa, D.M., "Contours of Karnataka's New Sixth Plan", *Southern Economist*, Vol. 19, No. 13, November 1, 1980.

Nanjundappa, D.M. and Goud, M.B., "Development of Backward Areas" *A paper presented at the Seminar on Design of Backward Areas Development*, Patna, January, 1979.

Nath, V., "Regional Development in Indian Planning", *Economic and Political Weekly*, Vol. II, Nos. 3, 4 and 5, Annual Number, January, 1970.

Pal, M.N. "Regional Disparities in the Level of Development in India", *Indian Journal of Regional Sciences*, Vol. VII, No. 1, 1975.

Pathak, H.N., "Policy Framework for Industrial Development in Backward Districts", *A Paper presented at the Seminar on Industrial Development of Backward Areas*, IDBI, Bombay, 1980.

Pitale, R.L., "Policy Perspectives for Industrial Development of Backward Areas", *A Paper presented at the Seminar on Industrial Development of Backward Areas*, IDBI, Bombay, 1980.

Pendse, D.R., "Balanced Regional Development" In S.H. Deshpande (ed.), *Economy of Maharashtra*, Samaj Prabodhan Sanshta, Poone, 1973.

Prabhakar Rao, P. and Sundaram, K.V., "Regional Imbalances in India — Some Policy Issues and Problems", *Indian Journal of Regional Science*, Vol. 5, No. 1, 1973.

Prasad, Bhagwan, "Backward Area Development with Special Reference to Weaker Sections and Decentralised Industrial Sector", *A Paper presented at the Seminar on Industrial Development of Backward Areas*, IDBI, Bombay, 1980.

Pred, A.R., "Industrialisation, Initial Advantage and American Metropolitan Growth", *Geographical Review*, 55, 1965.

Rao, Hemalatha, "Identification of Backward Regions and Trends in Regional Disparities in India" *Arthavijnana*, 1977.

Rao, S.K., "A Note on Measuring Economic Distances Between Regions in India", *Economic and Political Weekly*, Vol. VIII, No. 17, April 28, 1973.

Rosenstein-Rodan, P.N., "Problems of Industrialisation of Eastern and South-Eastern Europe", *Economic Journal*, June-September, 1943.

Rudra, Ashok, "The Rate of Growth of Indian Economy", in E.A.G. Robinson, and Michel Kindran, (eds.), *Economic Development in South Asia*, MacMillan and Company Ltd., 1970.

Sampath, R.K., "Inter-State Inequalities in Income in India, 1951-71", *Indian Journal of Regional Science*, Vol. IX, No. 1, 1977.

Sandesara, J.C., "Scale and Technology in Indian Industry", *Bulletin of the Oxford University Institute of Economics and Statistics*, August, 1966.

Sandesara, J.C., "Small-Scale Industry — Evidences and Interpretation", *Indian Planning and Economic Policies*, Gujarat Economic Association, Ahmedabad, 1981.

Sathe, M.D., "Industrial Imbalance in India", *Industrial India*, 1971.

Seers, Dudley, "Role of Industry in Development : Some Fallacies", *Journal of African Studies*, 1963.

Shah, S.M., "Growth Centres as a Strategy of Economic Development", *A Paper presented at the Seminar on Industrial Development of Backward Areas*, IDBI, Bombay, 1980.

Sharma, K.L., "Spatial Disparities in Rajasthan", *Indian Journal of Regional Science*, Vol. VII(i), 1975.

Sharma, Manojkumar and Bawa, R.S., "Sources of Inter-District Variations in Industrial Development in Punjab", *Indian Journal of Regional Science*, Vol XV, No. 2, 1983.

Singh, A.K., "States as Planning Regions", *Indian Journal of Regional Science*, Vol. 4, No. 1, 1972.

Singh, Manmohan, "Valedictory Address to the Eighth World Economic Congress — Excerpts", *The Economic Times*, Bangalore, December 18, 1986.

Stefan, R.H., "Regional and National Economic Development in India", *The Regional Science Associations (Papers and Proceedings, Sixth Annual Meeting 1959)*, Vol. VI, 1960.

Stohr, Walter, "Towards 'Another' Regional Development ? In Search of a Strategy of Truly 'Integrated' Regional Development", In Misra, R.P. and Honjo, M., (eds.), *Changing Perception of Development Problems (Regional Development Series)*, Vol. 1, UCRD, Maruzen, Asia, Singapore, 1981.

Streeten, Paul, "How Poor are the Poor Countries" in Seers Dudley and Joy Leonard, (eds.), *Development in a Divided World*, Penguin Books, 1971.

Sudarshan, P., "A Note on Inter-Temporal Differentials in Andhra Pradesh's Development", *Regional · Dimensions of India's Economic Development*, State Planning Commission, Government of U.P., Lucknow, 1983.

Sumithra, Gladys, "Some Aspects of Regional Development in Karnataka — An Inter-District Analysis", *A Paper presented at the Seminar on Regional Dispersal of Industries in Karnataka*, B.R. Project P.G. Centre, University of Mysore, January, 1984.

Sundaram, K.V., "Measurement and Analysis of Development at the Regional and Local Levels: Some Issues and Problems", *Regional*

Dimensions of India's Economic Development, State Planning Commission, Government of U.P., Lucknow, 1983.

Suri, Kamal, "Inter and Intra-State Disparities Widen", *Economic Times*, March 3, 1982.

Swarup, Anand, "A Methodology for Estimating District Domestic Product: A Case Study of U.P.", *Regional Dimensions of India's Economic Development, State Planning Commission*, Government of U.P., Lucknow, 1983.

Tandon, B.B., "Inter-State Income Disparities Since 1960-61", *The Asian Economic Review*, April & August, 1982.

Timothy, Raison, M.P., "The Meaning of Development", *Economic Digest — A British Review*, No. 21, Autumn 1983.

Tiwari, R.T., "Interregional Disparities in Levels of Development – Indian Experience", *Man and Development*, Vol. VI, No. 1, March, 1984.

Trapido, Stanely, "South Africa in a Comparative Study of Industrialisation", *Journal of Development Studies*, April, 1971.

Venkataramaiah, P., "Inter-State Variations in Industry, 1951-61: A Comment", *Economic and Political Weekly*, August 4, 1969.

Williamson, J.G., "Regional Inequality and the Process of National Development: A Description of Patterns", *Economic Development and Cultural Change*, Vol. XIII, No. 4, Part II, July, 1965.

C. Reports (Published and Unpublished)

Bureau of Economics and Statistics, Economic Development of Mysore, 1956-69, Government of Mysore, Bangalore, 1970.

—, Statistical Abstracts of Mysore/Karnataka (various issues), Government of Mysore/Karnataka, Bangalore.

—, Estimates of District Income in Karnataka, 1974-75, State Income Division, Government of Karnataka, Bangalore.

—, Sectoral Composition of State Income, 1960-61 to 1977-78, Government of Karnataka, Bangalore.

—, Sectoral Composition of District Income of Karnataka, 1960-61, 1970-71, and 1975-76, Government of Karnataka, Bangalore.

—, Mysore/Karnataka at a Glance (various issues), Government of Mysore/Karnataka, Bangalore.

Central Statistical Organisation, Statistical Abstract of the Indian Union, 1963 and 1964, New Series No. 12, CSO, 1965.

——, Statistical Abstract of India, 1975, New Series, No. 12, CSO, 1976.

——, Annual Survey of Industries, 1980-81, Summary Results for Census sector, Vol. 1, Part II, CSO, May, 1984.

Director of Census Operations, Census of India 1961, Vol. XI, Mysore, General Economic Tables, Mysore.

——, Census of India 1971, Series 14, Mysore, Economic Tables, Mysore, 1974.

Director of Census Operations, Census of India 1981, Series 9, Karnataka, Part II-B(i), Primary Census Abstract, General Population, Bangalore, 1983.

——, Census of India 1981, Series 9, Karnataka Part II — Special Report and Tables based on 5 per cent sample data, Bangalore.

Directorate of Economics and Statistics, Estimates of District Income in Karnataka for Selected Years (Revised Series), Government of Karnataka, Bangalore, 1986.

IDBI, Industrial Development of Backward Regions, Bombay, 1974.

——, Review of Ongoing Programmes for Development of Backward Areas with special reference to Industrial Development, Bombay, 1980.

——, Industrial Development of Backward Areas, Bombay, 1981.

National Committee on the Development of Backward Areas, Report on Industrial Dispersal, Planning Commission, Government of India, New Delhi, 1980.

NCAER, Techno-Economic Survey of Mysore, New Delhi, 1965.

Planning Commission, Third Five Year Plan, Government of India, New Delhi, 1961.

——, Identification of Backward Areas: Report of the Working Group, Government of India, New Delhi, 1969.

Planning Commission, Government of India, and the State Planning Institute, Government of U.P., Regional Dimensions of India's Economic Development, (Proceedings of the Seminar held at Nainital, April 22-24, 1982), State Planning Commission, U.P., Lucknow, 1983.

Planning Department, Economic Survey (various issues), Government of Karnataka, Bangalore.

Sardar Patel Institute of Economic and Social Research, Regional Variations in Industrial Development (A Project Report), Ahmedabad, 1972.

Special Studies Division, State Income Estimates of India: With Particular Reference to Karnataka, Planning Department, Government of Karnataka, Bangalore, March, 1985.

The World Bank, World Development Report, 1983.

The World Bank, *The World Bank Economic Review*, Vol. 1, No. 1, September, 1986.

——, The World Bank Economic Review, Vol. 1, No. 2, January, 1987.

UNO, Patterns of Industrial Growth, 1938-58, New York, 1960.

——, Industrial Development (Asia and Far East) Vol. II, New York, 1966.

INDEX